Arab Animation
Images of Identity

Omar Sayfo

EDINBURGH
University Press

Edinburgh University Press is one of the leading university presses in the UK. We publish academic books and journals in our selected subject areas across the humanities and social sciences, combining cutting-edge scholarship with high editorial and production values to produce academic works of lasting importance. For more information visit our website: edinburghuniversitypress.com

© Omar Sayfo, 2021, 2023

Edinburgh University Press Ltd
The Tun – Holyrood Road
12 (2f) Jackson's Entry
Edinburgh EH8 8PJ

First published in hardback by Edinburgh University Press 2021

Typeset in 11/15 Adobe Garamond by
Servis Filmsetting Ltd, Stockport, Cheshire

A CIP record for this book is available from the British Library

ISBN 978 1 4744 7948 6 (hardback)
ISBN 978 1 4744 7949 3 (paperback)
ISBN 978 1 4744 7950 9 (webready PDF)
ISBN 978 1 4744 7951 6 (epub)

The right of Omar Sayfo to be identified as author of this work has been asserted in accordance with the Copyright, Designs and Patents Act 1988 and the Copyright and Related Rights Regulations 2003 (SI No. 2498).

Contents

List of Figures		v
Acknowledgements		vii
1	Introduction	1
2	Mediating National Identities in Arab Animation	23
3	Arab Animated Sitcoms: Vehicles for the Mediation of Critical Notions of National Identities	105
4	Approaches to Pan-Arab Identities	138
5	Advocating Islamic Identities in Arab Animation	179
6	The Arab Spring of Animation	217
7	Epilogue: Can Arab Animation Go Global?	247
Bibliography		253
Index		275

For Armin

Figures

2.1	*Marco Monkey*: the first Egyptian animation, still regarded as foreign by critics	26
2.2	*Mish Mish Effendi*: the 'Egyptian Mickey Mouse'	29
2.3	*'Ali Baba*: a commercial by 'Ali Moheeb	35
2.4	*Bakkar*: a Nubian boy and a symbol of Egyptian identity	37
2.5	*Batal min Seena'* (A Hero from the Sinai): animating a glorious war	43
2.6	*Freej* (Neighbourhood): ladies from the hood	49
2.7	*Kaslan* (Lazy): from comic strips to the screen	54
2.8	*Ben wa 'Esam* (Ben and Izzy): a friendship between an American and a Jordanian boy	58
2.9	*Viva Carthago*: a Mediterranean journey through time and space	71
2.10	*Al-Jaza'ir Tarikh wa Hadarah* (Algerian History and Civilisation): reinventing history	80
2.11	*Shaykh al-Mujahedeen – Ahmad Yassin* (Sheikh of the Mujaheds – Ahmad Yassin): based on a true-ish story	91
2.12	*The Wanted 18*: the cows that joined the resistance	97
3.1	*Abu Mahjoub*: an average man from Jordan	112
3.2	*Shaabiat Al Cartoon* (Animation Neighbourhood)	117
3.3	*Bsant wa Dyasty* (Bsant and Dyasty)	119
3.4	*Al-'Ataak*: a tale of everyday struggle in Baghdad	122

3.5	*Youmiyyat Bou Qatada wa Bou Nabeel* (Everyday Stories of Bou Qatada and Bou Nabeel): a political take on Kuwaiti society	126
3.6	*Al-Masageel*: a Bedouin tribe's encounter with modernity	131
3.7	*Tunis 2050*: discussing the present through talking about the future	133
4.1	*Al-Kurat al-Qadam al-Amreekiyya* (American Football): the united Arab team beats America	143
4.2	*Al-'Amirah wal-Nahr* (The Princess and the River): an old tale in the service of Saddam Hussein	146
4.3	*Tuyur al-Yasmeen* (The Jasmine Birds): evoking Arabo-Islamic symbolism in animation	155
4.4	*Al-Jarrah* (The Jug): a moralistic tale of old Syria	158
4.5	*Za'toor*: a donkey for all people of the Gulf	164
4.6	*Saladin: the Animated Series*: a historical hero in a Disneyesque adventure	173
4.7	*Badr*: the first Arab anime	174
5.1	*Mohammad al-Fatih* (Mohammad the Conqueror): an idealised Muslim past	186
5.2	*Qisas al-Hayawan fil-Qur'an* (Stories of the Animals in the Qur'an): an Islamic identity for domestic consumption and export	198
5.3	*The 99*: homegrown Muslim superheroes	206
6.1	*Youmiyyat Zayn al-Abedine Ben 'Ali* (Everyday Stories of Zayn al-Abedine Ben 'Ali): JibJab meets the Arab Spring	224
6.2	*Al-Za'eem* (The Leader): an archetype of every (Arab) dictator	228
6.3	*Al-Khubz al-Siyasiyy* (The Political Bread): animated Tunisian democracy	230
6.4	*Egyptoon*: animating a time of political enthusiasm	234
6.5	*Qasr al-Sha'b* (The Palace of the People): animation with real stakes	242
E.1	*Bilal*: an Arab animation going global	249

Acknowledgements

Many people have helped me during the ten-year journey that has led to finalising this manuscript. My first expression of gratitude goes to my wife Anna Bakai and my good friend and colleague Zoltán Páll for their invaluable backing. I am especially grateful to my former supervisors Professor Sonja De Leeuw and Nico Landman, whose insightful suggestions and comments inspired me to choose Arab animation as a field of research. I am also greatly indebted to the Netherlands Interuniversity School for Islamic Studies (NISIS) and Utrecht University's Institute for Cultural Inquiry (ICON), and am beholden to Professor Christian Lange and Alexander Badenoch for their continuous support of this project.

I would like to express my gratitude to Professor Yasir Suleiman and Paul Anderson, who were the most generous of hosts during my visiting fellowship at the Alwaleed Bin Talal Centre of Islamic Studies at the University of Cambridge in 2014. I am also indebted to Professor Naomi Sakr, Professor Jeanette Steemers, Stefanie Van de Peer, Roxane Farmanfarmaian, Ehab Galal and Verena Hutter, who have shared my enthusiasm for Arab animation from the very beginning of this journey.

I am grateful for the support of Professor Miklós Maróth and the Avicenna Institue of Middle Eastern Studies, and the generous funding that I have received from Pallas Áthéné Domus Meriti Foundation that was essential in order to be able to conduct my research.

Last but not least, I cannot thank enough ʿAbbas ʿAbbas, Ashraf Hamdi, Ayman Jamal, Bassam Faraj, Didier Frenkel, Emad Hajjaj, George Khoury, Ghanem Elhersh, Mohamed Elmazen, Mohamed Ghazala, Mongi Sancho, Mustafa al-Faramawy, Mwaffaq Katt, Naif al-Mutawa, Omar al-ʿAbdallat, Omar Maghary, Osama Khalifa, Rashida al-Shafeʿi, Riad Ghariani, Sameh Mustafa, Sherif Gamal, Sulafa Hijazi, Tarek Rashed, Seddik Tayeb Cherif, Thamer al-Zaidi, Wafa Nabulsi, Zaidoun Karadsheh, Zainab Zamzam and all the other authors, producers, directors, animators and other dedicated members of the Arab animation industries who have inspired and assisted me during my fieldwork, shared with me their experiences and knowledge, and offered me their unique perspective on the exciting world of Arab animation.

Note on Transliteration

In the transliteration of Arabic proper nouns and titles, the form most commonly found in reputable written sources has been used. This includes names of people who are familiar to many speakers of English; for clarity, such words have normally been given a more simplified transliteration.

1

Introduction

Back in my childhood in the 1990s, when asked about their favourite cartoon, most Arab children would pick *Tom and Jerry*. The series created by William Hanna and Joseph Barbera had long dominated Arab children's television. As for me and my friends, our favourite cartoon was *Captain Majid* (Captain Glorious), the story of a heroic football team and its captain. While cheering the victories of Majid, it never occurred to us that his original name was Tsubasa and that the series was not an Arab production, but a Japanese one. This was not uncommon: Arab translators had long been trying to 'Arabise' cultural products aimed at children by giving foreign characters Arab names and adding culturally relevant phrases to the dialogues. However, all of these efforts did not change the fact that Arab audiences had been exposed to a one-way flow of foreign aesthetics and ideas.

Looking back on the summers I spent in Syria as a child, I can barely remember more than a handful of homegrown Arab animated cartoons. The first that comes to mind is the Egyptian series *Bakkar*, broadcast on the Egyptian state channel in the late 1990s, when satellite channels became widely available across the Middle East. At around the same time, a number of local religious and educational animations appeared on the screens. However, because of their poor visual quality and rather boring narrative, being the impatient children we were, we quickly switched to dubbed Disney cartoons when the titles of local pieces appeared on the screen.

My next encounter with Arab animation came more than a decade later in 2011, during a transcontinental flight. Browsing the video content offered by the onboard media system, I came across *Freej*, a beautifully animated 3D comical series of four elderly Emirati ladies struggling with the modern world around them. Enthusiastic about what I had found, during the following months I watched not only every season of *Freej*, but also a number of other sitcom animations from Egypt, Saudi Arabia, the United Arab Emirates and Tunisia. Thus I discovered an exciting, expanding world of Arab animation. As I kept watching, I began noticing how these animations, which at first seemed so innocent, were engaging in the negotiation of social, political and even religious identities. I also found that there was barely any scholarly engagement with the topic – the few relevant writings were largely restricted to short entries in encyclopedias about global animation and Arab cinema, popular articles on specific productions, and interviews with animators, authors and producers. At that point I decided to enter the then barely explored world of Arab animation.

My first fieldwork in Egypt in 2012 exceeded my expectations. Reading unpublished Arabic reports and conducting personal interviews with local art scholars, animators and producers, I realised that animated cartoon production in the Arab world is not a recent phenomenon, but dates back to the 1930s. Extending my research to other countries, I explored animation archives as well as contemporary productions from Algeria, Iraq, Jordan, Kuwait, the Palestinian Territories, Qatar, Syria, Saudi Arabia, Tunisia and the United Arab Emirates.

The first academic account of Arab animation was written by Giannalberto Bendazzi who included an incomplete list of producers and titles from Algeria, Egypt, Iraq and Tunisia, together with short descriptions of the narratives in his *Cartoons: One Hundred Years of Cinema Animation* (Bloomington, IN: Indiana University Press, 1994). In 2015, Bendazzi released an improved list of Arab animators from the Gulf and the Middle East and films in his three volumes of *Animation: A World History* (CRC Press, 2015). Stefanie Van de Peer's edited volume, *Animation in the Middle East: Practice and Aesthetics from Baghdad to Casablanca* (London: I. B. Tauris, 2017), became the first serious academic attempt to explore and analyse the realm of Arab animation. *Arab Animation* positions itself within the expanding literature on

Arab film and television, world animation and, as the format is often aimed at a young audience, children's media. In this regard, this book has parallels with Allen Douglas and Fedwa Malti-Douglas's *Arab Comic Strips: Politics of an Emerging Mass Culture* (Bloomington, IN: Indiana University Press, 1994) which besides performing thorough textual analyses of Arab children's comics, also investigates them within the broader political and social environment of their time. This book is even more closely linked to the extensive literature on Arab cinema, among others Viola Shafik's *Arab Cinema: History and Cultural Identity* (Cairo: The American University in Cairo Press, 2007) which reconstructs the history of Arab film production and investigates the ways culture and politics affected the formation of industries and identities. As television channels have been acting as a primary platform for distribution and main funders of animated shows, this book shares the focus of Lila Abu-Lughod's *Dramas of Nationhood – The Politics of Television in Egypt* (Cairo: The American University in Cairo Press, 2005) and other books investigating the politics and economics of Arab television, like Naomi Sakr's *Satellite Realms: Transnational Television, Globalization and the Middle East* (London: I. B. Tauris, 2001) and *Arab Television Today* (London: I. B. Tauris, 2007). This book also shares the production studies perspective of Joe Khalil and Marwan Kraidy's *Arab Television Industries* (London: Bloomsbury Publishing, 2017) in exploring the structural patterns, ownership, production, programming and the distribution of content. Linking animation with children's media, *Arab Animation* also connects to Naomi Sakr and Jeanette Steemers' *Children's TV and Digital Media in the Arab World: Childhood, Screen Culture and Education* (London: I. B.Tauris, 2017).

For many, animation production is a booming business for creating and selling marketable products. At the same time, it is also a cultural product that reflects the cultural values of their producers as well as the social conditions under which they were created. In sum, it is 'an industry that commercializes and standardizes the production of culture' (Belkhyr 2012: 704). As the extensive literature on Walt Disney cartoons and Japanese anime shows, animated cartoons have a strong potential to mediate and negotiate values, address issues of identity, and also present appropriations of socio-political issues.[1] Arab animated cartoons are no exception. The animation format effectively served different purposes, as it was adapted to in Middle Eastern and North African cultural and political environments. Formats in general and animated cartoons in particular are not the catalysts for cultural sameness or the loss of cultural diversity; on the contrary, adaptations provide opportunities for re-imagining nations and communities (Moran 1998). This book regards Arab animated cartoons as local champions challenging a decades-long hegemony of cultural authority imposed by imported animated cartoons and instead express socio-cultural, national and regional realities, and also mediate notions of identities. The goal of this book, then, is to explore how Arab animated cartoons mediate and negotiate notions of identity.

What Makes an Animation Arab?

Animation has emerged as one of the most influential creative forms of the twenty-first century. Though often used synonymously, there is a significant difference between 'animation' and 'cartoon' (Wells 2002). While the former is a fairly neutral term, describing a technological process and visual form used in films, industry, engineering, designing and advertising, the latter refers to a medium. Since the 1960s, 'cartoon' has become a loaded term, often connected to Saturday morning cartoons, and therefore implying a predominantly children's audience and whimsical content (Mittell 2001a: 18). Exceptions are the historical primetime appearance of *The Flintstones* in 1960, the subsequent appearance of mature animations and the popularity of sitcom animations like *The Simpsons* from the 1990s onwards.

In Arabic, the word 'cartoon' traditionally denotes animated films – either feature-length films or series – that are also defined as 'moving drawings' (*al-rusuum al-mutaharrika*). More than in the West, in Arab popular discourse both terms are generally associated with animations aimed at children, and are hence considered non-serious mediums.

In other words, we should be extremely careful to avoid generalisations when talking about 'Arab animation'. Animated cartoon production in the Arab world is culturally, economically, politically and structurally far too diverse to be described by a single or even a handful of production strategies. Moreover, 'Arab animations' are characterised by a wide range of narrative strategies, textual characteristics and visual styles. The production processes and business models also vary considerably and there is no single 'Arab way' of producing and distributing animations. Not only the Arab world as a whole, but also individual Arab countries – such as Egypt, the largest producer of animated cartoons in the Arab world – have had different periods of dominant cultural policies and stylistic influences that impacted animation both on the production and the textual level. This diversity is quite apparent when comparing animated cartoons produced during different decades and also when comparing contemporary productions. Even animations produced at the same time and in the same country display an amazing range of diversity in terms of visual characteristics and style. Therefore, 'Arab animation' in this book is used as an umbrella term for a variety of styles, narratives, textual characteristics, genres, and production and distribution models.

What, then, are the criteria for defining an animation as 'Arab'? 'Topic' comes to mind, yet there are a large number of productions made by non-Arab producers in non-Arab countries that deal with Arab themes or use Arab settings and scenery for their narratives, such as Walt Disney's *Aladdin* (1992), an adaptation of the Aladdin story of *The Arabian Nights* which was lambasted for indulging in orientalist fantasies and for promoting racist attitudes toward Arabs (Macleod 2003; Ostman 1996; Shaheen 2012). In defining the 'Arabness' of an animated cartoon we should take a closer look at the authorial background of the production. To put it simply, an animation is Arab if the authors are Arab. But who is the author of an animated cartoon that is often produced not by a single person but a larger group of people? Following Paul Wells' criteria for authorship in animation, this book regards producers, directors, concept artists and animators as individuals of creative authority over the text of an animated production.[2]

At the same time, in the case of animated cartoons produced by production companies or animation studios, more than one person can claim authorship. *Arab Animation* also considers the general cultural characteristics of Arab animation that make production a less democratic process and result in projects centred around influential producers claiming authorship. The criterion for labelling an animation as 'Arab' is straightforward: authorship claimed by Arabs, including diaspora communities.[3]

Animated cartoons should be considered as being 'Arab' even if their Arab authors highlight aspects other than national affiliation as identities of themselves or their productions. These include, for example, the so-called 'Islamic animations' that are predominantly produced by Saudi and Gulf individuals and institutions in order to provide Muslim children with morally appropriate animations. Even though the authors and producers stress the Islamic identity of their products, I read them as Arab animations, given the fact that their textual roots refer to specific Arab environments and understandings of Islam.

The Production of Arab Animated Cartoons

American animation appeared in Egyptian cinemas as early as the 1930s, where short films of Walt Disney and *Felix the Cat* were presented before popular films in the cinemas of Alexandria and Cairo. However, as children were not considered a primary target audience by Arab cinema owners, media owners and producers, cartoons by themselves were shown only occasionally in public cinemas for many decades.

Even after the introduction of television in the Arab world, children continued to be considered a secondary audience (Masmoudi 2006: 83). This is one of the possible reasons that very few animation studios were founded in the Arab world before the 1990s. Until that decade, terrestrial television channels were mainly owned by government institutions and their reach was largely limited to the national borders. Thus audiences were only able to see cartoons that had been approved by national censors. Choosing the sources of imported animations in the Cold War era was often a political decision, as socialist Arab countries such as Syria, Libya and Iraq favoured the products of France and the Eastern Bloc, while Saudi Arabia and the Gulf countries imported a great number of American series (Sayfo 2017a). Nonetheless, some animations such as *Tom and Jerry* were presented in both socialist and Gulf countries. Also, Japanese anime was admired by Arab media owners, regardless of political orientation: it was cheap to import and the narratives adhered to a strict moral code that made censorship unnecessary.[4] The first anime to achieve widespread popularity was *UFO Robo Grendizer*, a 1980s sci-fi series that later became a common point of reference among Arab producers who wanted to create a unique Arab or Muslim action hero (Al-Ghazzi 2018).[5]

Attempts to localise foreign animated productions became more prominent in the late 1980s and early 1990s when larger numbers of dubbed Japanese animes came to Arab screens. Arab studios not only translated but also culturally 'Arabised' most of the Japanese animations. One example is that of *Captain Tsubasa*, a Japanese anime from the 1980s that focused on the adventures of a Japanese youth football team and its captain. The first series were dubbed into Modern Standard Arabic (MSA) by a Saudi company in the 1990s and then aired on a number of Arab channels as *Captain Majid* (Captain Glorious), with the narrative focusing on the career of '*Fariiq al-Majd*' (Team of Glory).[6] This adaptability draws on a range of attributes, from the relatively low cost of dubbing to the lucrative merchandise revenues of existing property (Havens 2006). Imported productions also proved to have a long shelf life, a forward step for the distributing television channels, but a drastic blow for domestic production.

Following the satellite boom in the 1990s, enterprises, individuals, institutions and political parties launched their own channels in order to reach national and all-Arab audiences. The proliferation of satellite channels brought a growing demand for animated content. Once any free-to-air Arab channel purchased an animation, it became available to children across the entire Arab world. Due to the regionalising market, general expectations regarding layout and professionalism in the storyline grew. Therefore, homemade Arab shows in the 1990s were largely outnumbered by foreign productions on Arab screens; moreover, their visual quality was usually inferior to that of American and Asian productions.

From the early 2000s on, the spread of cheap videotapes and, later, DVDs, and the increasingly easy access to the internet meant that old and new Western animated films and series found their way to Arab audiences. Because of the complete lack of, or weakly implemented, intellectual property protection laws, street market vendors and shopkeepers in Cairo, Beirut, Damascus, Amman, Tunis and other Arab cities were selling Western animations to local customers. Therefore, 3D productions, among them Pixar's *Toy Story* (1995), DreamWorks' *Madagascar* (2005), Walt Disney's *Cars* (2006) and other blockbusters, were available in Arab countries shortly after their release. Again, this was an advance for the various distributors, but a blow for domestic production.

Theorising Arab Animated Cartoons: Cultural Resistance and Mediated Identities

While animation production is certainly a business for creating and selling marketable products, it is also a cultural production that reflects the cultural values of the animations' producers and the social conditions under which they were produced.

When watching foreign animation, Arab audiences were faced with a one-way flow of seemingly alien ideas and values that were disseminated. This fostered a desire to create their own productions (Sayfo 2014). The very first animation studio, established in Egypt by the Frenkel brothers in the 1930s, was in direct response to the popularity of American animations. Ever since, Arab animators and animation producers have drawn their inspiration from and even adapted foreign animated cartoons. At the same time, animation has the potential to become a platform for cultural resistance against foreign cultural impact: many Arab animation authors define their work as a 'cultural other' in contrast to American and Japanese animations that are still highly popular among Arab audiences.[7] Therefore, Arab animations are both a response to Disney and an adaptation of the global to the local, a localisation of universality to national and regional culture.

'Walt Disney. No other animation ever reached the quality of Walt Disney', answered Mustafa al-Faramawy, a leading producer of Egyptian Islamic animations, when I asked him about his main inspirations. 'On the other hand, it advocates a culture that should not be set as a model for our children', he added. This duality of simultaneously praising American animations for their technological and narrative excellence while rejecting their assumed cultural imperialism was repeated by most of the Arab producers I interviewed. Hence, Western animations serve both as models for and rivals to Arab productions, a phenomenon similar to Shafik's observations of traditional Egyptian cinema of the twentieth century (Shafik 2007b: 4). As American, European and Japanese producers have substantial advantages in selling the technology of animation production, the overwhelming majority of Arab productions reflect the visual style and narrative presented by global centres of animation. Arab producers often use well-developed formats and genres, and insert locality while leaving the basic concept unaltered. Despite this, Arab animations are not mere imitations of Disney and other foreign animations because globalised forms co-exist with and even promote local adaptations expressing unique local content. Moreover, the success of home-grown Arab animations shows the potential for a reaction of local/regional cultures and identities against global ones.

Arab Animation and Identity

The Arab world is a region of 400 million people living in twenty-two countries. The majority of Arabs share a common geography, religion, language, culture and history. Despite these common features, the Arab world is by no means homogeneous, as it incorporates several sub-regions, states and local cultures. Also, while the majority of the people follow Sunni or Shia Islam, there are numerous religious minorities such as Christian sects, Jews, Druze and others. In addition to religion, there are also significant ethnic minorities such as the Berbers, Kurds and Nubians. If we follow Stuart Hall's notion of identity as a 'production', which is never complete, always in process and always constituted within representation, we can see how the notion of identity in the Arab world is especially complicated due to its diverse socio-historical make-up (Hall 1990: 222).

Since the beginning of the Arab Awakening (*al-Nahda*) in the late nineteenth century, scholars have analysed the Arab world's constant search for identity (Hitti 1956). In this ongoing struggle, ideas of tribalism, nationalism, Arab nationalism, Islamism and Western ideologies compete and often blend with each other to create hybrid identities. Competing identities do not stand on their own, but extend to cultural production on the level of producers and to cultural consumption on the level of receivers. Beginning in the nineteenth century, many Arab writers and producers have been using imported Western literary genres such as the drama and the novel, and, later, media formats and genres such as film, soap operas, etc., to express and also to promote ideas on identity and belonging (Al-Musawi 2003; Siddiq 2007; Shafik 2007b).

Mass media plays a central role 'in re-imagining the dispersed and incoherent populace as a tight-knit, value-sharing collectivity, sustaining the experience of nationhood' (Higson 2005: 59). From the creation of Arab national states until the appearance of Arab transnational media in the 1990s, the media also reflected the localism/statism of the respective states. Because of the exclusive state control over media outlets, identity shaping was a privilege of Arab national governments. Therefore, televised media mirrored the political reality of national states as part of official propaganda, and Arab television continues to be the central platform for articulating the national.

The introduction of satellite channels in the 1990s challenged the propaganda monopoly of national governments. The flow of information and the transnational media revolution weakened the cultural hegemony of the nation-state and, at the same time, supported a trend of regionalism (Sakr 2001, 2007a). Along with other scholars, Khalil Rinnawi argues that a shared identity has been articulated in recent years, a phenomenon that he explains as an outcome of long- and short-term processes in the Arab world, as reflected by the failure of Nasserite pan-Arabism, a period marked by the isolation of states accompanied by foreign intervention, the rise of pan-Islam as an alternative to Arabism and the marginalisation of the secular Left in the Arab world. Rinnawi contends that the tensions between local (or, as he calls it, tribal) identities and global consumer conformity are articulated in a re-imagined pan-Arab identity, which he satirically dubs 'McArabism'. He distinguishes identities promoted by state-owned Arab media, serving national interests, and homogenising tendencies of regional identity constructions through content and format imitations of Western media outlets to refashion the orientations of local Arab-Islamic viewers. Thus, a new regional public identity is on the rise that involves a re-imagination of Arab and Islamic symbolism. The tensions on the structural-organisational level are reflected in the interests of political and religious elites, who control the flow of information via ownership and who represent social and religious values (Rinnawi 2006: 11–16). Therefore, a competition can be observed among Arab media elites as well as between Arab and non-Arab transnational broadcasters for audience. In spite of this tension, national structures still offer a potential for local cultural producers to pose challenges to global and regional producers, while regional structures also allow producers to challenge the global.

In cultural industries, local actors use globally distributed forms and genres to create cultural products to define and redefine national and local identities (Straubhaar 2007). Modern Western media technologies such as cinema and television have been fundamental tools in the Middle East for advocating competing identities of nationalism tied to Arab states, pan-Arab nationalism or Islamism (Gelvin 1999). At the same time, popular culture in general has the ability to produce and articulate feelings that can become the basis of an identity, and 'identity can be the source of political thought and action' (Street 1997: 10).

As a globally distributed format, animated cartoons have also become a popular instrument for mediating identities in the Arab world. Similarly to Arab films and television series, animation as a format and cultural text provides space for reproducing and, also, creating elements of national/regional/Islamic culture. Animations are texts in which different understandings of nation and identity are projected, defined and redefined against locally rival and imported formulas. Albert Moran has argued that formats are not catalysts for cultural sameness or the loss of cultural diversity, but rather providers of opportunities for re-imagining nations in various ways. Animated cartoons therefore provide spaces for the representation of local, regional and religious cultures through the adaptation of particular narratives, characters and values into basic formulas.

The Hybridity of Arab Animation

By the 1990s, critical studies on globalisation gave rise to theories on cultural hybridity. Early theories of cultural hybridity usually describe the interaction between centre and periphery as two or more cultures mixing with each other and creating a hybrid culture of mixed components. From a post-colonial perspective, hybridity regards colonial or imperialist traditions as dominating the suppressed indigenous traditions in any hybridised form. These theories were adopted in literary and media studies, analysing dominance and suppression in intertextual relationships.

Meanwhile, critical theories on cultural hybridity contend that Western hegemony has declined in the process of hybridity since hybridisation offers an opportunity for local and traditional cultures not only to survive, but also to become visible (Kraidy 2005). Homi Bhabha analyses hybridity in the context of the post-colonial novel and celebrates it as resistance put up by the colonised in the face of imperialist cultural domination, concluding that the process of relocation of ideas often inspires creativity and new expressions

(Bhabha 1994). In this process, a new hybrid identity arises that challenges the validity of any essentialist cultural identity.

For others, globalisation as hybridisation runs counter to models which view globalisation as a process of homogenising, modernising and ultimately Westernising (Pieterse 2004; Kraidy 2005). Cultures interact over time, mediated by technology, migration, and institutional and economic forms. Very often through this process, cultural products hybridise, with local and imported cultural elements blending to create new forms of culture (Straubhaar 2007).

In an Arab context, the phenomenon of media globalisation has accelerated localisation and cultural hybridisation since it enables vast numbers of local producers to encounter media content originally produced outside their immediate communities, and then to produce a new, locally or regionally relevant version of it. The process of the creation of Arab animations shares a number of similarities with cinematic and televised formats such as films, series, etc. Therefore, this book regards Arab animated cartoons as hybrid media forms, mainly following the arguments put forward by Kraidy and Pieterse. As cultural adaptations of a global format, Arab animations are hybrid media texts between the global and the local, or the global and the regional. As such, they usually transform foreign forms, ideas and topics to meet local cultural sensibilities.

The hybridity of Arab animation is not restricted to textual hybridity alone; genres and formats are cultural categories that surpass the boundaries of media texts and operate within industry, audience and cultural practices as well (Mittell 2001b). Hybrid media forms such as Arab animation are usually contemporary and economic as they reflect the strength of local production in terms of human and infrastructural background, and even economic status. Therefore, to understand media texts and production, we need to set them 'in their societal environment and disentangle various links, processes, and effects between communication practices and social, political, and economic forces' (Kraidy 2005: 7).

The majority of Arab animated cartoons provide a certain number of 'authentic' elements both in narrative and visual representation, which makes audiences accept and view the films as local, even if they carry global elements. The claim of textual authenticity can be a reference to local environment, local rhetoric, local cultural values and familiar stories based on collective memory. These local markers are intended to make local audiences accept the animations as their own. As Colin Hoskins and Rolf Mirus (1988) observe, the localisation of any format or content happens by two simultaneous movements: deleting foreign cultural markers that cause 'cultural discount', and adding local elements that give the programme a domestic identity. Therefore, to understand the hybridity of particular Arab animated cartoons, we need to examine the markers that were deleted or added by producers when creating homegrown animated cartoons.

Animation production in the Arab world has been largely led by the desire to create culturally relevant products and thus the 'Arabness' of most homegrown Arab content goes beyond the use of the Arabic language and includes other cultural references both in the narrative and on the visual level. Therefore, Arab animations are temporal reflections of local, national, and regional adaptation and appropriation of global patterns. The result can be a strongly localised adaptation of what is considered current or modern on the global level. Local and cultural elements often fuse into a global format that results in the creation of new genres and formats. In other cases, the result of interaction might be less than hybridisation, with local elements only slightly blending into foreign formats. Also, in some rare instances, interaction goes beyond hybridisation, with local cultures essentially extinguished.

Animation as Text – Visual Styles, Language and Identity

For producers, animation offers resources for designing 'reality', a space that projects images that may work towards articulating cultural identities, often structured around notions of 'self' and 'other' (Yoshida 2008: 15). Bill Nichols explains how ideologies disseminated through film shape the viewers as subjects. Introducing the concept of 'self-as-subject', Nichols argues that the fabrication of visual representations 'subjects' us to a specific way of seeing, by masking the conditions that underlie the surface appearance. The sense of 'self-as-subject', therefore, is often shaped by the visual codes that the dominant discourse provides, and compels viewers to seek positive identification with, or antagonistic opposition to, the other (Nichols 1981: 29–32). From a Western aspect, fluctuation of identities resonates particularly with animation, which has always embraced fluidity and the 'flux' of bodies, selves and worlds (Batkin 2017: 117).

Meanwhile, in the conservative Arab context – similarly to films and television series – animation as a format and cultural text provides primarily an imaginary space for reproducing and, also, for creating elements of national/regional/Islamic culture. Arab animated cartoons display characteristics defined by a complex set of markers that refer to existing or imagined identities, proposed by the producers. These markers have the potential to make audiences feel cultural proximity to the text, to accept it as their 'own' and to decode the encoded messages as intended by the author. These characteristics are largely defined by the production background and by potential markets. Given that the identities of individuals and societies are multi-layered and hybrid, media texts in general, and animated cartoons in particular, are also multi-layered and hybrid.

Arab Animation will investigate the identity of the text as such, as well as the identities promoted by animated cartoons from three interconnected aspects: the visual, the linguistic and the narrative. The decision to highlight these aspects is based on my interviews with authors, all of whom named the visual and the narrative as the two main aspects of expressing identity. I decided to include language as a third indicator of identity in line with the extensive academic literature on the role and symbolic value of Arabic in political rhetoric, public discourses, everyday life and the media.

On the visual level, considering my general observations from interviews with authors, I focus on the characters, analysing their appearance, colours and clothes as well as their environment.

Wells observed that large numbers of animation studios around the globe 'have insisted upon using their own indigenous fine art traditions, mythologies and cultural imperatives in order to differentiate their own work from what may be regarded as a diluted form of American artistic and cultural imperialism' (Wells 2002: 2)

Arab animation differs slightly from other animations. While figurative illustrations in traditional Chinese, Japanese, Indian and Russian visual arts have greatly influenced the styles of modern animation productions, figurative illustrations in traditional Arab visual arts are rare.[8] While many illustrated medieval Arab books do contain figurative scenes, the Arab illustrative arts are primarily dominated by non-figurative and calligraphic images (Contadini 2007). Arab animation producers have thus found it rather challenging to develop styles rooted in their own artistic traditions.

Wells notes that '[b]eyond fine art and socio-historical sources, one of the key aspects of visualisation may be the previously established graphic mode created by a particular studio' (2002: 18). For Wells, this is an aspect associated with the authorial signature of a major animation studio, which became a 'brand'. Given the fact that the Arab animated cartoon is not a homegrown format, but largely an adaptation, localisation and glocalisation of a foreign one, the visual styles of Western and Japanese animations were much more inspirational for Arab animators and producers than traditional Arab or Islamic visual arts. Since the style of Walt Disney had both a direct and indirect influence on Arab producers and animators, the majority of Arab animations recall Disney's 'orthodox hyper-realist styling, informed by close engagement with authentic, anatomically viable movement forms' (Wells 2002: 4).

Thanks to its enduring popularity, good reputation and visual quality, Walt Disney still constitutes a point of reference for many Arab authors. For those working in 3D animations, Pixar is a similar point of reference.

Since animated characters have no physical bodies, cartoons are able to achieve 'presence' though the implied body (Crafton 2012: 16). In creating characters, animation has more technical opportunities and fewer creative obstacles than cinema. Therefore, as Artz (2002; 2004) observed, Disney animation often thrives on the symbolic personification of values through its use of visual metaphors. Disney heroes, like Simba, the Sultan, Ariel, Pocahontas and others, exhibit youthful traits such as big eyes and round cheeks; they are drawn in curves, smooth, round, soft, bright and with European features (Lawrence 1986: 67). Villains like Scar, Jafar, the Hun, Ratcliffe and Ursula, however, are continually fashioned to be 'ugly' and are drawn with sharp angles, oversized and often in dark colours. In this regard, Arab animation often follows Disney's representation techniques (McGuire 2017).

Still, it would be nearly impossible to define an 'Arab animation style' in terms of visual layout and presentation. The same holds true when comparing the productions of individuals or companies coming from the same country. Due to different artistic backgrounds, inspirations and abilities, Arab authors rarely share a common visual style, even if they originate from the same country. While some similarities and influences can be occasionally observed, their frequency and consistency is insufficient for drawing general conclusions in this regard. Of course, in some cases, the adapted Western or Asian styles could create visual hybrids, when producers intend to revive traditional Arab and Islamic visual elements in their works.

Even though Arab animated cartoons have no common visual styles, visual content –which often reinforces the narrative – still remains a significant indicator of identity. Local, geolinguistic, Islamic and global identities can be largely defined by including or excluding particular visual elements like buildings, cityscapes, indoor and outdoor locations, and natural landscapes as well as characters, including their physiognomy and dress. However, it must again be stressed that visual markers of 'Arabness' alone do not make an animation 'Arab', as shown by Disney's *Aladdin*.

When it comes to language, I do not merely analyse content. Drawing on Niloofar Haeri and Yasir Suleiman's work, I view language as having a symbolic role. In this regard I examine what the choice of standard Arabic or dialects tells us about the identity of the text.

What is usually referred to as the 'Arab world' is a geolinguistic region where – besides culture and religion – common language is a primary unifier among those living in distant geographic locations. The usage of Arabic is characterised by diglossia: standard Arabic constitutes the formal or 'high' variety, while dialects represent the informal, or less formal, or 'low' variety (Suleiman 2003: 15).

In Arabic discourses, Classical Arabic is referred to as *al-lugha al-ʿarabiyya al-fusha* (the eloquent Arabic language) or *fusha* for short. Haeri notes that even though *fusha* cannot be labelled as a mother tongue as it is not spoken at home, it is 'the language of Islam, of the state, and of pan-Arab nationalism, and it is explicitly foregrounded as a central marker of "Arab" identity' (Haeri 2000: 61–87). Colloquial Arabic is referred to as *al-ʿammiyya* (the common) and is also the mother tongue of the vast majority of Arabic speakers. While *fusha* is widely understood, *ʿammiyya* has many local forms. It can be divided into regional language groups (Khaliji or Gulfi, Mesopotamian, Levantine, Egyptian and Maghrebi) that can be further subdivided into smaller groups (Egyptian, Lebanese, Syrian, Iraqi, etc.). These dialects do not always coincide with the borders of the modern state after which they are named. Further, on the level of individual states, a number of local dialects co-exist. Spoken language is a main indicator of the possible identity of its speakers: it shows whether they come from the city or from the rural areas of a particular country, and it often carries connotations of their level of education. In many Arab countries, differences in dialect usually reveal whether the speaker is of Bedouin origin or Arabic.

Thus, language plays a crucial role in the construction of identities (De Swaan 1991). As a driver of the politics of inclusion and exclusion, language also remains a pillar of cultural identity in an increasingly globalised world (Anderson 1991). In the Arab world, language plays a central role in the formation of nationalisms and national identities (Suleiman 1994; al-Khalidi et al. 2003). Regarding the formation of different notions of Arab nationalisms in the twentieth century, Suleiman points out that language is the 'most important of all systems of functional and symbolic expression' in the study of nationalism (Suleiman 2001: 3).

Language also plays a crucial role in the dissemination of identities through media: 'broadcast language could be understood as a way in which nations are daily reproduced'; television, therefore, 'normalizes the ties between language and nations'. Likewise, the media 'contributes to the perpetuation of national cultures by spreading a vernacular and reinforcing linguistic bonds among populations' (Waisbord 2004: 359).

Media productions are then instrumental in identity construction, given that they are often used by producers to promote cultural, political and religious identities in everyday life. In the case of Arab cinematic and media productions, language is a similarly vital factor in reproducing social and political struggles, and the choice of language in Arab media productions has a symbolic value. As cultural and media productions, animated cartoons using national languages or dialects thus provide – whether intentionally or not – an arena for the representation of local and regional struggles over identity, while productions using *fusha* largely refer to identities broader than the national.

When exploring the links between language and animation, the characteristics of the 'Arab world' should be taken into consideration. In the last decades, there has been a marked tendency for television flows to articulate around 'geo-linguistic markets' (Sinclair et al. 1996). Similarly, in the case of the Arab world, language in the media delineates cultural boundaries that articulate flows of television programming. As Sakr observed with regard to the Arab world, '[l]anguage differences from one country to the next increase the "cultural discount" to which media flows across borders are already subject because of variations in taste and customs. Media flows are thus facilitated where language is shared' (Sakr 2007a: 109).

Traditionally, Egyptian film and television industries have benefited from this wider Arab market. The proliferation and popularity of Egyptian cinematic productions since the mid-twentieth century made the Egyptian dialect a widely understood lingua franca in the Arab world. The spread of Egyptian colloquial Arabic also reflected Egypt's unique role in trans-Arab cultural as well as in political discourse (Haeri 2003).

Since the emergence of Gulf-based pan-Arab television channels in the 1990s, MSA has become widespread. This new language of transnational broadcasting and television production is based on Classical Arabic, with a simplified grammar system and the inclusion of contemporary terms. Rinnawi observed that MSA has become perhaps the most widely understood language in the Arab world, as it is the written language taught throughout school systems (Rinnawi 2006: 22–3). Because both 'Classical Arabic' and 'MSA' are concepts largely used in Western discourses, I prefer to use *fusha* when referring to the language of productions, in order to highlight the identities promoted by Arab authors.

When analysing productions dubbed in dialects, my approach is more practical. Rather than designating the dialects by their original Arab name such as *Masri* (Egyptian), *Shami* (Syrian), *Khaleeji* (Gulf Arabic) and so on, I label them by reference to the particular country as a political entity whose identity is advocated in the text. This choice is led by the fact that Arabic definitions of dialect do not always overlap with the borders of contemporary countries. Speech can also provide indications of the age, ethnicity, gender identity, region of origin and socio-economic status of the characters in animated cartoons (Dobrow and Gidney 1998). Presenting characters that speak a dialect other than the local one can also serve as a marker of otherness. The choice between *fusha* and a local dialect can often be understood as a statement made by the author with reference to national versus regional identities.

Therefore, as we will see, Arab animated films and series generally use local dialects when their authors intend to target local (national) audiences and create a sense of belonging and unity.

Kraidy has pointed out that the creation of MSA as a pan-Arab lingua franca by influential Arab satellite channels led to 'the emergence of a pan-Arab imagined community with converging concerns and a sense of regional belonging' (Kraidy 2002). Notwithstanding the consolidation of MSA as a lingua franca, the linkages between language and nation are still significant to Arab media owners and producers. As many Arab governments still view the media as a primary tool for nation-building, using local dialects is increasingly widespread in local television productions. The tendency of a return to local dialects can be observed in the case of national animation production. The use of local dialects by animation authors can also be understood as a resistance to what Rinnawi defined as the 'McArabism' offered by pan-Arab satellite channels such as Al Jazeera.

Needless to say, the choice of local accents can pose a barrier in the trade of animations to other Arab markets as audiences are not used to each other's accents. For this reason, Maghrebi cultural and media productions are barely purchased in the eastern Arab world, and productions dubbed in a particular Gulf dialect are often exclusively distributed on local television channels.

Generally, the cross-border flow of animations dubbed in *fusha* is significantly more common than that of those using local dialects. Animated cartoons using *fusha* essentially target general Arab audiences since they create a sense of neutrality and cultural proximity compared to Western animated cartoons, and are therefore more attractive to other national markets.

In addition to market considerations, the use of *fusha* is also often related to identity issues. In the case of animated cartoons produced in Baathist Iraq and Syria, I will explore whether *fusha* could be viewed as a vehicle for stressing a pan-Arab identity, and whether such considerations apply in the case of animations produced by pan-Arab children's television channels such as Al Jazeera Children's Channel (JCC) and MBC3. I will also investigate the role of language in the case of films and series that stress Islamic identities. As a language stemming directly from the Qur'an and as the official language of Arab Islamic discourse, *fusha* can also serve as a symbol for advocating Islamic identity as well as a proof of the authenticity of the texts. Similarly, by using *fusha*, the language of Arab classrooms, educative animations can reinforce the authority and intended educational goal of the content.

Structure of the Work

This book consists of six main chapters, with a narrative that is built around several case studies. Chapters 2 to 6 examine how Arab animated cartoons mediate and negotiate different notions of identities: the 'national', the 'critical national', the 'pan-Arab', the 'Islamic' and the 'revolutionary'. Each chapter is made up of sub-chapters which cover a certain country or particular producers and explore how animation production and distribution operate in the media and political environment of individual Arab countries, or, in some cases, in transnational media spaces.

Chapter 2 describes how notions of 'national' identities are mediated in Arab animated cartoons. Here, the focus is on animation production of countries whose regimes tend to focus on domestic issues and therefore maintain media and media industries that principally address a 'national' audience: Egypt, Jordan, UAE (Dubai), the Palestinian Territories and Tunisia. After providing an overview of the historical and cultural context, I use case studies to show how animated cartoons are integrated into the cultural discourses and production hierarchies of their times.

Chapter 3 investigates how dominant notions of national identities are negotiated in sitcom animations, presented on television channels with relatively weak links to local and political hierarchies. Looking at the most prominent cartoons produced in different Arab countries, I show how productions are integrated into local media systems and how they express criticism of social and, occasionally, political issues, articulating a critical approach to national identities.

In Chapter 4, I explore the mediations of regional/pan-Arab identities. The analysis starts with the productions of countries with declared pan-Arab agendas, specifically Saddam Hussein's Iraq (1979–2003) and Syria after the 1990s. While the Iraqi feature-length project *Al- 'Amirah wal-Nahr* (The Princess and the River, 1982) was both a local attempt at nation-building as well as a war propaganda film, Syrian feature-length animations and films such as *Al-Jarrah* (The Jug, 2001), *Khait al-Hayat* (Yarn of Life, 2007) and *Tuyur al-Yasmeen* (The Jasmine Birds, 2009) often reflect Baathist

Pan-Arabist visions, as a result of the co-operation of the public and private sectors in production processes. The analysis continues with transnational organisations. First, it follows the establishment and subsequent rise of the Gulf Cooperation Council's (GCC) Joint Programme Production Institution (JPPI) in the late 1970s to become a prominent producer of animated cartoons. The closing sections of the chapter investigate the role played by pan-Arab satellite channels such as JCC and Saudi MBC3 in the expanding animation production, and how these channels advocate a new breed of 'pan-Arabism' via particular productions.

Chapter 5 focuses on Arab animations mediating Islamic identities. The first sub-chapter analyses self-defined 'Islamic animations' created mainly by producers from the Gulf, such as *Mohammad al-Fatih* (1995) and *Tareq ibn Ziyad* (1999), produced by Ella, a Saudi-owned production company. The second sub-chapter explores Egyptian animated cartoons revolving around Islamic topics. After investigating the religious policies of the Egyptian state and the nature of the advocated Islamic identities in the *Qisas al-Qur'an* (Stories from the Qur'an, 2011–) series, the chapter concludes with *The 99* (2011), a Kuwaiti-American superhero series with the declared goal of addressing children of the Muslim Diasporas. I suggest that the production articulates a hybrid Islamic identity.

Chapter 6 shows how cheap means of animation and increasingly easy access to the internet from around 2008 onwards enabled young creative individuals to bypass traditional hierarchies of media production and distribution. Through the case studies of the Jordanian *Kharabeesh* and producers from Tunisia, Egypt and Syria, I show how various notions of revolutionary identities were mediated in short, edgy animations distributed online, and how they led to the 'Arab animation spring'.

Conclusion

One of the ambitions of *Arab Animation* is to promote an understanding of eighty years of animation production in the Arab world. To do so, this book blends different approaches such as political studies, cultural studies and textual analysis to provide an insight into how this genre is used in specific cultural and political contexts.

This research also hopes to add a non-Western perspective to the study of identity issues. In this respect, it analyses how 'national', 'alternative national', 'pan-Arab', 'Islamic' and 'revolutionary' Arab identities are advocated in both direct and allusive ways in Arab animated cartoons visually and through language and narrative, and ponders the potential of Arab animation to expand its viewership around the globe.

Notes

1. On Walt Disney and politics, see Henry A. Giroux and Grace Pollock (2010) *The Mouse that Roared: Disney and the End of Innocence*. Plymouth: Rowman & Littlefield. See also Steven Watts (1995) 'Walt Disney: Art and Politics in the American Century', *The Journal of American History* 82.1, pp. 84–110.
2. Wells lists eleven so-called 'textual' and sixteen 'extra-textual' definitions to describe the author in animation production. When put into practice, definitions marked as 'textual' overlap with the functions of the director, concept artists and animators, while definitions marked as 'extra-textual' describe the functions of the producer.
3. The single exception is the Egyptian *Mish Mish Effendi*, created by the Frenkel brothers. Despite the fact that the Frenkels were Russian-Jewish immigrants who neither claimed 'Arabness' nor obtained Egyptian citizenship, their activity is emblematic of the characteristic traits of Egyptian cinema industries of the early twentieth century.
4. Personal interview with Sulafa Hijazi (Copenhagen, 18 June 2014) and Mustafa al-Faramawi (Cairo, 6 September 2012).
5. *UFO Robo Grendizer* is a Japanese anime of the Mecha subgenre, written by Go Nagai, which originally ran from 1975 to 1977 on Japanese television.
6. *Captain Majid* was distributed by Saudi al-Sharika al-'aalamiyya lil-I'lam wal-Tawzi'. The first series was dubbed by Studio al-Sharq al-Adna lil-Intag al-Fanniyy (Saudi Arabia) and the second series by al-Zahra (Syria).
7. This was a recurring claim made by Arab animation authors I interviewed.
8. The majority of figurative illustrations in Islamic art can be found in cultures which have a long tradition in illustration, such as Turkey, India and Persia. On the other hand, classical Arab storytelling focuses on oral traditions rather than illustrations. See John Renard (1999) *Islam and the Heroic Image: Themes in Literature and the Visual Arts*. Macon, GA: Mercer University Press.

2

Mediating National Identities in Arab Animation

The efforts of nation-building that followed the end of colonialism and the formation of Arab states in the twentieth century principally called for the creation of a common identity that would unite different population groups forced to live together within the new 'national' borders. The formulation of the concept of 'nation' was unique in each country, varying according to local circumstances, social landscape, historical traditions and also the priorities of the elites.

Nations are linked to narratives. In other words, national identities are created, sustained and challenged in the imagination of peoples through narratives which validate particular national myths and symbols, constructing a common popular culture memory that defines the identity of a group of people (Bhabha 1990: 1–8). Narrated national identities embody national ideals, symbols and myths, making nationality itself a particular 'cultural artifact' (Anderson 1991: 4). In this respect, media productions, including animated cartoons, often serve as a means for 'national' elites to create and maintain the 'imagined communities' sharing common identities (Bennington 1990: 121–37).

Speaking about Egypt, Lila Abu-Lughod asserts that television is one of the essential institutions in creating national culture due to the role it plays in 'producing nations and national feelings and in shaping national imaginaries' (Abu-Lughod 2005: 8). Given the prominent role of television across the entire Arab world, this contention is also valid for other countries. The vast majority of animated cartoons presented on television channels linked to governments express ideas, whether directly or indirectly, about national identities. In addition, they often deal with political issues that serve as the cornerstones of the legitimacy of particular regimes.

Animated cartoon production in different Arab countries fits into the broader strategies of mediating local (national) identities, as power operates locally through media production to reproduce social hierarchies and inequalities at the level of daily interactions (Mayer 2009: 15). Productions presented in Arab cinema and television, especially if they use government funds, largely reproduce the existing social and political struggles in their imagery, spectacles and narratives.

Egypt

The Beginnings of Egyptian Animation in the 1930s

Egypt was the only Arab country that had developed a national film industry before it gained independence. From the early twentieth century, Egypt acted as the geographical centre of Arab cinema production. By 1908, Cairo and Alexandria already had five cinemas, screening mainly subtitled foreign films. A year later, the production of local news films started. As Viola Shafik notes, the Egyptian film industry remained relatively undisturbed by colonial authorities and the flourishing cultural life of multicultural Alexandria also attracted a large number of foreign professionals (Shafik 2007b: 10–14).

The heyday of Egyptian cinema began with the production of sound movies. Smaller studios produced over forty films between 1930 and 1936. The financial opportunities offered by cinema were quickly discovered by nationalist-oriented entrepreneurs. In 1925, industrialist Tal'at Harb established the Misr Company for Cinema and Performance (*Sharikat Misr lil-Sinema wal-Tamtheel*), to produce commercials and information spots. In 1934–5, Banque Misr, under the management of Harb, established Studio Misr, a studio equipped with modern technology which employed European specialists and also sent Egyptian professionals on scholarships to Europe. By 1948, six more large studios were established, and by the start of World War

II, cinema had become the second most profitable industrial sector after the textile industry (Shafik 2007b: 12–14).

The eighty-year history of Arab animation starts with the Frenkel brothers.[1] After fleeing the city of Jaffa, the Russian-Jewish family consisting of Betzalel, Gnissa and their six children (three brothers and three sisters) settled down in Alexandria, which offered a livelihood for newcomers of the time, and lived there until Betzalel's death. Being foreign-born Jews, the Frenkels had little chance of becoming Egyptian citizens (Beinin 1998: 38).

The three brothers, David (1914–94), Hershel (1905–74) and Salomon (1912–2001), moved to Cairo in 1935, where they started a successful furniture business. Like many young people of their age, the Frenkel brothers were greatly attracted to cinema. The first imported American animated cartoons premiered in Egyptian cinemas in 1930. Disney's *Mickey Mouse* was followed by *Felix the Cat* a few years later; both were a huge success. The Frenkel brothers were enchanted by American cartoons and wanted to create something similar, so they started their own animation business called Frenkel Pictures.

As Frenkel Pictures did not receive any outside funding, the brothers were forced to make sketches and drawings of their planned animations after finishing their work for the day. Lacking the opportunity to learn from foreign professionals, the Frenkels reinvented the frame-by-frame technique and used Disney as their main inspiration. The traditional, hand-drawn celluloid technology used by the Frenkels was rather time-consuming, as one minute of animation required 1,500 sketches. From 1,600 metres of film they created a four-minute animation on the adventures of Marco Monkey. It was by no means a localised production, but a copy of the Disney genre, using characters and backgrounds similar to those of American animated cartoons.

The rise of nationalist sentiments in Egypt during the 1920s and 1930s was also reflected in the stories and plots of the period's Egyptian films (Shafik 2007: 17–18). Although people involved in the cinema industry came from the most diverse backgrounds, the preferences of local audiences led to a tendency to localise the subject matter. Therefore, even directors from a foreign background chose to produce films with narratives rooted in local culture and history in order to reach wider audiences. This tendency for localisation affected the reception of *Marco Monkey* rather negatively.

Figure 2.1 *Marco Monkey*: the first Egyptian animation, still regarded as foreign by critics. 1935 © Didier Frenkel.

Although *La Bourse égyptienne* hailed *Marco Monkey* in a front-page article as 'Mickey Mouse's Egyptian brother' (1935), *Al-Ahram*, Egypt's most prestigious newspaper, criticised the awkwardness of the motion and the poor voice quality, mocking the creators as incompetent.[2] A later article in *Al-Ahram* was even more scathing in its criticism, advising the Frenkels to focus more on local Egyptian culture and to at least attempt to create a local cartoon character.[3] Realising both their technical shortcomings and the demands of the local market, the Frenkels decided to create characters and stories localised to an Egyptian environment.

The Birth of Mish Mish Effendi, *the 'Egyptian Mickey Mouse'*

The Frenkels approached the various studios of the cinema industry, seeking technical and financial support, but time and again, they were turned away. One anecdote – whose accuracy cannot be verified – reveals that when asked for financial support, one producer answered, '*Mafish fa'ida*', literally meaning 'There's no benefit'. After the brothers once again tried to persuade him, the producer flatly refused, answering, '*Bukra fil-mishmish*', which meant 'in the future', i.e. 'when pigs fly'. This incident is said to have been the main inspiration for the Frenkels' new character, whom they named Mish Mish Effendi.[4] As *mishmish* means 'apricot' in *fusha* Arabic, it also gave the title character a funny edge. This anecdote is, however, contradicted by the fact that Mish Mish was a comic character David Frenkel had painted in *Al-Barquqa* magazine years earlier.

The first four-minute episode of *Mish Mish Effendi* debuted in Cairo on 8 February 1936 (*La Bourse égyptienne* 1936). The episode entitled *Mafish Fa'ida* (It's No Use), most probably a reference to the producer's refusal, was shown before a film called *Nashid al-Amal* (The Song of Hope).[5] From the very beginning, *Mish Mish Effendi* was presented as a production with a strong Egyptian identity, for example in its self-description as a '*Film Mutaharrik Misriyy*' (Egyptian animated film) in the title sequence. A number of episodes also showed the Egyptian flag beside the portrait of Mish Mish in the titles. The narrative takes place in Egyptian locations, with tall buildings, and urban and rural scenes. Similarly to other Egyptian productions, the characters used the Egyptian dialect. The success of the first episode inspired the Frenkels to produce eight more *Mish Mish Effendi* adventures, the final one appearing in 1950. *Mafish Fa'ida* was produced entirely by the three Frenkel brothers.

The Frenkels' limited experience meant that their cartoon visuals suffered from various inadequacies, which can be observed in all episodes. One example is the style in which the character of Mish Mish Effendi was drawn. In some scenes, he is portrayed like a caricature, with movements reminiscent of Mickey Mouse, while other scenes are dominated by a more realistic style. The transformation from one style to another was often random, but in some cases, the intention to convey an extra message cannot be ruled out. The episode *Bil-Hana wal-Shifa'* (Bon Appetit), made in 1946, revolves around Mish Mish's infatuation with a celebrated actress. During the episode, Mish Mish is consistently drawn in a caricature style, but the actress in a realistic style. In the end, Mish Mish wins the actress's heart and the style in which he is drawn changes to a realistic one. I assume that such a 'transformation' was not merely done for aesthetic reasons, but that the Frenkels synchronised the visual representations of the actress and Mish Mish, so they could form a matching couple.

Mish Mish Effendi can largely be considered as a hybrid between American cultural forms and Egyptian culture. Disney's influence is present in the style of the characters, as the eyes, round body shapes and gloved hands, frame rates and even Mish Mish Effendi's movements all recall Mickey Mouse. The Frenkels also adopted Disney's hyper-realist styling, characterised by a close engagement with authentic, anatomically viable movement forms. The title sequence of the cartoons, showing the head of Mish Mish Effendi surrounded by stars, clearly recalls the similar portrayal of Mickey Mouse at the beginning of Disney animations. The influence of *Felix the Cat* is also visible, as the unrealistic movements of the characters were intended to be a source of amusement, and the rules of physics were often ignored. The visual layout of *Mish Mish Effendi* also, however, seems to reference al-Misri Effendi, a cartoon character appearing in a number of Egyptian magazines during the 1930s and 1940s, who represented the average Egyptian as 'a concept of national identity symbolized by the very fact of his being an effendi' (Ryzova 2005: 131–3). Similarly to al-Misri Effendi, Mish Mish Effendi wore a European suit and tie together with an Ottoman-style fez on his head, indicating that the character was both modern and Egyptian. The modernism is also highlighted by the protagonist's love interest, Bahiyya, an Egyptian adaptation of Betty Boop.[6] As with contemporary American animations, the episodes also included comical animal characters such as Mish Mish's donkey, whose visual style also resembles Disney animations.

Mish Mish Effendi was accompanied in the episodes by his friend Fayyoumi, presented as a large comic character of Nubian origin. Fayyoumi's portrayal as a black character distinctly recalls Disney's racist representations of African-Americans in the 1930s, as well as the character of Othman the Nubian, developed by stage and film comedian ʿAli al-Kassar (Tam 2020).

Besides Fayyoumi, various episodes of *Mish Mish Effendi* feature several other African characters, presented as simple people, mainly in the roles of musicians and servants. In this respect, *Mish Mish Effendi* recalls not only American cartoons, but also contemporary Egyptian cinema. As Shafik notes, Nubians in Egyptian cinematic traditions prior to 1952 were largely

Figure 2.2 *Mish Mish Effendi*: the 'Egyptian Mickey Mouse'. 1940 © Didier Frenkel.

represented as honest, but naive and funny characters, often cast in the role of servants (Shafik 2007b: 73, 85).

In May 1936 Mussolini invaded Ethiopia, causing fear among the Egyptian elite. World War II was also seen by King Farouk (r. 1936–52) as an opportunity to loosen British rule. Realising the immense popularity of animated cartoons, two years after the debut of the first episode of *Mish Mish Effendi*, the Ministry of War ordered a propagandistic episode from the Frenkels in order to support the loan requested by the Egyptian government for the army. The result was a fifteen-minute film, *al-Difaʿ al-Wataniyy* (National Defence), released in 1938.

The opening scene shows contemporary Giza, with its traditional one-storey houses, palm trees and the three pyramids. Riding a cart pulled by his donkey, Mish Mish Effendi is heading to his girlfriend's house to serenade her with traditional love songs. The following scene is set at a local bar where female dancers perform a belly dance. The American cartoon tradition of bringing inanimate objects to life finds its counterpart in the dancing hookahs.

The episode makes references not merely to local, but also to global, popular culture, as the animators included the characters of Warner Bros.' *Bosko and Buddy* as well as using animated versions of contemporary Hollywood stars such as Laurel and Hardy, Eddie Cantor and Charlie Chaplin, all dressed in local Egyptian garb.[7]

When Mish Mish Effendi arrives at the bar the music stops, and a news programme comes on the radio informing the clients in the bar about the serious events of the war. Mish Mish Effendi jumps on a table chanting patriotic slogans, receiving applause from the audience. The scene then changes to an Egyptian street with a band marching and singing a patriotic song. The musicians are followed by a cart and an ancient Egyptian coffin, a reference to the glorious past and national identity, with donations for the war being collected.

The second part of the film shows Mish Mish Effendi riding to war on his donkey, and then fighting side by side with the Allies. He is injured and taken to hospital, where a doctor, portrayed as a crazy genius, heals the wounded arriving on a conveyor belt by replacing their lost limbs and, occasionally, even their head with new ones from a closet, and offering them a magic potion from a teapot, in a possible reference to James Whale's *Frankenstein* (1931). The next scene shows the soldiers rejoicing and returning to the front. Mish Mish Effendi also returns to the front with a home-made radio-like contraption that emits thunderbolts, enabling him to blow up hostile planes, tanks and cannons, and so forcing the enemy to surrender. After the victory, Mish Mish Effendi becomes a celebrated hero. The episode ends with he and Bahiyya romantically gazing at the cityscape of Cairo.

Later presentations of the character of Mish Mish Effendi show fundamental differences to the one portrayed in the propaganda episode commissioned by the Ministry of War. In the 1946 episode *Bil-Hana wal-Shifa'* (With Contentment and Healing), he is presented as a broken man, pursued by his creditor, and in *Mish Mish al-Shatir* (Mish Mish the Clever), made in 1949, he is portrayed as a pitiful comic character, an object of ridicule for being pursued by policemen, dumped by Bahiyya and beaten up by her lover, who happens to be a boxer. With *Bil-Hana wal-Shifa'* the Frenkels basically created an animated Egyptian comedy by building on tropes of social inequality, failed love affairs and experiences of the lower-middle classes.

After releasing the first episode of *Mish Mish Effendi*, the Frenkels produced one animation film every year. In 1937, the Ministry of Agriculture commissioned the Frenkels to produce a four-minute educational animation to encourage peasants to stamp out cotton parasites. Between 1938 and 1948, the Frenkels also produced a number of animated commercials (spots of two to four minutes) for al-Nadi al-Malakiyy Lil-Sayyarat Bi-Misr (the Royal Automobile Club), and for Egyptian commercial products such as Sabun Sunlight (Sunlight soap), Vim al-Munazzaf (Vim scouring powder) and Saboun Ward al-Neel (Flower of the Nile soap).[8] As the Frenkels' prestige grew, they also lined up celebrated Egyptian cinema stars to lend their voices for the animated cartoons. Later episodes of *Mish Mish Effendi* featured the animated characters of famous stars such as Camilia, Sabah and other popular female performers. Using a rotoscoping technique, the Frenkels mixed animated shots with live actors, resulting in Mish-Mish Effendi dancing with the popular singers and belly dancers of his time. All in all, *Mish Mish Effendi* became an integral part of Egyptian popular culture and its Egyptian identity remains indisputed.

However, the political turmoil of the 1940s put an end to the thriving business. Violence against Jews started in the mid-1940s, and after the founding of Israel in 1948, the attacks became more frequent (Krämer 1982: 127). In less than a decade, 40 per cent of the 75,000 Jews living in Egypt left. Because of an amendment to the Egyptian Companies Law dated 29 July 1947, requiring that 40 per cent of a company's directors and 75 per cent of its employees be Egyptian nationals, the Frenkels' films were now stigmatised as foreign productions and their financial sources dried up (Shamir 1987: 33–67). As the situation worsened, the Frenkels decided to leave Egypt. In 1951, the three brothers and their families left for France and settled near Paris, never to return to Egypt. David created a studio in the basement of the new family home and continued to make animated commercials for Egypt, commissioned by the Lever Brothers. He did not give up the concept of *Mish Mish Effendi* however; he replaced the fez of the Egyptian character with a French beret and renamed him Mimiche, which sounded more authentic to French ears. These productions were no longer distributed in cinemas, but were sold as family TV shows. In 1964, David made *Le Rêve du beau Danube bleu* (The Dream of the Beautiful Blue Danube) which remained his single major production in Europe (Bendazzi 1995: 103). The Frenkels obtained French citizenship and spent the rest of their lives in their new European homeland. Though their influence on the native Egyptian animators of the 1930s and 1940s was never truly acknowledged, their position as the pioneers of Egyptian and Arab animation is undeniable.

The First Generation of Native Egyptian Animators in the 1930s and 1940s

Egypt was the first Arab country to institutionalise higher education in the arts. The Madrasa al-Funun al-Jamilah (School of Fine Arts) was established as early as 1908. After the Free Officers Coup on 23 July 1952, it was renamed Kulliyyat al-Funun al-Jameela (Faculty of Fine Arts). In 1975, the institution became part of Helwan University. The first generation of Egyptian animators was mainly made up of graduates of the High School of Fine Arts. Due to the lack of both equipment and teaching staff, these educational institutions did not have animation departments. However, they later proved to be important social spaces for young artists with an interest in animation.

After the release of *Marco Monkey*, interest in animation began to grow. With the financial support of a wealthy producer, ʿIssa ʿAbd al-Hamed, a group of graduates from the High School of Fine Arts – Robert Tyba, Antoine Salim, Ahmad Salim and Ahmad ʿAbdul-Fattah – opened a Cairo-based studio in 1937 (Eskandar and al-Mallah 1962: 85–6). In a bid to produce the first Arab animation, a few days after the Alexandria premiere of *al-Difaʿ al-Wataniyy*, Anton Salim presented his animation film *Haboub wa Haboubah* (Haboub and Haboubah) in Cairo. After Robert Tyba later left the group, the remaining members completed a four-minute work entitled *Hilm Fallah* (A Peasant's Dream) in 1938.

Antoine Selim decided to start his own project in 1939. His main works were stories centring on a character called Daqdaq, envisioned as an 'Egyptian Mickey Mouse', released in 1940 (Sulayman 1975: 88). Gabriel Nahhas, owner of Nahhas Film Studio, ensured that Selim's animations were presented in the Corsal Cinema of al-Jawhar.[9] Inspired by the success of the first film, Nahhas signed a contract with Selim to produce more episodes of *Daqdaq*. However, his dream of creating an animation show with an Egyptian identity did not come true, as Selim accepted Michel Talhimi's offer to work for al-Ahram Studio instead and to produce cinema tricks and title sequences for films.[10]

The Second Generation of Native Egyptian Animators in the 1950s and 1960s

The introduction of terrestrial television in 1960 offered new opportunities for Egyptian animators. In 1952, Gemal ʿAbdel Nasser and the Free Officers Movement overthrew King Farouk. President from 1956 to 1970, Nasser regarded television both as the main platform for reaching out to the people of Egypt and for advocating pan-Arab ideas, and as an important medium for nation-building (Abu-Lughod 2005: 10). During the early years of television, the Egyptian government installed hundreds of sets in rural and urban cultural centres (Boyd 1999: 52). To provide television access in rural areas, the government even subsidised television sets for cooperatives and village councils. Public information was kept under tight state control: both the representatives of the Egyptian Radio and Television Union, and the television sector chairmen were appointed by the Minister of Information. Television became a key institution for the production of national culture in Egypt (Abu-Lughod 2005: 8).

The animation scene of the Nasser era was obviously largely dominated by individual artists, who were integrated into Egyptian media and academic hierarchies. Production emerged slowly and local practices developed, dependent on decision-makers, small-scale advertising and credit sequences for local films. The majority of animated productions were commercial spots for local products. Despite their commercial nature, these animations simultaneously advocated local Egyptian identities through the use of Egyptian colloquial Arabic and references to the immediate environment. However, animators also had the chance to create their own short productions. Though Egyptian animators received some smaller commissions – mostly commercials and film title sequences – from other Arab countries, their main partner remained Egyptian Television and the cinema industry. The texts of the productions – similarly to cinematic ones – therefore mainly expressed national identity by using Egyptian dialect and locally relevant narratives, characters and scenes.

This period is characterised by a high number of unfinished projects such as those of Mustafa Hussein (b. 1935) and Mohamed Hakeem (b. 1929), both graduates of the Faculty of Fine Arts. In 1958, together with ʿAbd al-Haleem al-Bargheeneyy (b. 1930), they produced *Tete*, a short animated film with a local theme, about a child in Pharaonic Egypt called Tete who comes to life from a scene in a wall painting, climbing down a pillar to dance, play and have fun until he is ordered back into his place. After this project, the creators stopped working with animation, as it was proving a time-consuming and costly passion project (Bendazzi 1995: 391).

The most significant animators of the Nasser era were ʿAli Moheeb (1935–2010) and Sameeʿ Rafeʿ, both students of Jusuf Sayyeda at the Faculty of Fine Arts.[11] Together with his brother Hosaam al-Deen (1930–96), ʿAli Moheeb began creating his own works in 1960, producing commercials in the Iskandar Nadheer Studio.[12] Sameeʿ Rafeʿ also had foreign experience, as he had travelled to Poland for a four-month study trip in 1959 to work in animation studios, where he had met Norman McLaren.[13] After returning to Egypt, he produced title sequences and credits for feature films. The visual style of Moheeb's later works, defined by sharp lines and the abstract, caricature designs of characters, were influenced by animated films of the Soviet Union and socialist countries of Eastern Europe.

On 13 May 1961, the Moheeb brothers invited ʿAbdelkader Hatem, Minister of Education (1962–4), to their studio to show him their work. Very soon, the idea of establishing an animation section at Egyptian Television was born.[14]

ʿAli Moheeb gathered students from the Faculty of Fine Arts and invited them to work at Egyptian Television.[15] The team began working in the television studios under the supervision of Hosaam Moheeb. The animation department acquired modern equipment and, in order for its members to gain experience and grow, they welcomed foreign professionals.[16]

One of their most significant creations was a propaganda piece, *Nas Fawq wa Nas Taht* (People Above and People Below) that recounted the heroic struggle of the Egyptian people which led to the downfall of King Farouk, and the events of the so-called July Revolution. Although Moheeb produced a number of artistic projects – the most significant among them being *Al-Khatt al-Abyad* (The White Line) in 1962, which featured a twenty-five-minute animation combined with live action in the style of a musical – his best-known works were commercials and title sequences for television productions.[17]

Figure 2.3   'Ali Baba: a commercial by 'Ali Moheeb. 1964 © Moheeb Animation Studio.

The presidency of Anwar al-Sadat (1973–81) heralded a period of free market policy and capitalism, and pan-Arab causes were no longer priorities. The *infitah* (economic open-door policy) introduced in the 1970s reversed the former processes of nationalisation and state production. As restrictions on foreign imports were lifted, foreign goods entered the Egyptian markets (Abu-Lughod 2005: 135). The *infitah* policy was the primary cause of the end of the local animation industry. Animated commercials that accounted for the greater part of all animated production in the Nasser era took too long to produce to meet the demands of competing advertisers, who chose to commission live commercial spots for their products rather than investing in more expensive and slowly produced animations. Imported animation films and programmes – notably from the United States – appeared on Egyptian television in large numbers, which made local productions of lower quality uncompetitive. Although the animation department of Egyptian Television was not shut down, artists focused on small personal projects and on supplying the local film industry with title sequences and other animated content.

The Revival of Egyptian Animation in the 1990s

The revival of Egyptian animation was sparked by the introduction of CGI. Although the technology itself was introduced in the United States and Western Europe in the 1960s, it only reached the Arab world in the 1990s. Due to the high costs of computers at the time and the talent-intensive nature of CGI technology, the pioneers of CGI animation remained integrated in Egyptian academic and media hierarchies. One of the most prominent individuals in this field was Mona Abu al-Nasr (1952–2003),[18] a student of 'Ali Moheeb who had graduated from the Faculty of Fine Arts at Helwan University in 1975. She received her PhD in 1988 in the United States, and produced her first animated work there. *Al-Muntaser* (The Survival), a ten-minute film about the universal message of peace, won the Silver Plaque at the Chicago International Cinema Festival in 1989. As al-Nasr's personal favourites were *Tom and Jerry* and other Disney cartoons, the imagery in her later works was heavily influenced by American animations.

After returning to Egypt in 1988, al-Nasr taught at Helwan University and decided to establish her own company, Cairo Cartoon. The enterprise was largely funded by Radio and Television Union, and also received support from al-Nasr's husband, a wealthy construction entrepreneur.[19] After producing a number of animated commercials, she started work on her first animated series. In 1989, she produced *Kanee wa Manee* (Kani and Mani), a children's programme combining live and animated spots that ran for three seasons. Although the stories avoided engagement with political and religious affairs, parts of the stories were visually localised to Egyptian and Arab environments. In 1996, al-Nasr released *Hekayat Sindubad al-Bahreyy* (Stories of Sindbad the Seaman), a mix of animation and live content. The plot featured a traditional storyteller, played by the popular TV announcer Sameya al-Tarbee, telling stories from *The Arabian Nights* for a group of children gathered around her. While the frame was recorded with real actors, the stories were animated. Beginning in 1993, Cairo Cartoon also produced short animations for the newly established ART children's channel.

Bakkar, *an Icon of Egyptian Identity*

The birth of Egypt's best-known animation hero came about as an attempt to preserve Egypt's leading role in Arab media and to extend its influence to children's television. In 1993, ART, owned by Saudi businessman Sheikh Salih Kamel, became the first television network to launch a channel targeting a children's audience. Egyptian authorities, proud of their country's long tradition in Arab media, were wary of seeing non-Egyptian players dominate Arab children's media. Concerns over the decline of Egyptian cultural influence increased the willingness of the Egyptian media authorities to support local productions aimed at children. Thus, when in 1995 Mona Abu al-Nasr came up with the concept of creating an Egyptian animation hero, the idea was readily accepted by Egyptian Television. Very soon, the character of *Bakkar*, the Nubian boy, was born.[20] Preparations for the first season took three years. In addition to the technical aspects, the producers also undertook substantive cultural research. To ensure the authenticity of the text, members of the Cairo Cartoon crew travelled to Nubia to study the environment and

Figure 2.4 *Bakkar*: a Nubian boy and a symbol of Egyptian identity. 1998 © Cairo Cartoon.

the people, and they also hired Nubian advisers to train the actors who gave their voices to the characters.[21]

Bakkar ran for nine seasons, with thirty episodes aired each year until 2007. In subsequent years, *Bakkar* grew from a cartoon character into an Egyptian brand used to sell snacks and other products aimed at children.

The animations were produced in 2D, while the background was 3D. The *Bakkar* series was a blend of Egyptian traditions and elements of Disney productions. Bakkar, the main character, is an idealised, good-hearted, sometimes naive boy, aged around ten to twelve. His sidekick Hassouna resembles the character of Donald Duck, a similarity accentuated by his hoarse voice. The two are often accompanied by their classmates Hamaam and Faris, as well as a younger girl, Haniyya. Like most Disney heroes, Bakkar has a pet, a goat called Rashida. The producers also took care to please older audiences, introducing adult characters also. One of these is Bakkar's uncle, Sidon, a friendly character struggling to find a job and make ends meet. Another adult character is Masraf, a devious looter of ancient graves, who is often outsmarted by the kids.

The story takes place in a Nubian village. The plots and characters highlight the traditionalism and forgotten values of the Upper Egyptian region. The majority of the stories are set among the mud huts of Nubia and Pharaonic temples. In some episodes, however, the heroes travel to Cairo, which is presented as a stereotypical image of the crowded capital. All of these locations were chosen with the aim of linking people from urban areas in the north and rural people in the south (Khallaf 2000).

Similarly to the vast majority of Egyptian cinematic and media productions, *Bakkar* was dubbed in Egyptian colloquial Arabic. By choosing this dialect, the authors acknowledged that their aim was to provide a localised production that was an alternative to foreign animations mainly dubbed into *fusha* Arabic. Conforming to their background, the protagonists have a Nubian accent and even use some Nubian words. Ehab Galal claims that the rationale behind the Nubian language being largely excluded was that it is less marketable than colloquial Egyptian. As Galal put it, an 'Egyptianized Bakkar is marketable contrary to the minoritized Bakkar' (Galal 2017).

As Shafik and Smith note, Nubians had long been discriminated against both in Egyptian society and in the media (Shafik 2007a: 68–73; Smith

2006: 399–413). Prior to 1952, the majority of Egyptian films – as we have seen in the case of the Frenkels' *Mish Mish Effendi* – cast Nubians in the role of servants and musicians, subservient to lighter-skinned Egyptians, and they were usually portrayed as honest, naive, funny and, on occasion, foolish people (Shafik 2007a: 68–73). In contrast, *Bakkar* presents Nubians as equal to other Egyptians and an integral group of society without detailing their history or special identity. As a Nubian, *Bakkar* symbolises not a group of people, but the unity of Egyptians. The presentation of Nubians in this manner fitted into the national narrative in the media under Mubarak. Ethnic and religious minorities, according to the framing, were an essential part of the Egyptian nation. *Bakkar*'s debut in 1998 came during a politically sensitive period; after the violent clashes between the army and Islamist forces in the early 1990s there was an urgent need for national harmony, tolerance and unity.

Abu-Lughod (1993) asserts that media and cinematic productions under the presidency of Mubarak (1981–2011) were used as instruments in the creation and mediation of a common national identity, an aim also reflected in the promotion of a common national language. The proposed identity of *Bakkar* and the textual identity of the series are Egyptian, as is the theme song, performed by the famous Egyptian singer Mohamed Mounir. The theme song could be understood as a slogan of the production, with a refrain leaving no doubts about the intentions of the authors: 'ever since he [Bakkar] was young, he has known in his heart and soul that he is Egyptian; that the Nile runs in him; that his country's history is in his blood'.[22] To highlight the patriotic message, and to connect a modern Egypt to its past, the video clip accompanying the theme song shows national symbols such as the Egyptian flag, and emblematic scenes and buildings such as the Nile, the National Museum in Cairo, the pyramids, Egyptian soldiers and fighter jets.

Most episodes of *Bakkar* carry a moral narrative that fits the national context.[23] Presented through the naive character of Bakkar, the series dealt with important social problems such as illiteracy, solidarity with disabled people and personal vendettas to improve children's social responsibility. One case in point is an episode that shows the children going after a greedy businessman whose agents sold sandwiches made with rotten meat in front of the school; one of the children's friends had bought one and had got sick.[24]

The moral values presented in *Bakkar* are both universal (honesty, hard work, responsibility) and particularistic, such as patriotism for the homeland (Galal 2017).

Abu-Lughod and Shafik both note that in Egyptian television productions, Islam is generally presented not merely as a religion, but as an essential part of life (Abu-Lughod 1993: 16–17; Shafik 2007b: 17, 34, 45–55). Regarding religious identity, the character of Bakkar conforms to the general Egyptian trend, representing a localised Islam presented as an ingrained element of national identity. The visit of Bakkar and his friends to the Al-Azhar mosque in one of the episodes was designed to highlight Egyptian religious authority. Another episode revolves around the celebration of a local saint's birthday (*mawlid*). By presenting a tradition rejected by Islamists as a legitimate part of Egyptian culture, the authors took a firm stand in the cultural debate.

Although *Bakkar* promotes a local Egyptian identity for children, it also deals with Egypt as part of the global community. While neither the Islamic nor the Arab heritage of Egypt is overly stressed in the narratives, there is a clear emphasis on general human values. One case in point is an episode in which a social researcher from Cairo arrives to interview the children as part of a United Nations project. In the episode, there are statements about the importance of the United Nations and the necessity of education for children.

Characters are presented from a wide range of Egyptian backgrounds, indicated by accents, clothes and skin colour. Instead of scapegoating a particular group of people, villains are presented as characters with diverse backgrounds such as tricksters from Cairo, southern Egyptians and fishermen from the north. The portrayal of people from different backgrounds once more serves to emphasise the national unity of Egyptians.

Owing to the boom of satellite channels in the mid-1990s, producers strove to reach beyond the borders of Egypt. Thus, in some episodes, Bakkar visits other Arab countries such as Morocco, Yemen, Sudan and Syria.[25] In these episodes, the otherness of non-Egyptians is indicated through dialects, while national idiosyncrasies are presented by showing Bakkar marvelling at the differences between Egyptians and other Arabs.

Bakkar ended with the untimely death of al-Nasr in 2003, which also put an end to the production process of the feature-length project *Bakkar wal*

Bahth 'an Qalb al-Malik Tout (Bakkar and the Search for King Tut's Heart). Bakkar was resurrected in 2015, thanks to al-Nasr's son, Sherif Gamal, who turned the story into a 3D production, but left the concept and the popular title song unchanged.

The Fourth Generation of Native Egyptian Animators

Cairo Cartoon was an important base for young animators to gain experience in the animation industry. After the death of al-Nasr, Sherif Gamal became CEO of the company, while many of her students and co-workers launched their own businesses. These producers and animators benefited from the traditionally liberal policies of the Egyptian government that allowed private entrepreneurs to set up on their own. One of them was Mona Abu al-Nasr's student Mustafa al-Faramawy, who established CartooNile, a company that produced animations such as *Youmiyyat al-Ustaz Sahlawi* (Everyday Stories of Mr Sahlawi), a 2008 edutainment series revolving around the adventures of a lizard who travels through Egypt, providing viewers with information about the different plant and animal species of particular regions. While the overall style has Disneyesque tropes, it also recalls Franklin the Turtle (1997–2003) and other European children's animations. The series was broadcast on Egyptian television and was also purchased by Egypt Air to show as in-flight entertainment. Later, CartooNile also produced a successful series of animated stories from the Qur'an (see Chapter 5).

As a result of increasingly easy access to computer-based 3D technologies in the early 2000s, around fifty animation companies began operating. Due to the production process of 3D animation, newcomers were no longer fully dependent on local media as potential customers because they now had the chance to sign with foreign production companies. The increase in demand led to a growth in production that resulted in talent being poached between studios, contributing to rising labour costs and placing an upper limit on revenue.

Egyptian animation studios with modest experience in whole production processes focused on supplying foreign production companies with animation content. One of the most significant animators in this regard is Tarek Rashed, a mechanical engineer and owner of Tarek Rashed Studio. While some of his animations were premiered on local channels, his most profitable, such as *Bou Qatada wa Bou Nabeel* (Bou Qatada and Bou Nabeel) and *Youm wa Youm* (Day after Day), were produced for well-paying customers from Kuwait and Oman.[26] These productions were stripped of any Egyptian identity and focused solely on the national identities of the producers who headed up the projects. As Tarek Rashed Studio was the first company focusing exclusively on 3D animation, it attracted a lot of young talent who later started their own 3D studios and production companies.

In 2007, Zamzam Media, owned by Zainab Zamzam, a renowned producer of clay animations on Islamic topics, released *Batal min Seena'* (A Hero from the Sinai). The 15x10 2D animation series, defined by its aims of realistic visual representations of characters and environment, shows the adventures of a young boy, Saleh, and his father Sheikh Hamdan as they spy on the Israeli occupants on behalf of the Egyptian secret service after the 1967 war. The timing of this celebration of the Sinai people's patriotism came in the wake of terrorist attacks carried out by radical Sinai-based Islamist groups such as al-Tawhid wal-Jihad in the early 2000s, provoking an aggressive counterterrorism crackdown by the security forces from 2004 to 2006, fuelling tensions between local people and regime forces (Aziz 2017). The Sinai identity of the protagonists of *Batal min Seena'* is highlighted by their Bedouin clothes and Sinai dialect. However, presenting Saleh and his father as true Egyptian patriots supported by a group of dark-suited Egyptian officers gathering around a conference table with a portrait of President Nasser behind their backs gave the show a definite Egyptian identity. This patriotic Egyptian approach is further highlighted in the series' finale, which revolves around Egypt's peace with Israel, framing it as a victory for Egypt. The closing montage shows shots from Saleh's future as he joins the army, grows up and sits at an office desk as an officer with an Egyptian flag and a portrait of President Mubarak in the background. *Batal min Seena'* was followed by *Batal min Boursa'eed* (A Hero from Port Said) in 2011, a 12x13 2D series with the same production background and on a similar topic, telling the story of a boy called Sameer during the 1956 conflict in a comic manner.

Animation shows by artists and producers Mona Abu al-Nasr and Zainab Zamzam were well received by national critics and celebrated in the official press and media as a symbol of Egyptian modern cultural production. All of al-Nasr's productions were honoured with national awards and were selected

Figure 2.5 *Batal min Seena'* (A Hero from the Sinai): animating a glorious war. 2008 © Zamzam Media.

to represent Egypt in twelve international festivals. Similarily, Zamzam's art has never been challenged or faced any criticism in official media, as it represents images of an Egyptian nation as it is imagined by the state and gatekeepers of the national media.

Regardless of critical and popular reception, *Mish Mish Effendi*, *Bakkar* and the heroes of *Batal* are local champions in a global Disney-dominated market, participating in the creation and maintenance of the Egyptian imagined community united by language, symbols and narratives.

The Impact of the 2011 Revolution on Egyptian Animation Production

By 2011, a dynamic Egyptian animation scene had evolved. Local animation industries, however, still suffered from too few employees. Due to the lack of education in 3D animation, animation and production companies either trained their own crews or hired self-taught people. The lack of animation professionals also led to stiff competition to employ the most talented workforce possible.[27]

Until Mubarak stepped down in 2011, Egyptian Television remained the main customer for local animation companies, spending over 100 million Egyptian pounds per year on animated content. Animators and producers with good contacts in decision-makers at Egyptian Television, and even newcomers with creative, innovative ideas, could land contracts that largely covered production costs. Financial predictability even allowed many companies to produce self-funded demos or entire projects to find customers in other markets.

However, the aftermath of the Mubarak regime in 2011 came as a setback for the Egyptian animation industry. TV budget cuts also pushed back contracts with animation companies. Simultaneously, more affluent producers and production companies from the Gulf started to turn to Indian animators due to the political uncertainty in Egypt.[28] Almost all companies were affected by the Egyptian budget cuts, and only those that had tapped into alternative sources of income outside Egypt could avoid losses.[29] In contrast, companies with well-developed transnational networks of cooperation, mainly with partners from the Gulf, remained relatively unaffected.[30]

Dubai and the United Arab Emirates

Changing Social Realities in Dubai and the United Arab Emirates since the 1980s

At first glance, the cityscape of modern Dubai could give the impression that the futuristic city of skyscrapers had risen straight out of the desert. Before the 1950s, however, Dubai was a British protectorate, a sleepy, traditional town whose 20,000 inhabitants lived off fishing, trading and pearl diving. Unlike some other Gulf settlements, the society of Dubai and the other Emirate states (Abu Dhabi, Ajman, Fujairah, Ras al-Khaimah, Sharjah and Umm al-Quwain) was by no means homogeneous at the time. The influx of foreigners began with the transport of slaves from East Africa in the nineteenth century (Ricks 1988). Later, in the early 1900s, Iranian traders – referred to as *al-'ajam* – arrived and became a part of the merchant class of *khaleeji* societies (Fuccaro 2005).

Following the oil boom in the 1960s, Dubai and the United Arab Emirates (UAE) attracted a continuous inflow of populations from countries all around the globe. The slight growth between 1975 and 1995 was followed by a population explosion; the number of inhabitants doubled, exceeding 1.6 million by 2008. Today's inhabitants of the Emirates are descended from over 200 nationalities, with the majority originating from the Middle East, South-East Asia and Europe.

During the past decades, both Dubai society and the city itself have changed dramatically. The construction boom of the 1990s resulted in Dubai emerging from the desert as an ultramodern city, whose cityscape is characterised by innovative urban design, urban regeneration and place-branding strategies. Historic city centres and traditional neighbourhoods were pulled down to make space for modern infrastructure projects. Conceptual islands, extravagant skyscrapers, theme parks and media cities have given Dubai a newly crafted identity, while the physical demolition of traditional homes has led to a gap between the past and the present (Khalaf 2006).

Samir Dasqupta sums up the effects of globalisation on local cultures and traditional values as follows:

> [t]he widening gap between the rich and the poor and rampant commercialization and commoditization of social life undermine the social integration . . . and also threaten the moral, ethical and economic fabric of those societies. As a result, anxiety over the loss of cultural, social and economic identity and the weakening of ethnic and communal solidarity and social harmony seems widespread. (Dasqupta 2004: 126)

In the case of the modern UAE in general, and Dubai in particular, there is a clear gap between the cultural traditions and social practices that were once of utmost importance, and the commercial and economic pressures and realities that have since moulded the community as a whole. The change in economic, environmental and social realities, namely the destruction of traditional places coupled with the influx of immigrants, has impacted the lives of young Emiratis and led to a growing dependency on commercial products and lifestyles, while moving them away from the traditional norms of life (Hurriez 2002: 56).

On the other hand, despite the influx of immigrants, traditional social and tribal networks have continued to structure the lives of native citizens and have thus remained untouched. Familial bonds, tribal affiliations and religion are not only important factors that shape the identity of native local populations, but also the most important indicators of status in society (Heard-Bay 2001: 254–72). However, changing lifestyles has led to a sense of dependency on foreigners and to feelings of a cultural threat that resulted in a vigorous shift toward nationalism (Khalaf 2006). At the same time, Sally

Findlow contends that nationalism, as interpreted in the UAE, represents a 'positive turning inward' rather than a 'negative turning outward', in the sense that hostile attitudes towards neighbouring countries or foreigners living in the UAE, or a sense of 'superiority' of the 'own' is not part of a collective identity that binds Emiratis (Findlow 2000: 16). To be sure, while xenophobia or physical atrocities against foreigners are uncommon in the Emirates, the exploitation and abuse of foreign workers remains an issue of concern. Moreover, naturalisation of foreigners is practically non-existent.

This Gulf society is an excellent example of the dual characteristics of rapid economic modernisation and the preservation of traditional politico-legal and cultural dimensions (Khalaf and Alkobaisi 1999). The protection (or creation) of a national identity, culture and way of life have become a priority both in social development and in politics. UAE and Dubai governments have supported a protectionist policy by maintaining a tribal nature and excluding foreigners from political life as well as limiting their rights and participation in social life. Controlling national wealth, the government is also able to control national development and maintain its paternalistic hold over citizens, while also connecting to the global economic system.

Aware of the impacts of globalisation and the threat of losing national identity, UAE governments perceived the need for an imagined political and cultural community (Anderson 1991: 1–9). Hence, to create a sense of belonging among native Emiratis, an imagined past was created and revived to provide nationals with a sense of 'Emiratiness'.

Since the late 1990s, concerns over loss of identity and cultural heritage (*turath*) resulted in government policies referred to as heritage revival (*ihya' al-turath*). UAE governments established institutions such as the Abu Dhabi Authority for Culture and Heritage in order to promote traditional Emirati cultural heritage. They also used the media to publicise a national agenda, and national flags started to be flown not only over state institutions, but also over private and government schools (Lawson and al-Naboodah 2008).

(Re)constructing sites of remembrance, central and local governments began to establish cultural centres and heritage sites where locals and tourists alike can learn about the traditional Emirati culture and way of life (Hurriez 2002: 65). These efforts include the creation of heritage institutions such as historical villages and museums as well as the organisation of cultural events.

One of the most important social spaces for Emiratis in the pre-oil days was the traditional neighbourhood (called *freej* in the local dialect), where a relatively small number of inhabitants provided a sense of social security. A typical example of these was recreated in Dubai Heritage Villages, founded in 1996 as a project of the Dubai Society for Heritage Revival and the Emirates Society for Pearl Diving. It is located in old Dubai's Shindagha quarter – an artificial site where visitors can stroll back in time and see the traditions of old Dubai.

Sulayman Khalaf (2002) sees these cultural and ideological enterprises not as a negation of globalisation, but rather as its affirmation. As he notes, '[s]ince globalization threatens indigenous cultures, a national cultural revival gains credible rationale, as well as a particular symbolic meaning and ideological capital. Equally important, this national revival fosters politico-cultural support that generates its continuous production'. Others remain sceptical about the heritage revival, considering it 'illusive history', a phenomenon similar to Hobsbawm's notion of 'invented traditions' (Elsheshtawy 2010).

The Development of Media Industries in Dubai

Responding to the challenges of diversifying an oil-based economy, ruler Sheikh Rashid bin Saʿeed al-Maktoum (1958–90) implemented liberal economic policies that were designed to turn Dubai into a free market economy. Since then, Dubai has adopted a cluster-based development strategy by developing themed free zones and industrial clusters with the explicit intent of building a strong base in strategic industries.

Dubai Media City (DMC) was opened in January 2001, with the declared objective of turning Dubai into a regional media hub (Sakr 2007a: 195). Indeed, the foundation of DMC had a fundamental impact on the growth of both the local and the regional media industry, as it attracted not only local but also regional and international media companies (McGlennon 2006). Within a few years, DMC had grown into a regional hub for media organisations and it now hosts a number of media groups, television channels and production studios. DMC has not only an economic but also a cultural mission. While one of its goals was to promote the Arab and Islamic culture of the Gulf, its establishment also led to Dubai's further integration into the global media market and cultural industry. In addition to its economic benefits, DMC has also had an enormous cultural impact, as cultural industries convey lifestyles with both a social and entertainment function (Chaker 2003). As an open economy, Dubai witnesses an inflow of foreign cultural products, making it also a centre of great potential for building film industries and for animation production.

Film industries in general, and animation production in particular, are fundamentally linked to developments in technology, human resources and regulation. Although they operate in the dynamics of transnational geography, location is nonetheless a critical factor in the industry's development. Building a strong centre for the film industry and particularly for animation production requires a variety of factors, most notably the existence of a critical mass of production companies, their proximity to broadcasters, the availability of a skilled workforce, strong pre/post-production capacities and, occasionally, even government support (Lee 2010). The Dubai government proved to be a generous patron for local cultural producers, providing funds for Emirati filmmakers who intended to highlight the local culture in their productions.

Freej, *a Symbol of Emirati Identity*

Freej (Neighbourhood, 2006–) was the first technically advanced mature animation in the Arab world and the first 3D animated series produced by an Emirati. The brainchild of Mohammed Saʿeed Harib, a Dubai producer, *Freej* can be considered one of the pioneers in Arabising the genre of sitcom animation as well as the main model for subsequent productions in various Arab countries.[31] The project started as a six-page study book in 1998 that was shelved until 2003. However, the creation of DMC and the government funds offered to young entrepreneurs in the 2000s gave local creative industries a much-needed boost. Harib's Lammtara Pictures was by no means independent of local hierarchies as it was funded by Sheikh Mohammed Bin Rashid's Establishment for Young Business Leaders in 2005.[32]

International clusters such as DMC became a meeting point for people with different cultural backgrounds that stimulated the growth of a new generation of globalised Emirati youth (Mourtada-Sabbah et al. 2008). Mohammed Saʿeed Harib represents this generation of Emiratis. The crew and production process of *Freej* could be viewed as a mirror of Emirati society and division of labour. Harib himself as well as the leading actors who lend their voices to the animated characters are Emirati nationals, whereas the greater part of the creative work is performed by an international crew and the labour-intensive animation process has been outsourced to India.

The first season of *Freej* premiered during Ramadan 2006 on Dubai TV and Sama Dubai, and became popular among audiences of both sexes and all ages from children to grandparents (Baldwin 2010). It was not long before *Freej* moved beyond the borders of the UAE and gained popularity in the entire Gulf region. In Dubai, *Freej* became a national icon and a part of local popular and even commercial culture. In 2011, a special one-minute TV spot celebrating the National Day of the UAE was produced, alongside an onboard safety video for the flydubai airline. Apart from the series, a twenty-eight-episode quiz show, *Kitab al-Alghaz* (Book of Riddles), was aired during Ramadan 2009. One year later, Harib and his crew also produced a theatrical show, *Freej Folklour* (Freej Folklore), and in 2013, a *Freej* theme park was opened.

While the basic idea of *Freej* was inspired by American sitcom animations, the original idea was developed by Dubai writers. At first glance, the 3D animated style of *Freej* recalls the visual traits of Pixar animations.

Figure 2.6 *Freej* (Neighbourhood): ladies from the hood. 2006 © Lammtara Pictures.

However, unlike in many Arab productions, the appearance of the characters does not echo Disney or anime traditions, but is a recreation of Emirati types. Through the intensive incorporation of local visual elements, the authors created a unique visual world.

Freej could be easily viewed as a 'televised animation museum', where cultural representations are presented to viewers as discourses on Emirati and Dubai national culture. While the series is produced by a Dubai company, *Freej* is not a symbol or embodiment of Dubai alone, but of the UAE as a whole. The national flag of the UAE is frequently seen flying in outdoor scenes and there are also many references to other UAE member states, carefully avoiding criticism or negative stereotypes.

The creation of *Freej* was preceded by in-depth research on local cultural heritage by students from Zayed University who volunteered to take pictures of traditional buildings and collect proverbs, cultural sayings and old songs (Saffarini 2006). The material gathered was used as references for the drawings and was incorporated into the scripts and dialogues.

The show is set in an old, fictional neighbourhood of Dubai (referred to only as *Freej*), resembling traditional Dubai areas such as Shindaga and Bastakiyya. At the same time, the cityscape in the background references modern UAE and its iconic buildings.

The plots revolve around four elderly ladies, Umm Sa'eed, Umm Salloum, Umm 'Allawi and Umm Khammas, whose lives are challenged by the ever-expanding city and the increasingly modern world around them. Umm means 'mother', and Arab women are traditionally addressed by the name of their eldest son. Salloum and 'Allawi are nicknames, while Sa'eed and Khammas are real names. Umm Sa'eed was most probably modelled on Mohammed Sa'eed Harib's grandmother, and her character represents tradition. All four ladies wear local clothes and the traditional *battoulah*, a typical Emirati metal mask. Most scenes are set in the *majlis* (traditional lounge) in Umm Sa'eed's house, where the friends gather to drink *gahwa* (black coffee) and chat about personal and social matters. Given that *majlis* are an important space for elderly Emirati people, this can be seen as a clear intention to present *ihya' al-turath* (Rehman 2008).

The four characters represent a cross-section of Dubai society in the pre-oil days. Umm Sa'eed, the central character, has a thick Bedouin accent and a passion for traditional poetry. The incorporation of traditional poetry through Umm Saʿeed is a tribute to Emirati culture, in which poetry is considered one of the most prestigious of all arts. Public and government concerns of losing *turath* are frequently mirrored through the character of Umm Saʿeed. One example is an episode in which she phones a local radio show to complain about rising prices. Becoming emotional, she recites a poem, written in traditional verse, which condemns materialism and mourns the loss of tradition and *turath*.[33]

Umm Salloum is an overweight, absent-minded lady. Her accent suggests a non-Bedouin Arab origin, and the character is a simplified portrayal of elderly Emiratis.

The third character is Umm ʿAllawi, a thin old lady who wears glasses. Her Persian accent and frequent use of Persian phrases indicate her *ʿajam* background, as does her affinity for business and her fascination with modern technological devices such as computers and smartphones. Despite the constant quarrels between Umm Saʿeed and Umm ʿAllawi on modernity and tradition, there is a strong bond of friendship between them, a symbol of the need to find harmony between *turath* and modernity.

The fourth lady is Umm Khammas, whose hot-headed character is a source of many comic situations in the series. Her dark skin tone, her love for *Maʿlaya* songs (a music genre of the slave communities in the Gulf) and her knowledge of *Zar*, a traditional East African magic (Khalifa 2006), suggest that she is of African descent.

The friendship between the old ladies of different backgrounds reflects the concerns of the producers and the funders with regard to nation-building, and their intention to present the social groups of the traditional UAE as blending into one nation. The role of language as an indicator of such unity is particularly important, as all four ladies speak the same dialect, reflecting the unity of Emiratis of different backgrounds.

Conforming to the dominant national discourse of the UAE, *Freej* presents a positive view of the different backgrounds and nationalities portrayed. Even though foreign nationals – whose otherness is clearly revealed through accents and visual characteristics – are shown regularly, the plots are free of negative stereotypes. One case in point is an episode about Margaret, an elderly British lady who moves to the *Freej*.[34] Her appearance and calm voice imply a likeable character. Margaret runs a tidy house and leads a healthy lifestyle. After she sends a cake to the four ladies as a sign of friendship, they return the gesture by bringing her traditional Emirati foods. As their friendship unfolds, Margaret continues to promote her healthy ways among the ladies, but finds herself gaining weight and neglects her once-tidy house as she adapts to the Emirati lifestyle.

One of the central issues of *Freej* is the changing lifestyle of modern-day Emirati people. The producers of the show are relatively bold in their social criticism, expressing their concerns about the loss of traditional values and weakening social ties. One episode, for example, asserts that younger Emiratis neglect their parents because of the changing family structures after the oil boom.[35] In the story, Umm Salloum's eldest son, Salloum, and his wife return from a trip to Oman and express their regret at having left her behind – but only because there was no one else to look after their daughter when they were busy.

On the other hand, integrated as it is into the Emirati media system and being an advocate of local culture, *Freej* rarely gets involved in political criticism. Nor does the show engage in crude humour and it avoids sexual references altogether. It does, however, preserve reflexivity on social issues and it addresses local traditions. At the same time, most jokes are built on the different personalities and contrasting reactions to particular events.

A few episodes that denounced religious extremism drew sharp criticism. In one episode, *Al-Blagh al-Kadheb* (The False Announcement), Umm Khammas becomes fervently religious after being told that she will die soon. She declares herself a *sheikha* (a female sheikh) and starts giving religious advice (*fatwa*) to women. At the end of the episode, it turns out that the doctor was wrong and everything returns to normal. The episode was criticised by some Islamic clerics because of its assumed mockery of religious authorities. The episode was not repeated after its first showing and nor was it included in the DVD collection.

Although rather cautious as far as local affairs are concerned, *Freej* is more daring with references to regional political events. An episode aired during Ramadan 2011 contained obvious references to the Arab Spring. Agha, the owner of the local grocery shop, becomes greedy and begins to abuse his monopoly by charging higher prices. The locals eventually get fed up and begin a demonstration in front of the shop, chanting, '*Freej* wants a change in the shop' and '*Erhal!*' (Go away!), similar to the slogans sweeping across the countries gripped by the revolution, such as Tunisia, Libya and Egypt. The shopkeeper replies by inventing a conspiracy theory of large supermarkets fuelling the discontent that led to the demonstration and then offers ridiculous discounts. As the ladies keep calling for his departure, Agha responds with an impromptu fireworks show for the crowd and promises that he will hunt down the opponents: '*Shibr-Shibr, Bayt-Bayt, Sikka-Sikka*' (inch by inch, house by house, alley by alley) is an obvious reference to Qaddafi's infamous speech.[36] In the end, the four ladies enter the shop's secret storeroom where the customers' bills and the fireworks are kept, and they blow it up. At the conclusion of the double episode, the sky is lit up by fireworks celebrating the revolution and freedom.

All in all, *Freej* advocates for a modern Emirati national identity that fuses traditional values with modern achievements. In the series, a clear distinction is drawn between 'us' (Emiratis) and 'them' (foreign nationals). However, it also calls for tolerance towards others. When religion is discussed, Islam is largely portrayed as integral to the construction of local identity and part of the cultural heritage.

Emirati Children's Animation

Freej impacted Arab animation production in two ways. On the regional level, it started a trend of sitcom animations (see Chapter 3), while on the national level it became a vanguard for local authors, backed by liberal Emirati entrepreneurship and creative industry policies, together with a consistent *ihya' al-turath* and nation-building strategy that continued to create funds for productions celebrating Emiratiness.

By the mid-2000s, Arab children, long neglected by producers, became a target audience. As a response to the emergence of pan-Arab children's television channels, like the powerhouses Saudi MBC3 and JCC, Emirati authors produced an increasing number of high-quality animations of local relevance. One of the most ambitious projects has been an animated reworking of the popular comic strips of *Majid*, an Emirati children's magazine. Published weekly, it targeted the Gulf and Egyptian markets. *Majid* has been the most widely read children's magazine in the Arab world, and was dependent on the

Al-Ittihad newspaper and thus on the Ministry of Information of the United Arab Emirates.

The magazine claimed a relevance beyond the national borders, featuring moralistic stories of universal validity and visually referencing the region's folk art, especially textiles (Douglas and Malti-Douglas 1994: 150–1). Similarly to other Arab children's magazines, *Majid* participated in generating regional hybrid identities that are simultaneously Muslim and modern, Arab and cosmopolitan, child- and consumer-oriented (Peterson 2005).

Majid himself, a young, black-haired boy in a traditional white *thaub*, who appeared throughout the magazine, became the central character in a series. The 2D animation revolved around him and his friends, with their identity clearly indicated by their Emirati dialect and the actual locations of today's Emirates. Majid and his friends experience a wide range of adventures of educational potential, such as treasure hunting at historic locations or chasing illegal animal traffickers with the help of his drone and local police.

By the early 2000s, in line with the nation-building policies of the Emirati government, *Majid* had shifted its focus from a hybrid regional to an explicit Emirati identity. Such shifts can be best traced by the events preceding the UAE's National Day on 2 December, when major characters, whose particular national affiliation had not previously been highlighted, started to wave Emirati flags and wear baseball caps in the national colours.

Figure 2.7   *Kaslan* (Lazy): from comic strips to the screen. 2015 © Majid.

In 2015, Abu Dhabi Media, the official media organisation of the Government of Abu Dhabi, set up Majid Entertainment with a mission to extend the Majid brand to the screens. In September of that year Majid TV went on air and online, with a number of animation shows, mainly drawing on characters and visual styles from the comic strips (Sakr and Steemers 2017: 9). Upon their release, the channel broke a regional record by producing seventy hours of animation in a six-month period, mainly adaptations of the magazine's popular comic strips. With the aim of becoming an introduction for Emirati children to their national identity and *turath* through edutainment, Majid TV left the pan-Arab focus of the magazine behind. This can be observed in the numerous animated video clips outright celebrating Emiratiness. Among them is a children's choir singing the patriotic song *'Eishee Beladee* (Live My Land), illustrated by flags, maps and picturesque landscapes.

While the UAE were looking at the creation of their nation-building past and their efforts to preserve their identity amidst Western influences, some producers in Jordan were using animation to advertise a Western friendly past.

Jordan

The Formation of Jordanian Identity and the Struggle for Political Legitimacy since the 1980s

The Hashemite Kingdom of Jordan is a lower-middle income country with a relatively small population compared to neighbouring Arab states, where neither national wealth nor the size of the market (as in Egypt) called for the establishment of a strong centre for cultural production.[37] Unlike in the Gulf States, there had been no influx of immigrants, necessitating the support of cultural production in order to reinforce the population's national identity. At the same time, the Jordanian government's concerns over the political economy and the regime's legitimacy eventually led to development strategies that enabled media producers to set up their enterprises.

Jordan can be best described as a dynastic authoritarian regime with a traditional elite – mostly of urbanised Bedouin heritage – and a tribal loyalty in politics towards the dynasty. At the same time, over half the population is made up of citizens of Palestinian origin who immigrated after the establishment of Israel in 1948 and during the Arab–Israeli war in 1967. Jordanian foreign policy under the reign of King Hussein (1952–99) was fundamentally fuelled by concerns over the regime's legitimacy, consolidation and survival (Salloukh 1996). Lacking natural resources or an advanced agriculture and industry, the regime largely relied on foreign aid and investment.[38] Being aware of this fact, the United States offered to cancel Jordan's debts and promised aid for building a solid economy in exchange for the country signing a peace treaty with Israel. This promise led King Hussein to sign the peace treaty with the Jewish state in 1994. Needless to say, the decision was not particularly popular among the citizens of Palestinian origin and was criticised by the Islamic Action Front (*Jabhat al-'amal al-Islamiyy*), a major opposition party, and the Jordanian branch of the Muslim Brotherhood.

Since ascending the throne in 1999, King Abdullah II, King Hussein's son, has strengthened the country's ties to Western powers such as the United States and the European Union (Ryan 2004). The political uncertainties of the early 2000s, including the 2003 Iraq war, made the Jordanian government even more wary of becoming embroiled in diplomatic and economic conflicts. This led to the strengthening of diplomatic and political bonds with the United States, despite local opposition to involvement in the war against Iraq. As Ryan writes:

> Jordanian foreign policy, therefore, must be seen as walking the tightrope between domestic, regional, and even global constraints. But by the same token, the regime's interest in the economics of its own security tends to take precedence in both domestic and foreign policy over all other considerations. (Ryan 2004: 47)

The Economic Opening and Media Policies in Jordan since the 1990s

The foundations of Jordanian political openness and economic liberalisation were laid down by the initiatives of King Hussein between 1989 and 1993. However, these reforms were somewhat limited; they were essentially responses to political and security threats. From 1993 to 1997, a national economic and social plan was implemented. As part of this initiative, the government took significant steps towards building a knowledge-oriented society, with an emphasis on information and communications technology (ICT) as well as on research and development, and scientific and technological services. Since 1999, King Abdullah II has also taken a series of measures to lessen his country's dependence on foreign aid. The ruler has regarded foreign investment and joint ventures as an important means of boosting information technology and productive private capital, and as a key to economic development. Therefore, strategies for further improving domestic economic productive capabilities have been introduced alongside the liberalisation of the environment for private investments (Djeflat 2009).

The economic policies of King Hussein and, later, of King Abdullah II paved the way for the establishment of a number of media companies, which in turn led to a boom in Jordanian cultural and media production, principally in animated cartoons. Since the early 2000s, a number of animation companies have been set up, working not only for the local market but also forming production networks on the geolinguistic and global level.

Ben wa 'Esam *and the Mediation of a Pro-Western Jordanian Identity*

Ben wa 'Esam (Ben and Izzy, 2006) was the first Jordanian 3D animated action adventure cartoon.[39] The thirteen-episode series was produced by Rubicon Group Holding, a private digital content publishing company. Initially called Jordanian Training Technology Group, the company was founded by Jordanian businesswoman Randa Ayyoubi in 1994, taking advantage of the policies created by King Hussein between 1989 and 1993. In 2004, it was renamed Rubicon Group Holding and its profile expanded to include digital content production (*Arabian Business* 2012). The company received funding from the King Abdullah II Fund for Development, which was established by royal decree in 2001 as a non-governmental organisation for funding investments in technology and other ventures.

In 2010, Rubicon signed partnership deals with American Turner and Emirati Etisalat. The former opened the gates for Rubicon's animated cartoons – *Ben wa 'Esam* among them – to be presented on Cartoon Network Arabic, a subsidiary of the American company airing Arab animations for child audiences in the Middle East and North Africa. Rubicon is one of the few Arab companies in the animation business to produce animations for

Western companies by doing animation work for episodes of *Postman Pat* and *The Pink Panther* (Cherian 2007).

Ben wa 'Esam was Rubicon's most ambitious project, given its $6 million budget, quality and mobilised marketing powers. The series shows a clear desire to imitate Pixar's visual style, and was produced by a crew whose members came from Jordan, Iraq and the Palestinian Territories. The executive producer is David Pritchard, an American who worked as a producer on *The Simpsons* and *Family Guy*.

The *Ben wa 'Esam* project was supported by the Jordanian state not only on the institutional and financial levels; it was also introduced at an extravagant gala in New York's Metropolitan Museum of Art in 2006 to attract global media attention (Steinberg 2006). The most prominent supporter of the project was Queen Rania; the Jordanian royal couple makes concerted efforts to maintain the image of an open-minded, modern family as part of the country's foreign policy. Both King Abdullah and Queen Rania were admirers of American animations such as *The Simpsons*. However, such productions had little impact on either the humor or the narrative of *Ben wa 'Esam*, which represents a conservative Middle Eastern approach that generally rejects crude humour and instead presents characters who are supposed to be role models for the young audience.

Figure 2.8 Ben wa 'Esam (Ben and Izzy): a friendship between an American and a Jordanian boy. 2006 © Rubicon GH.

The authors of *Ben wa 'Esam* did not create a unique visual style, but opted for a generic Jordanian and Middle Eastern environment. The Jordanian identity is highlighted in the narrative. The plot revolves around the friendship between two eleven-year-old boys, one American, the other Jordanian. Ben is presented as a blonde, blue-eyed boy, while Izzy is drawn as an Arab character with brown eyes, and dark hair and skin. While the series was produced in Jordan, it was first released in English and then dubbed into Arabic in 2008. In the Arabic version, the characters speak Modern Standard Arabic and not even Ben, the American character, has a foreign accent. Similarly, in the English version, the main characters do not have accents, only the real-life historical figures. The subtle message here is that there are few differences between the two boys, despite their appearances and cultural backgrounds. This is unsurprising, since the goal of the series is to promote a cross-cultural understanding between the Arab world and the West, and to persuade children from both cultures to reject prejudices. The characters represent the stereotypes of their homelands. The official promotional materials describe Izzy as 'slight of build, sinewy and studious', but 'on the downside, Izzy can be a little too serious, self-righteous, superior, even devious'. The American Ben, on the other hand, is 'energetic', but 'on the negative side, he is a bit xenophobic, self-centered, needs-to-win competitive'. The creators also add that '[l]ike his native land, he sometimes blunders into situations without thinking' (Steinberg 2006). At first, the boys are not too keen on each other. However, during their travels and their fight against an unscrupulous antiques dealer named Clutchford Wells, they learn to cooperate with and respect each other. It is important to note that while they portray cultural differences, the characters do not engage in political or religious debates of 'real' life.

The boys meet through their grandfathers who are working on an archaeological excavation in Jordan. They find a magic lantern from which Yasmine, a genie, emerges, who takes them on adventures through both time and space. In the first episode of the series, the three travel back in time and meet Mark Twain visiting the ruins of the ancient city of Petra. In one of the scenes, Mark Twain turns to Izzy, saying, 'I see you and Ben don't get along too well', to which Izzy replies, 'He is annoying. Americans are so brash and full of themselves.' Mark Twain smiles and says, 'He is one of God's creatures, and all of God's creatures should be respected.' To which the writer later adds, 'Don't judge the country, son. Judge the man.' He uses the word *Allah*, a name used by Muslims, rather than *Al-Rabb*, the term preferred by Arab Christians. By referring to Allah, the producers are claiming religious legitimacy for the message of tolerance, challenging widespread stereotypes fuelled by Islamist political and religious discourses in Jordan after the invasion of neighbouring Iraq by the United States.

Beside its message of tolerance, the series also has an educational mission. The boys travel back in time and meet historical characters from the Arabic and Middle Eastern past such as Dido, the Phoenician queen, Ibn Sina, the medieval philosopher, Ismail al-Jazari, the Muslim inventor and mathematician, among others. When meeting these people, Izzy uses his smartphone to find out more information about the person and their deeds that were inspirational for both Eastern and Western cultures. By promoting this kind of knowledge, the series fulfils a twofold mission. First, it creates a sense of pride in young Arab audiences and counters the dangerous tendency of praising radicals as role models.[40] Second, it acts as a counterbalance to the stereotypical Western view of Arabs and Muslims as being backward or radical by showing the English-speaking audience that the Arab world has been rich in scientific innovations and cultural achievements. As he travels through time, the American Ben is presented as a 'Western eye', a curious and open-minded boy who does not know much about the history of the Middle East.

The episodes focus on adventure and – besides the basic information and facts – do not claim to be historically accurate as they involve genuine historical characters in fictional adventures and even magical situations. At the same time, the past is presented in a way that aims to mould present-day identity; a collective Jordanian past is presented as integral to the Arab and Muslim world, which are shown to be realms of science and tolerance. The positive critical acclaim and the strong political background of the production did not, however, translate into success. Though originally twenty-six episodes were planned, *Ben wa 'Esam* ended after the release of only thirteen, and Rubicon stopped animation production for reasons that remain unverified.

Tunisia

Tunisian National Cinema

With the French colonisation (1881–1956), Tunisian cinematic production has been connected to the French cinema industry since its very beginning. Tunisian films – starting with the first local production, the 1922 film *Zuhra* – involved collaboration and co-production with French professionals, Tunisians remaining outside the domain of cinematic production (Shafik 2007b: 12). The establishment in 1946 of cinemas and Studios Africa in Tunis by the French paved the way for further institutional Tunisian-French collaborations in cinematic production (Shafik 2007: 17). At the same time, a cinephile movement, emerged with members of the local elite establishing film clubs, regarding cinema as a tool of national struggle against imperialism.

This struggle went hand in hand with the struggle for national identity. The French colonisation resulted in a reimagining of the community based on the dichotomous formula of 'us' (Tunisian) versus 'them' (French). In this regard, the French presence played a fundamental role in pushing a community to be imagined among groups of diverse backgrounds and thus creating a new breed of ethno-nationalism. Sraieb concludes that, against a background of traditionalist and pan-Arab tendencies, 'Tunisian-ness' had to be invented as a legal construct and a national identity (Sraieb 1987). However, as Sadiki observes, for many early Tunisian politicians and thinkers, this kind of ethno-nationalism also overlapped with ethno-religiousness (2002: 501). Habib Bourguiba, a French-trained lawyer who was Tunisia's first president, governing from from 1957 to 1987, was an advocate of French-style secular politics (Moore 1988). His party advocated a territorially defined identity that incorporated ethno-nationalism, but regarded ethno-religiousness as secondary.

The French influence did not cease after the country's physical departure in 1956, as Habib Bourguiba and the new Francophile political elite maintained strong ties with the former colonial powers (Micaud 1964: 74–5). After gaining independence, Tunisia even tried to copy the French economic and education model when making plans for modernising Tunisia that also included the development of cinema and its associated trades and professions (Zghal 1991). Despite fundamental differences, the political elite of the Bourguiba regime and the left-wing cinephile elite shared the same goal: to develop a vivid national cinema scene.

Independence proved to be a catalyst for national filmmaking. In 1957, the government established the Société Anonyme Tunisienne de Production et d'Expansion Cinématographique (Tunisian Company for Cinematic Production and Expansion – SATPEC), gathering Tunisian and Western agencies working in the field of production. In 1962, the Association des Jeunes Cinéastes Tunisiens (Association of Young Tunisian Filmmakers – AJCT) was created by a group of amateur filmmakers, becoming the Fédération Tunisienne des Cinéastes Amateurs Tunisian Federation of Amateur Filmmakers – FTCA) in 1968. A year later a decree was issued that transferred to SATPEC the monopoly over the production, import and distribution of films (Shafik 2007b: 21). Owing to limited local resources, Tunisian producers searched extensively for Western co-producers. Government initiatives with regard to creating an institutional and infrastructural background for film production, such as the establishment of SATPEC and building the Gammarth film laboratory in 1967, were essentially political decisions with the goal of creating an independent national cinema (Kchir-Bendana 2003). This was supported by the founding by the Tunisian Ministry of Culture of the Kélibia International Festival in 1964 and the Carthage International Film Festival two years later, which had the declared intention of creating an institutional platform not only for local filmmakers, but also for those to the north and south of the Sahara, and improving Tunisia's authority in regional film affairs (Brahimi 1997: 61–4). Later, the Tunisian government was involved in the creation of a number of production and distribution organisations as well as in the setting up of local and international festivals. The vision was that this film industry would enable the articulation and mediation of a national identity and the creation of 'national cinematic aesthetics' (Hunebelle 1980: 67). Despite these ambitions, notions of Tunisian 'national identity' as mediated in local cinematic productions often remained characterised by biculturalism and a pluralistic identity (Kchir-Bendana 2003: 40). Zine al-Abidine Ben Ali's takeover of the presidency in 1987 did not change the situation. Even after the late 1980s, the search for identity in Tunisian cinematic productions remained confined to the mediation of local Arab and Tunisian themes, and the retelling of old narratives (Brahimi 1997: 101).

Generally speaking, animation in Tunisia was until the 2000s, represented by short, one-off productions, with screening generally limited to art cinemas and local film festivals. Productions tended to only occasionally appear on local television channels and did not manage to become part of national popular culture.

The History of Animation Production in Tunisia since the 1960s

Early Tunisian animation was pioneered by individual animators, producing short films, who received only limited support or none at all from government sources. Just like the local film industry, animation production has been defined by strong cultural and professional links with European countries, particularly with France. In one respect, Tunisian authors have been fortunate, as local film festivals offered an opportunity to showcase their productions. Since then, film festivals – whether local or international – have continued to be the main forums for the introduction of homegrown animation productions.

While authors generally denied that their productions had any political content, their texts reveal a sensitivity with regard to local issues and allusive reflections on political trends of the time. Further, under the presidencies of both Bourguiba and Ben Ali, Tunisian animated productions articulated 'national' identities by mediating folkloric, fictional or real-life topics from the territory of modern Tunisia. On the other hand, a Francophone cultural impact is also evident as title sequences were often in French, and the dubbing was into either French or a local dialect.

One of the pioneers of Tunisian animation was Mongi Sancho (1948–2017) who worked as a photographer at the Secrétariat d'Etat à l'Intérieur (Ministry of the Interior). In 1965, after renting a 16mm camera, Sancho produced a puppet animation made from a series of photos taken of penicillin bottles with stuck-on eyes and moustaches, called *La Rentrée des Classes* (Back to School). The four-minute film features a young schoolboy trying to escape the first day of school and being chased around the city by a policeman. Both the penicillin bottles, with their moustaches and fezzes, and the location of the film articulate a Tunisian identity, and could be regarded as a reaction to Bourguiba's reform that made education free and compulsory. Such an identity is also highlighted by showing a blackboard in the school with the first letters of both the Arabic and the French alphabets on it.

A year later Sancho released *Le Chien intelligent* (The Intelligent Dog), a celluloid production telling the story of an old man in traditional Tunisian clothes, who returns from work to his home in the Medina, the old quarter of Tunis, and falls asleep with a cigarette in his hand that subsequently starts a fire. Luckily, his dog had earlier deposited money in the local branch of the Societé Tunisienne de Banque so the man's fortune is saved. Though *Le Chien intelligent* could be read as a commercial or a lighthearted educational film, Sancho insisted that he had received no funding either from the government or the bank.[41] *Le Chien intelligent* won first prize at the Kairouan Festival of Engaged Cinema. The success helped Sancho to win a scholarship to study at the Bulgarian National Cinematographic Centre where he learned animation from Todor Dinov, the godfather of Bulgarian animation (Khlifi 1970: 190–2). Returning to Tunisia in 1967, Sancho presented a project to SATPEC: a plan to establish an animation studio. This, however, was turned down. Undaunted by the refusal, Sancho continued to work on his own projects and started to teach at l'Institut Technologique d'Art et d'Urbanisme (Technological Institute of Art and Town Planning). In 1967, Sancho released his Bulgarian graduation film, *Le Marchand de fez* (The Fez Merchant), a coloured celluloid production in a minimalist style that tells the story of monkeys stealing a farmer's fez, trying to imitate him but ending up not only losing the fez but also their own coconuts. As Maya Ben Abed observed, this story serves as an allegory to Tunisia's failed experience with economic socialism, as the monkey's attempt to imitate the farmer could be regarded as a symbol of the government's experiment with adapting a socialist-style collectivist land policy despite the refusal of the *fellahin* (small landowners), then the bigger landowners.

Le Marchand de fez was followed by *L'Homme et le rocher* (The Man and the Rock) in 1969, and by *Le Pain* (Bread) in 1972, a story of a poor man's Tom and Jerry-like chasing after a loaf of bread, which is also a reference to the Tunisian expression 'to run after bread' (to make ends meet). Inspired by the works of Émile Cohl, Sancho planned to promote social animation and exploit its gags for their educational potential (Bachy 1978: 334–8). During our interview, Sancho claimed that he was apolitical and that his aims in animation were purely artistic. While consciously focusing on topics of local relevance, he denied any intention of entering into political discourses, including those related to identity. On the other hand, he admitted being an admirer of former president Habib Bourguiba for his 'modern views on Tunisia and the Tunisian nation'.[42]

Another significant member of the first generation of Tunisian animators was painter and cartoonist Nacer Khemir (b. 1948). After releasing *La Fleur* (The Flower) in 1970, *L'Homme qui dort* (The Man Who Sleeps) in 1971 and *Le Bûcheron* (The Woodcutter) in 1972, he also collaborated with the Polish-French director and animator Piotr Kamler and in 1972 participated in the production of *Le Mulet* (The Mule),[43] the story of a mule who believes itself to be better than the other mules. In 1973, Khemir worked on the preparations for a movie with French producer Jean-Marie Drot and on a project about the children in the Medina of Tunis. Similarly to his live films, his animations largely revolved around topics connected to Tunisian culture, indicated through characters and scenes (Shafik 2007b: 53). Khemir later stopped working on animations and turned to live films, focusing on Muslim history.

An even more straightforward political commentary can be observed in *Mohammedia*, a short cut-out by cameraman and director Ahmed Bennys and animator Mohamed 'Abdennadher released in 1974 at the fifth Carthage Film Festival. Combining cut-out technique with live action, the animation tells the story of Ahmed Bey I (1786–1851), the nineteenth-century ruler of Tunis who failed to introduce much-needed reforms, eventually paving the way for the French occupation decades later. *Mohammedia* focuses on Ahmed Bey's megalomaniac project of building a palace to rival that in Versailles, featuring live footage from today's Mohammedia villages and animated spots from the times of the extravagant ruler, a clear reference to Bourguiba's failed economic reforms and large-scale construction projects in Tunis.

Amateur filmmaker and AJCT member Mohamed Charbagi focused on the darker side of the Tunisian experience, exposing European racism and mediating an us-versus-them narrative with a focus on the individual's struggle for identity and recognition. While in France in 1974, he released

L'Histoire d'un œuf (The Story of an Egg), which shares many similarities with Sancho's *Des Caprices de poupons* (The Whims of Dolls), as it incorporates genuine eggs with eyes and mouths painted on them. The plot addresses the cultural differences between African and Arab immigrants to Europe and their different fates. The protagonist is a brown egg living in a poor country. As he struggles to survive, he decides to emigrate to a country of white eggs. Initially turned back, he nonetheless manages to enter the white eggs' country. Attracted by the charms of this new civilisation, and after meeting a white female egg, he too wants to be white. Despite all his efforts, he continues to be rejected by the white community. He heads back to his home country, where he also faces rejection by his own community for no longer being himself. After a failed attempt to find his identity, he throws himself from the top of a dune and smashes.

By the early 1980s, Tunisia was facing a political and social crisis as a result of the failed economic policies of the regime, leading to popular uprisings in 1984, known as the 'bread riots', and undermining the authority of the Bourguiba regime. It was at this time when Zouhair Mahjoub (b. 1945) left for what was then Czechoslovakia to master puppet animation. He was bold in his use of different techniques such as drawing-based animation, puppet animation and paper cut-outs. Similarly to his colleagues, Mahjoub's main interest was Tunisian identity, and he largely focused on stories from local folklore. However, like many other authors, he chose to dub his animations in French. In 1970, he participated in the animation of letters for *La Calligraphie arabe* (Arabic Calligraphy), a short film by Hamida Ben ʿAmmar, and released parts of *Les Aventures de Hajji* (The Adventures of Hajji) a year later. In 1974, he wrote the scenario for an animated cut-out adaptation of one of the stories of the eighth-century Persian thinker Ibn Al Mouqaffa, which he entitled *Les Deux souris blanches* (The Two White Mice), released in 1976.[44] In the story, a witch named Kira turns a royal couple, Jameel and Jameela, into white mice, telling them that they will only regain their human form when another human discovers the most powerful person in the world, one who can conquer fire.

Unlike many of his colleagues, Mahjoub remained active in the animation field. While in Czechoslovakia in the early 1980s, he created *Le Petit hibou* (The Little Owl), a short animation based on a medieval legend, released in 1984. The same year saw *Le Guerbagi* (The Water Vendor), an animated puppet story of an old, blind water vendor, set in the 1950s during the struggle for independence from France. The water vendor spied on collaborators and helped the revolutionaries by distributing leaflets for which he was killed by a policeman. The approach of empowering a simple man who turned into a hero was challenging the official narrative of Bourguiba as the leader of the national struggle. In 1992, Mahjoub released *Fleur de pierre* (Stone Flower). The story revolves around a Berber woman watering a dry flower in a magical world resembling southern Tunisia. During the same year, he also produced a twelve-episode TV series, *Les Aventures de Hatem, le courageux cavalier Zlass* (The Adventures of Hatem, the Courageous Horseman of the Zlass), an animated adaptation of a legend from the North African region of Zlass. In 2009 he released *La Goutte miraculeuse* (The Miraculous Drop), which tells the story of a boy called Salah, born in one of the villages perched high in the Tunisian mountains. As there is no water in the village, Salah goes down to the foot of the mountain several times a week to ensure his family have a regular supply. One day, he waters a flower dying of thirst, and all of nature begins to smile.

Given the lack of institutional support and encouragement by SATPEC, many Tunisian animators released only a single project, for example, Ezzeddine Harbaoui, who created *La Cigale* (The Cicada) in 1986. Samir Besbes (b. 1949) released a two-part production, *Les Aventures de Jahjou* (The Adventures of Jahjou) in 1983 and 1985, based on the story of Jahjou, son of Jha, the North African version of the Middle Eastern character Juha, the 'wise fool'.

Local issues and identity were also among the core interests of Mustafa Taieb (b. 1961) who started his career as a painter before taking up amateur filmmaking (Bendazzi 1995: 392). From 1981, he was assistant director, designer, animator and illustrator of a number of short animations, including *L'Enfant et l'avion* (The Child and the Aeroplane), a reflection on the war in Lebanon, *Artiste comme la cigale* (The Artist as a Cicada), and *Jahjouh, il était une fois* (Jahjou, Once Upon a Time). In 1986, he directed *Secourez-la* (Rescue Her, She is in Danger). He released *Le Calligraphe* (The Calligrapher) in 1987, *Le Soulier* (The Shoe) in 1989 and *Le Déluge* (The Flood) in 1992. In 1994, he moved to Rome, returning to Tunis in

2008 to found 2MT Productions. In 2010, he presented a new animated short, *Châteaux de sable* (Sandcastles), produced by 2MT Productions,[45] the story of Anise, a small boy who is passionate about the history of Tunisia. He sets off on an imaginary journey on the trail of a mysterious horseman who introduces him to the major periods and events in the history of the country. The characters move among realistic settings, representing regions of southern Tunisia.

Bourguiba's rule ended on 7 November 1987. The new president, Ben Ali, and his promise of change were initially welcomed with enthusiasm. However, the Tunisian Spring ended in 1990, successively becoming more and more authoritarian (Erdle 2010).

The privatisation then closure in 1994 of SATPEC was a huge blow for Tunisian animation production and pushed authors to search for alternative sources of finance. Still, Sancho managed to release a coloured version of *Bread* in 1994. A year later, Bennys released *Les Ficelles* (The Thread) which continued in the same vein he had started with *Mohammedia*, this time criticising the dynastic system of Bey-era Tunisian history, a thinly veiled allegory for Ben Ali's regime. In spite of these difficulties, Mahjoub recruited a group of young talent and started an ambitious project, *Le Sous-Marin de Carthage* (The Carthage Submarine), work on which continued from 1993 to 1999.

Political allusions to the Ben Ali regime are explicit in the works of Nadia Rais (b. 1967), and Alaedine Boutaleb, two leading members of the younger generation of Tunisian animators. Nadia Rais gained experience while working on Mahjoub's *Le Sous-Marin de Carthage*, and in 2009 released *L'Ambouba* (Ambouba), a nine-minute animation recounting the story of a woman named Ambouba who is desperately rushing to keep a 5 p.m. appointment with two friends, while the hands of a clock turn faster and faster. The surrealistic story is set in an urban Tunisian environment with avant-garde music, spinning clocks and erratic movements. The film won prestigious awards at several festivals, including best short film at the African Festival of Meknes in 2010. A politically laden production, *L'Mrayet* (The Glasses), followed in 2012, combining animation with rotoscoping. The eleven-minute production – also characterised by *L'Ambouba*'s surrealistic style – is a dystopian portrait of a totalitarian state, in which freedom of expression is non-existent and people are oppressed. The hero, Boum Mrayet, is a member of a society where people are made to wear glasses as soon as they are born. Once an adult, he is employed in a company responsible for writing the future. One day, he becomes aware of the system, removes his glasses and informs the other officials, who leave their office to overthrow the regime. The use of sound and images in *L'Mrayet* offers an experimental and satirical perspective on a totalitarian state, also reflecting on the Tunisian revolution of 2011. The symbolic repetition of the number 7 and the colour purple may be regarded as an allegory of the Ben Ali regime. The calendar present at Boum Mrayet's birth shows the date as 7 November 1987, the date of Ben Ali's coup. The number 7 also returns as a close-up on a clock, resembling the great clock at Bourguiba Avenue in Tunis, built by the Ben Ali regime. The film was produced with funding received from the Organisation Internationale de la Francophonie and the Tunisian Ministry of Culture and Heritage Preservation. It was screened in the official selection at Annecy in 2012 and in festivals in Italy, Mexico and Egypt.

Alaeddine Boutaleb's *Coma* (2009) was possibly inspired by the six-month mining revolt of Gafsa in 2008, which was brutally oppressed by the regime (Gall 2014). The seven-minute production tells the story of several skeletons come back from the dead and longing to exist once again. They are confrinted with a black-suited monster that stomps on them with its heavy boots. One of the skeletons grows wings and defeats the monster, and in the last shot we see the skeletons rising from the ground and floating into the air.

This overview of the history of animation in Tunisia reveals that prominent animators like Sancho, Khemir, Mahjoubi, Taieb and Rais were sensitive to local social and political issues, and this is also reflected in their productions. Identity-wise, some of these animations are neutral in the sense of completely excluding representations of Tunisian/Arab/Islamic environments and characters, using the French language and featuring an ostensibly neutral narrative. However, an equally significant number of productions reflect a Tunisian national identity that could be regarded as 'Westernised' in the sense that the narrative is set in local environments with characters who speak French or a local Tunisian dialect.

A Mediterranean Approach to Tunisian Identity – Viva Carthago

Early in his presidency, Habib Bourguiba tasked Tunisian academics with creating a new Tunisian identity that would break both with the immediate colonial past and with the memory of the Husainid dynasty between 1705 and 1957. Post-independence Tunisian historiography therefore goes back to the Phoenician period and describes Tunisian identity as the result of a solid mixture of different civilisations (Abbassi 2005). This approach fundamentally contradicts pan-Arabists who link the country to the Arab world, and Islamists who regard Tunisians as an integral part of the Muslim community (*'ummah*).

Though President Ben Ali focused more on Islamic and Arabic history, he did not deviate radically from Bourguiba's notion of Tunisian-ness. Such notions of identity formation can also be observed in *Viva Carthago*. The production is one of the most ambitious Tunisian animated cartoons regarding both the number of people involved and the budget. The 6 million-euro production consists of a feature-length animation, *Les Naufragés de Carthage* (The Castaways of Carthage), and a series, *Viva Carthago* (Viva Carthago, Figure 2.8), comprising thirteen episodes, each twenty-six minutes long, targeted at children aged between eight and fourteen. It was produced by Cinétéléfilms, a Tunisian company, with the participation of French, Italian and Belgian co-producers. The main crew members – such as executive producer Mohamed Habib 'Attia and producer Ahmed Baha 'eddine 'Attia – are Tunisian, while the drawings were sketched by a design team headed by Algerian artistic director and artist 'Abdelkader Belhadj Slah Hamzaoui and the director, Fabrice Ziolkowski, was French-American. Around 20 per cent of the animation was outsourced to South Korean studios, while the dubbing was done in Lebanon. Mohamed Habib 'Attia acknowledged that choosing *fusha* Arabic over the local Tunisian dialect as the language for dubbing was driven by the ambition to sell the production to other Arab countries. The plan succeeded. The film was sold to Algeria and Morocco, as well as to Établissement de la Radiodiffusion-Télévision Tunisienne (ERTT, the state broadcasting association), its co-producer, Canal+ (the Planète+ network) and RAI Jazeera Children's Channel. *Les Naufragés de Carthage* has participated in international festivals in Tunisia, Canada, the Netherlands and Portugal. In 2007 the company released *Ségou Fanga* (The Birth of Ségou), a

Figure 2.9 *Viva Carthago*: a Mediterranean journey through time and space. 2005 © Cinétéléfilms.

Tunisian-French-Malian co-production about a seventeenth-century Malian legend.

The five-year project to produce *Les Naufragés de Carthage* and *Viva Carthago* began in 2000, when the United Nations Fund for Children (UNICEF) signed a partnership with Cinétéléfilms in Tunis for 'producing the animated feature film that traces the history of the Mediterranean, its culture, its people and the characters who shaped it' (L'UNICEF 2006). The production of both the movie and the series was funded mainly by the European Commission, within the framework of the Euromed Audiovisual programme.

The production of *Les Naufragés de Carthage* and *Viva Carthago* shares many of the characteristics of what Miller et al. describe as 'treaty co-productions', involving artists, technicians, funders and the more or less active participation of government officials from two or more countries. As a consequence, treaty co-productions are formal affairs that fall within the realm of international relations and involve issues of national identity and cultural policy (Miller et al 2001: 84). Even though governments were not directly involved, *Les Naufragés de Carthage* and *Viva Carthago* nonetheless conform to Miller's main criteria as 'treaty co-productions' due to the involvement of semi-governmental organisations.

The funders and producers had slightly different priorities with regard to the identity of the text. Jean-Michel Delmotte, the representative of UNICEF Tunisia, explained their goal as follows: '[b]y partnering with Cinétéléfilms, we wanted to expand our collaboration with actors of the modern media who share our values of universality, solidarity and commitment to a more just world' (L'UNICEF 2006). The producer's vision was that the film would recount the ancient history of the Mediterranean and Carthage in terms of its creators and thinkers, and of its ordinary people. In an interview, executive producer Mohammed Habib 'Attia welcomed the opportunity to provide a medium for 'southern historians' to air their views. In 'Attia's view, northern historians (Europeans) tend to cast Hannibal in the role of a 'bloodthirsty warrior' and to portray Phoenician merchants as 'chauvinists only interested in trade and money', while for southerners like himself, Hannibal was 'a hero and a great military strategist' and the Phoenicians were a 'creative people'.[46] In order to prove their point, the producers also involved Tunisian academics. Historical accuracy was verified by consultant Dr Hassine Fantar, Professor of Ancient History and Archaeology at Tunis University.

The plot of *Les Naufragés de Carthage* and *Viva Carthago* begins in 146 BCE, in the midst of the battle of Carthage. The city, shown as a cultural and commercial centre, faces a violent attack by the Roman imperial forces. Séfrou, a wise old man, is dying. He is anguished to see his beloved city falling prey to destruction and is beset by fears that his life's accomplishment is at risk. Séfrou's last hope is his grandson Seddiq, a cheeky, resourceful ten-year-old boy, whom he tasks with recovering the scrolls that will save knowledge for future generations. Seddiq is accompanied by four fellow adventurers: the enigmatic Cid from Numidia; Ghada, a former slave girl of thirteen who fled from her master during the battle of Carthage; Kothar, a grumpy twenty-year-old sailor, who found himself in the adventure quite by accident; and Hamoura, a wise donkey. While the human characters represent a cross-section of Carthagian society regarding age, gender and socio-economic background, they work together in order to achieve their common goal. They board a ship called *Carthago*, and thus begins their magical journey over the Mediterranean. *Carthago* is no ordinary ship, as it has a special power that allows it to slip through the cracks of time; simply by passing through a mysterious cloud it can find itself in a different place and era. Driven by their mission to explore and record their history, Seddiq and his friends travel through ancient times aboard their ship. When in trouble, Séffrou's soul appears as a spirit, uttering enigmatic sentences to help his grandson. Their journey introduces them to the history of the Mediterranean. Thus, 'The Wayward Carthage I' covers three episodes of the *Viva Carthago* series, namely 'The Forgotten Kingdom', about an encounter with Admiral Hanno on the banks of the Niger; 'The Wrath of Serapis', about the Lighthouse and the Library of Alexandria; and 'The Mask Amarascos', about the pirates of the Mediterranean. After these first three episodes, *Viva Carthago* continues with other episodes recounting stories from ancient history, such as 'The Survivors of the Alps', an encounter with Hannibal during his crossing of the Alps; 'The Wind of Destiny', an introduction to the world of gladiators; or 'Pearl of the Orient', about the inventions of ancient Greece. In the telling of these stories, both *Les Naufragés de Carthage* and *Viva Carthago* mediate a 'Mediterranean Tunisian' identity that highlights Tunisia's contributions to Mediterranean culture, without explicitly mentioning its ties to the Arab or Muslim world. Thus, both productions present a secular approach to Tunisian identity. This approach largely conforms to both the political discourse of the Ben Ali era and the concept of the European Commission's Euromed Audiovisual programme, as well as to the identity of the local Francophone elite. This identity is reinforced by the French title of the film and the series as well as by the language of the production, which was originally French and was then dubbed into *fusha* Arabic with a slight Tunisian accent, a language that is also used in Tunisian television newscasts.

Visually, both *Les Naufragés de Carthage* and *Viva Carthago* adopted the hyper-realist, non-caricaturist style typical of French series of the late 1980s such as *Les Mondes engloutis* (Spartakus and the Sun Beneath the Sea, 1985–7), created by Nina Wolmark, and *Bleu, l'enfant de la Terre* (Blue, the Earth Child, 1986), by Philippe Druillet, as well as those of the 1990s such as *Kirikou et la Sorcière* (Kirikou and the Witch, 1998), by Michel Ocelot, and *Le Château des singes* (A Monkey's Tale, 1999), by Jean-François Laguionie. Seddiq's facial features also bear similarities with those in *Avatar: The Last Airbender* (2005), an American animated television series, and has anime-like visual traits. This style is used to evoke authentic medieval characters and environments, and to articulate a Mediterranean Tunisian identity.

Algeria

Nation and Identity in Algeria

Algeria's bid for independence was one of the most violent decolonisation struggles in the Arab world. The war between colonial France and the Algerian independence movement lasted from 1954 to 1962, leaving an estimated 200,000 dead (Windrow 1997: 3). Even after gaining independence, the idea of national unity was overshadowed by the violent clashes of 1962 and the coup d'état in June 1965.

From the moment Algeria gained independence, and especially since the 1970s, the country's governments have devoted much of their efforts to write and rewrite the country's official history as decolonisation strategy (Remaoun 2003). Both the French and the francophone intellectual elite had used historical narratives to legitimise their presence in Algeria (Vatin 1974; Lucas 1975; Leimdorfer 1992; Soufi 1997). To highlight Algeria's European ties, the ancient Roman, Latin and Christian periods were emphasised in education, while the Berber-Arab and Ottoman periods were referred to as the 'dark ages' of barbarism (Remaoun 2003).

How a society publicly remembers its past is a political act, and how institutional leaders remember the past is neither innocuous nor preordained. Literature, theatre, films and even animations about historical topics participate in what Foucault defined as the 'manipulation of popular memory', awakening and developing nostalgia for an idealised past that never existed (Foucault 1975: 25). Since the popular media shape popular memory, and thus knowledge of past struggles, film and television are useful in the dynamics of history making. Accordingly, it is important to be critical not only of how history is told, but also of how the media construct 'history' as a category of popular memory.

Driven largely by ambitions of self-legitimisation, the Algerian state was intent on seizing the monopoly over historical memory. To strengthen its position, the National Centre for Historical Studies was founded in the 1970s, and was later attached to the Ministry of Interior (Remaoun 1994). Strongly institutionalised, Algeria entered a period of writing and rewriting history (Manceron and Remaoun 1993). There were two major strands in the rewriting of pre-colonialist history: proving the continuity of the Algerian nation and rectifying the assumed falsifications made by colonial historiography (Haddab 1984).

The Islamic past and its major events such as the conquest of the Maghreb, and the Almohad and Ottoman periods, became central, as did Andalusia, which was under Muslim rule from 711 to 1492, and came to be remembered as a 'lost heaven' (Remaoun 1994). Narratives of the Algerian War of Independence were accorded the highest priority because of their direct impact on power relations in independent Algeria. Therefore, such narratives became the backbone of the political legitimacy of post-independence governments as well as one of the most important factors in shaping modern Algerian identity (Branche 2011). Under the presidency of Shadli Bendjedid (1972–92), the Organisation nationale des moudjahidin (National Organisation of Mujahedeen – ONM) won the monopoly on collecting and archiving documents on the War of Independence and was hence authorised to write its own version of that particular historical period. In January 1994, a national research centre was founded to study the national movement and the revolution of 1 November 1954, and was placed under the supervision of the Ministry of the Mujahedeen.[47]

From independence until 1988, the ideological glue of the political system was a combination of etatist, nationalist, revolutionary, socialist and collectivist elements, which provided a basis for a social contract between the regime and society, with the former taking care of the population's wellbeing via distribution of goods, and the latter accepting exclusion from power in exchange (Werenfels 2007: 32–3). On the government's side, there were attempts to create an identity through the transformation of a multiethnic, multilingual and culturally diverse society into an Arab-Islamic one, with Islam as the state religion and Arabic as the official language (Remaoun 1994). The constitution declared Islam as the official religion, although this actually implied 'the subordination of Algeria's religious leaders to the nation-state' (Roberts 2001).

In the late 1980s, oil revenues shrank, financial difficulties grew and government propaganda sources ran low. The disillusioned middle class began to lean towards the Islamists, and in the autumn of 1988, a revolt shook the country. The regime reacted to this with liberalising policies and allowed the establishment of new parties. Private foundations were created that engaged in gathering documents on the War of Independence, challenging the state's monopoly on creating historical narratives.

Following the victory of the Islamic Salvation Front in the first round of the 1991 legislative election, the military intervened in 1992 and nullified the election result. Bendjedid resigned, and a state council assumed power. This was followed by the outbreak of a bloody civil war between the government and Islamist rebels that lasted for eight years. The civil war increased the need for a common national narrative – the state turned to the past in order to bolster its legitimacy and find common ground for national consensus. Schools remained the main platforms for teaching history.[48] Ever since then, successive presidents and governments of Algeria have struggled not only with economic problems, but also with the lack of legitimacy among a part of Algerian society.

Language and Identity in Algeria

After Algeria declared independence in July 1962, its new leaders decided to eliminate the differences between various social groups in order to engage in a process of 'nation-building'. In doing so, unifying the language was a primary tool (Benrabah 2004). An Arabisation process was soon declared, affecting all spaces of public life previously monopolised by the French language (Berri 1973). The first National Conference on Arabisation, held in May 1975, recommended the Arabisation of all sectors of life, with the goal of restoring Classical Arabic as the symbolic language of Arabo-Islamic identity. Classical Arabic was specified as the country's official language in the Algerian National Constitution, and became prominent in schools, particularly in the teaching of history.[49]

Today, Classical Arabic is still viewed as being of particular importance in all aspects of Algerian public life as well as in the media. At the same time, however, a diglossic situation exists, characterised by the use of Classical Arabic and French as 'high varieties', mainly used in formal and public domains, while colloquial dialects (Algerian Arabic and Berber) are considered 'low varieties' for informal situations (Mostari 2004).

The History of Animation Production in Algeria since the 1960s

The history of Algerian animation production dates back to the 1960s. Western art forms, formats and genres mostly found their way to Algeria through the local francophone-educated elite during the colonial period and later. French authors and productions were a major source of inspiration for early Algerian animated cartoons.

Early Algerian animation can best be described as having a minimal engagement with social and political affairs; artists and producers were both driven by artistic goals rather than by making profit or engaging in politics. The very first known Algerian animation was *La Fête de l'arbre* (The Tree Party) by Mohammed ʿAram (1934–2020), released in 1963, just one year after the country gained independence (Bendazzi 1994: 392–3). The plot does not engage with local politics directly, as it conveys a message of peace and non-particular identity with its plea for replanting forests destroyed by napalm. Therefore it serves both as a memento to the peace movement that was then in its early days in response to the horrors of the Vietnam War, and as a reference to the Algerian villages that were burned down with napalm by the French army.

Mohammed ʿAram taught himself animation and produced his black-and-white celluloid animations with no funding from local government or from cinema authorities. Although he did not develop a personal style, ʿAram's animations are visually localised productions, set in local environments. His narratives largely revolve around topics particular to the region, with a respect for its cultural sensibilities and traditions. Locality is also indicated by the titles of ʿAram's productions: *H'Mimo et les allumettes* (H'Mimo and the Matches, 1965), *H'Mimo et le babtême* (H'Mimo and the Baptism, 1966), *Douieb au Sahara* (Douieb in the Sahara, 1967), *Fertoh et le singe* (Fertoh and the Monkey, 1971), *Les Couleurs du diable* (The Devil's Colours, 1975), *L'Olivier justicier* (The Olive Tree Who Loved Justice, 1978), *Adrar* (1979) and *Sema* (1983).[50]

Aside from working as an animator, ʿAram also trained a team with whom he produced around twenty largely self-funded short productions between 1963 and 1999. Similarly to his early work, his later animations had an educational dimension too, dealing with illiteracy in *Ah, s'il savait lire* (Oh,

If Only He Could Read, 1963) and with urban health problems in *Microbes des poubelles* (Bugs in the Bins, 1964) (Bendazzi 1994: 392–3). In 1967, 'Aram returned to television, and in 1976 he opened his own studio. Two members of 'Aram's team also contributed their own projects: Mohamed Mazari, who was working as a director, directed *Mariage* (Wedding) in 1966, while Menouar Merabtene, a comic-strip designer, directed *Le Magicien* (The Magician) in 1965. These were followed by *Gasba et Galal* (Gasba and Galal) and *Bouzio dans le train* (Bouzio on the Train). Similarly to 'Aram, his students too focused on narratives with a local relevance.

From the early 1990s onwards, several Algerian animators were employed in European and Arab animation industries.[51] Still, animation production in Algeria remained on a modest scale for various reasons, among them the political instability of the time. In contrast to Egypt, the relatively small size of the domestic market meant that animated productions did not attract investors, while the inward-turning nature of Algerian politics did not encourage pan-Arab cultural production either (unlike in Syria and the Gulf). The stagnation lasted until the introduction of modern computer animation technologies. From the mid-2000s, a number of private enterprises began to operate in the animation business, even though government support remained minimal.[52]

Al-Jaza'ir Tarikh wa Hadarah – *Animating Algeria's History*

Because of the violence and tensions with the Islamist opposition, the Algerian state kept a tight control on television programming (Hadj-Moussa 2003). The government-run Enterprise Nationale de Télévision (ENTV) for a long time enjoyed a monopoly as the sole TV channel. While the lifting of the ban on satellite dishes in 1987 finally provided an opportunity for locals to access channels from other countries, privately owned TV stations are still not allowed in Algeria. In 2009, two other channels were launched: Rabi'a, a Berber-speaking channel, and Al-Qur'an, a religious channel, to provide people with a national religious identity that would be an alternative to radical views (Belamry 2009).

Al-Jaza'ir Tarikh wa Hadarah (Algerian History and Civilisation) aired on ENTV in 2012 as the most ambitious animation production ever made in Algeria. The fifty-two-episode series (each lasting approximately twenty-six minutes) offers a chronological overview of the history of Algeria from the creation of the kingdom of Numidia in antiquity until the end of French colonial rule in 1962. Production and animation work was done by the Algerian Al-Bouraq Studio, a private company established by Seddik Tayeb Cherif, and lasted for five years.[53] The 50 million-dinar (approximately $600,000) production was largely funded by the Ministry of Mujahedeen and the Ministry of Culture (Grande 2012).

As a historical animated cartoon, *Al-Jaza'ir Tarikh wa Hadarah* presents an alternative past, written from an Algerian nationalistic, anti-colonialist point of view, while offering a textual and visual reworking of traditional narratives. It offers a site where representations of history are remediated, and hence re-appropriated and challenged. It must here be noted that *Al-Jaza'ir Tarikh wa Hadarah* is not a pioneer in adapting a Western cultural form to use it as a site of resistance and a platform for discourses over history for children. Comic strips had similarly been a popular format for presenting narratives both on pre-colonial history and on the War of Independence (Douglas and Malti-Douglas 1994: 182–8).

(Re) Defining Algerian Identity in Al-Jaza'ir Tarikh wa Hadarah

The institutional background of the production indicates that *Al-Jaza'ir Tarikh wa Hadarah* advocates the official viewpoint in Algerian discourses on local history and national identity. An analysis of the content shows that the series is a work of propaganda whose aim is to stir up pride in the people. One of its visible goals is to create a sense of continuity in Algerian history from antiquity to the twentieth century. At the same time, targeting primarily an audience under 18, *Al-Jaza'ir Tarikh wa Hadarah* does not provide an in-depth historical analysis of the local and regional history, but rather offers a general overview, with a special focus on Algeria's national identity. Visually, the influence of anime on the producers is quite obvious. Instead of creating local aesthetic forms, animators used a Japanese style for animating characters and drawing backgrounds, although certain French traits are also evident. Localism is only represented by backgrounds of actual places and by characters with local visual characteristics.

The language of the series is generally *fusha* Arabic, most probably in order to add an extra dimension of reliability to the series as a source of historical knowledge. However, the episodes covering the struggle for independence in

Figure 2.10 *Al-Jaza'ir Tarikh wa Hadarah* (Algerian History and Civilisation): reinventing history. 2012 © Studio El Bouraq.

the twentieth century are dubbed in local Algerian dialect in order to allow viewers to better identify with the characters. Unlike the colloquial dialect of modern Algeria, the dialect of these particular episodes is generally stripped of French phrases in order to stress the country's cultural uniqueness.[54]

The episodes in the series have a visual style and a framed narrative similar to Albert Barille's French animation series *Il était une fois . . .* (Once Upon a Time . . .), seven series of which were made between 1978 and 2008.[55] Each episode includes an animated narrator, a professor-like man with a beard who wears glasses, a yellow shirt and a green tie, standing by a chart that shows either the title or actual maps. Following a short explanation of the historical period, the narrative moves back in time and is acted out by animated historical characters.

The proposed identity of the series goes beyond Algerian nationalism and highlights the Islamic identity of the country by referring to modern Algeria as a geographical and cultural unity rather than a nation-state. In this sense, the series mediates a cultural citizenship that includes religion as an integral part of national identity as well as an indicator of the 'own' and the 'other'. The historical events presented are not restricted to what happened in the territory of modern Algeria, but rather they encompass the entire Maghreb region, with a special focus on Algiers and the wider territory of modern Algeria.

Islamic identity is highlighted at the beginning of each episode, when an animated narrator greets the audience with 'Salam ul-llahi ʿalaykum' (May Allah's peace be with you!). Adding Allah's name to the traditional Arab-Muslim greeting 'as-salam ʿalaykum' (Peace be with you) is a clear indication of the producers' Islamic commitment. Further, when talking about particular events, the narrator uses the dates of the Islamic calendar in addition to those of the Western calendar.

The aim to position Algeria as an integral part of the Muslim world is most obvious when one analyses identities and the terminology used for labelling different periods of local history, alluding to what is accepted as 'own' and what is regarded as 'other'.

When talking about non-Arab Muslim leaders or groups, ethnic origin is neither concealed nor highlighted. Instead, their Islamic identity is stressed, for example in the episodes on the Almohads. Even though their Berber ethnic background is mentioned from the very beginning, they are referred to as 'Muslims'. This is unsurprising; while the Almohad dynasty has been the main historical reference to Berber ethnic identity in twentieth-century Algerian discourse, after independence, the elaboration of Algerian 'official culture', history and nationhood were mainly based on the doctrine of an essentially Arab-Islamic Algeria (McDougall 2003). President Abdelaziz Bouteflika (1999–2019) did not give in to the Berbers' demand for cultural equality, and the Berber opposition, particularly in the region of Kabylia, has been facing continued repression (Holm 2005).

When talking about the non-Muslim rulers of the present-day territory of Algeria, the narrator defines them in terms of *ihtilal* (occupation) or *istiʿmar* (colonisation), while the Muslim rules are labelled as *ʿahd* (period), regardless of their ethnic background or sectarian affiliation. In this regard, the Algerian and Sunni Muslim producers accept the Ottoman Turks and Shia Fatimids as legitimate rulers of the country.[56] When recounting the battles between the Ottomans and the European powers, the Ottoman army is referred to as a 'Muslim army' (*jays al-muslimeen*), and its victories, such as Hasan Agha's (ruler of the Regency of Algiers from 1533 to 1545) defeat of Christian pirates, are celebrated with a sense of pride.[57] The episodes do not engage in theological discourses; the sectarian affiliations and beliefs of particular Muslim characters and groups are not challenged. One case in point is the episode about the Fatimid imam Abu ʿAbdullah al-Shiʿi, an Ismaili cleric who wielded great influence on the Fatimid dynasty, and who is described by the Sunni producers as a man of justice and wisdom who won the heart of Berber pilgrims to Mecca.[58]

The moral superiority of the Muslims is often highlighted. The Berbers' conversion to Islam is explained by their recognition of its justice, ignoring the fact that the arrival of Islam to Algeria was followed by fierce Berber resistance and tensions within Berber societies themselves (Maddy-Weitzman 2011: 21–39). The moral superiority of the Muslims is also acknowledged by non-Muslims and even by their foes. In one episode about Tareq Ibn Ziyad and his Spanish ally, Count Julian describes Muslims as 'men of justice' (*rijal al-ʿadl*). Muslim leaders are generally presented as tall and handsome; for example Emir ʿAbdelkader is portrayed as a good-looking bearded man with lighter skin and a deep, reassuring voice.

The official Algerian nation-building strategies are also apparent in several cases when tribal loyalties (*ʿasabiyya*) are highlighted as the core problem that enabled foreign powers of the past to divide and conquer Algeria.

Presentations of the 'Other' in Al-Jazaʾir Tarikh wa Hadarah

Unlike many 'Islamic animations' of Saudi Arabia and the Gulf (see Chapter 5), *Al-Jazaʾir Tarikh wa Hadarah* does not demonise hostile non-Muslims. While the visual markers of the otherness of the European characters are indicated by traits such as blond hair, their appearance is not paired with 'evil-looking' features. However, non-Muslim characters, like Frankish rulers who oppose the Muslims, are presented as arrogant.[59] The religion of the 'other' is not a target of mockery, nor is it labelled heretic. Whilst the Christianity of the Europeans is often mentioned, their faith is not challenged.

Following the official rhetoric, the periods under non-Muslim rule and attacks by non-Muslims such as the French and the Spanish are defined as an occupation (*ihtilal*) or colonisation (*istiʿmar*). Explanations of the motives governing the actions of European powers remain rather superficial. Even though the narrator avoids direct assertions, the lack of any obvious rationale behind the Europeans' actions suggests that they – unlike the Muslims – were led not by a cultural mission but by mere imperialistic ambitions. One case in point is the narrative about the beginning of French colonialism in the eighteenth and nineteenth centuries. The series presents the pirate activities of the Barbary States against European and American ships (referred to as *al-jihad al-Bahriyy*, the maritime *jihad*) as a legitimate strategy for retrieving previous loans that the French governments had refused to pay back.[60] The narrator consistently defines the Muslims' battles – such as that of Emir ʿAbdelkader – as *jihad*. However, the term does not primarily refer to a religious struggle, but rather to a nationalist one, a '*jihad* for Algeria'.[61]

While foreign enemies are not demonised, their local collaborators are cast in a rather unfavourable light. Muslims who cooperate with foreign powers against their own people are labelled traitors (*khawana*; sing. *khaʾen*) and presented as weaklings with an unpleasant countenance and shady morals. One example is an unnamed leader of the Tawair and Zmala tribes in the episode recounting the rise of Emir ʿAbdelkader.[62] The collaborators are portrayed in the style of a caricature, with large eyes, round shoulders and a potbelly. They grovel before the French and when given orders, they merely squeak, '*Oui Monsieur, oui Monsieur*'. It is important to note that only the leaders are accused of treachery. Their kinsmen are presented as weak or ignorant folk who obey their leader even if they disagree with him. The portrayal of traitors largely fits into the Algerian post-colonial political discourse, where accusing opponents of being traitors was an effective tool for delegitimising them.[63] Political opponents routinely accuse each other of being descendants of the *haraki*s (Muslim Algerian loyalists to the French, equivalent to traitors). *Haraki* or 'son of a *haraki*' is still a major insult in all walks of social and political life (Branche 2011). The call for unity within a people, especially when faced with occupation, is not just found in Algerian historic animations, but is also a theme in many Palestinian animations.

Palestinian Territories

An Introduction to Palestinian Animation

Like Palestinian cultural and media productions in general, animation has been linked to the political struggle both between Palestinians and Israeli occupants, and between different Palestinian factions. Palestinian animation is largely serious, and expresses the social and political realities of a people living under physical and digital occupation on the part of both the Israelis and their own leaders. Palestinian animation is therefore often dominated by realism, capturing subjective realities and representing rival notions of Palestinian identities.

The establishment of the State of Israel in 1948 and the fate of the Palestinians living under occupation has inspired countless filmmakers from Palestine and across the entire Arab world. While animation producers of Palestinian origin are now beginning to tell their own stories, the majority of higher-budget animation productions dealing with the Palestinian cause have been made not by Palestinians, but by Arabs and Muslims from other countries.

With no state or national film fund, and the absence of a strong local audience, until the late 2000s the Palestinian people were mainly spoken for by non-Palestinian animators and producers. Two notable cases, both by Saudi producer Osama Khalifa and his company, OK Toons, are *Hilm al-Zaytun* (Olive Dream, 2008), the epic story of Miryam, a Palestinian girl who fled the small city of 'Ain Karem in 1948, and *Shahid al-'Aalam* (The Martyr of the World, 2003), which tells the story of a Palestinian boy, Muhammad al-Durra, who was shot by an Israeli soldier in 2000.

Because of the harsh economic circumstances and the different political priorities of those living in the Palestinian Territories, it took a long time before Palestinian authors began producing their own animated cartoons. Still, Palestinian animated cartoon production remains weak compared to that in other Arab countries, in terms of both quality and output. Given the diverse nature of Palestinian politics, identity formation in Palestinian animation should not simply be seen as a tool for advocating the Palestinian cause, but also needs to be analysed taking the complexities of cultural and media production in the Palestinian Territories into account. A significant difference compared to productions made by non-Palestinians is that the purpose of Palestinian animations is not always to address an international audience by 'Arabising' or 'Islamising' the Palestinian cause, but is often to communicate with its own people and mobilise them for particular domestic issues, the latter reflected in the tendency to use local dialects, present local places and people, and include local intertextual references.

One common characteristic of Palestinian animated cartoons is the lack of a developed visual style, which can be ascribed to the severe economic situation and the lack of opportunities. The vast majority of animators are self-taught and struggle to create a sustainable business model that allows them to produce more than one animation, or a few at best.

Media and Media Industries in the PLO-controlled West Bank

After the Israeli occupation of the West Bank and the Gaza Strip in 1967, a military regime was established and restrictions were imposed on the freedom of the press (Nossek and Rinnawi 2003). As Palestinians were forbidden to create an indigenous broadcasting industry, the population of the West Bank and Gaza could only view television channels broadcast from neighbouring countries, including Israel, Jordan and Egypt. Until the Oslo Accords of 1993, Palestinians were exposed to a one-way flow of foreign cultural productions. In the wake of the 1993 agreement between Israel and the Palestine Liberation Organization (PLO), administrative powers were partly transferred to the newly established Palestinian Authority (PA), which passed new laws and regulations that expanded its control over local media (Najjar 1997). Local media and early television production soon became vehicles of the nationalist struggle. Meanwhile, the focus against Israel also led to an internal self-censorship in order to prevent outsiders from gaining insights into the weaknesses and fissures within Palestinian society (Nossek and Rinnawi 2003: 187). The Palestinian Broadcasting Corporation (PBC) was established immediately after the implementation of the Oslo Accords. Soon afterwards, due to the spread of satellite technology, Palestinian media proliferated, and the number of local channels – including private ones – grew to over thirty (Salama 2006). Because they were entertainment channels, they not only discouraged political discourse, but were also objects of self-censorship. As Tawil-Souwi put it, the neoliberalism that followed the Oslo Accords resulted in a 'digital occupation', imposed by Israel, and reinforced by rival Palestinian governments of the PLO and Hamas, who regarded digital networks as spaces of control (Tawil-Souri 2007: 16).

Ever since then, broadcasting rights have been part of a political struggle between Palestinians and Israelis as well as different Palestinian factions (Tawil-Souri 2007: 7). PA-run state institutions such as the Ministry of Information, the Ministry of the Interior and the Ministry of Culture have a fundamental role in the regulation of broadcasting and television production.

The PA uses media regulations and censorship as a means of securing its own hegemony over local rivals (Rubin 1994; Jamal 2000). Therefore, media productions, including animated cartoons, presented on local PA-run channels either have to be politically neutral or supportive of the PA in order to gain support for production and receive approval for broadcast.

These conditions affected the identity formation of PA media on a broader level. Tawil-Souri notes that Palestinian broadcasting largely fails to fulfil the role of a public sphere that could help to shape and (re)create an 'imagined community', either as an entertainment or educational resource, or as an integral part of cultural production or self-expression (Tawil-Souri 2007: 16). On the contrary, Palestinian media tends to prevent unity because it is used as the mouthpiece of rival political factions.

Nationalist Identities Proposed by Animations in the West Bank

In the post-Oslo period of the mid- to late 1990s, numerous international NGOs entered the Palestinian Territories promoting financial, educational and cultural projects in support of Palestinian civil society. Animation production was appreciated for its capacity both as a creative industry and as a format for children's education. With funds from the British Council, the Gaza College of Applied Science's Animation and Games Unit was established in 1998, followed by the Palestine Information and Communications Technology Incubator programme in 2004, distributing funding from international donors like the European Commission, Oxfam, USAID and Wamda to a number of small studios both in Gaza and the West Bank.

Despite the flow of foreign funds, Palestinian animation production can best be described as an individualistic scene of authors and small start-up companies, often with a short life span, working on one-off projects.[64] Even if they receive professional training and financial support from local or international donors, most companies generally shut down after completing the project they received support for. One representative case is *Humum Mutaharrikah* (Moving Issues), a sitcom-like miniseries of five episodes that aired on Filastin, a PLO-controlled channel, in 2007 (Mutaharrika 2007). The production was a result of cooperation between the University of Birzeit and the British Council. The series was actually produced by Zan Studio, a small Ramallah-based company set up by university students. The series strongly advocated a Palestinian identity: the plot revolved around a young man from the West Bank dealing with everyday life and social problems. Despite promising first steps, Zan Studio was unable to stand on its own feet and ceased operation.

The animated cartoon format was also discovered by the PA, which used it as a propaganda tool. *Bhibbak ya Baladna* (I Love You, Oh Our Country), a series of thirty episodes each lasting two minutes, was produced by the Jordanian Sketch in Motion Studio on behalf of the PA in 2008. Benefiting from USAID funding, the animation was part of a campaign in cooperation with Media Plus that also included radio spots and newspaper comic strips, whose goal was to foster more positive attitudes among the Palestinian people towards both their homeland and the PA.[65] The series promoted a Palestinian identity by using a Palestinian dialect, and it involved characters with different social backgrounds in order to stress the unity of the people.

Identity and Media Politics of Hamas

While animations from the West Bank mainly focus on artistic quality, productions from Hamas-ruled Gaza tend to prioritise the message.

Hamas, literally meaning 'zeal', is the acronym for *Harakat al-Muqawama al-Islamiyya* (Islamic Resistance Movement). It was founded as the underground armed wing of the Muslim Brotherhood in the Gaza Strip at the beginning of the first Palestinian uprising (Intifada) in 1987 (Abu Amr 1994: 62–3). Hamas cited Islam as the alternative to the failed nationalist and secular ideologies, and called for the establishment of an Islamic society in Palestine (Abu Amr 1994). The organisation formulated its ideology in rivalry with secular national Palestinian factions, and presented an alternative in both ideology and identity, fusing Islam and nationalism in the Palestinian-Israeli conflict. Lybarger noted that Hamas came up with a 'Palestinianised' Islam that incorporates nationalist elements in order to be competitive with mainstream Palestinian nationalism (Lybarger 2007: 7–14). In less than two decades, Hamas grew into the main rival force to the PA, and Hamas-led press and media outlets became tools for domestic battles for power and public approval.

According to Atef Alshaer, Al-Aqsa TV was established in the context of the rising political power and social influence of Hamas in the Gaza

Strip. It began broadcasting in January 2006, right after Hamas's victory in the Legislative Council. The channel was established by Fathi Ahmad Hammad, the previous leader of the Izzedeen al-Qassam Brigades in North Gaza, a Palestinian Legislative Council member and chairman of Al-Ribat Communications and Artistic Productions, a Hamas-run company that also produces a number of other Hamas media including the Voice of al-Aqsa radio station and its biweekly newspaper, *Al-Risala*. Later, Hammad became Hamas Interior Minister, responsible for security within the Gaza Strip. The establishment of Al-Aqsa TV was a response to the dominance of rival Fatah in the Palestinian media. Very soon, Al-Aqsa TV became a forum for mobilising Hamas supporters against both Israel and Fatah. Following the Hamas takeover in the Gaza Strip in August 2007, the government blocked television channels controlled by Fatah, preventing them from broadcasting into Gaza. Since then, Al-Aqsa TV has become an important platform for criticising the PLO's policies, including its willingness to cooperate with Israel and introduce security measures against Hamas.

The increasingly easy access to technology enabled young artists in the Gaza Strip to produce short animated spots on local channels. Similarly to other television and cinematic productions produced in the Gaza Strip, animated cartoons often wage a dual propaganda war, against both the Israeli authorities and local rivals (Alshaer 2012).

Islamist-Nationalist Identities Proposed by Animations in Gaza

One of the most prominent Hamas animations presented on al-Aqsa TV is a caricature-style miniseries entitled *'Esabaat Dayton* (Dayton's Gangs), created in 2010 by animators affiliated to al-Aqsa TV. The title is a reference to Lieutenant-General Keith Dayton, US security coordinator for Israel and the Palestinian Authority between 2005 and 2010, who was in charge of overseeing the creation of three Palestinian battalions recruited in the West Bank, trained in Jordan and then deployed in the occupied territory with the task of maintaining peace between Arabs and Israeli settlers. Dayton decided that the Palestinian units would be primarily used against two targets: criminal gangs and Hamas. In turn, official Hamas propaganda quickly accused those participating in the project of betraying the Palestinian cause. *'Esabaat Dayton* follows this narrative. The animation was produced by a small company called Required Vision. The scenarios and dialogues were written by a local Hamas activist, Baha' al-Deen Yaseen, who was also responsible for the animation. The theme song, sung by a men's choir, encapsulated the essence of the production's message with its militaristic undertones:

> We swear that we will not be terrorised by Dayton.
> You will leave, oh Dayton.
> We swear that we will not be terrorised by Dayton.
> The occupation will not stay and enjoy the quiet.
> Oh West Bank, persevere.

The main character of the series is a Palestinian militant called Bahloul, whose name is an allusion to a dim-witted character of folk tales. Bahloul has a straggly moustache, a potbelly and an ugly patch on the back of his trousers. His adversaries, the Israeli soldiers, are portrayed as tall, handsome men, broad-chested and clean-shaven. As a collaborator, Bahloul is despised by the Israelis, who train him and often also beat him. The dialogues reflect Bahloul's betrayal of his fellow Palestinians. In one of the episodes, the Israeli officer asks him, 'If you get orders to arrest your father or your uncle, would you do so?' to which Bahloul answers, 'Yes'. Next, the Israeli asks him, 'What if you get orders to shoot your brother?' to which he responds, 'I will'. Another scene shows Bahloul shining and kissing the shoes of an Israeli soldier.

The series shows Israeli settlers in an unfavourable light. One scene has an elderly settler visualised as an Orthodox Jew sending his armed son, a thin young man with unpleasantly sharp features to Hebron, saying, 'Go, drink from their blood and come back safely'. When the father offers his son a map of Hebron so that he will find his way, the son replies, 'I won't need it, I am not Gilad [Shalit], and the West Bank is not Gaza.[66] Calm down. Shalom, father.' The following scene shows the young settler massacring Palestinian children. After seeing what he has done, Bahloul speaks to the settler: 'Listen you ... You Jew, you got yourself lost, you killed my people right before my eyes. I will respond with ... with more peace. Are you done?', then offers the settler a white dove and carries him on his own back to his home.

In another scene, Bahloul tortures a young boy who threw stones at Israelis. After being handed over to the Israeli authorities, the boy turns to

Bahloul: 'Hey, man, are you going to turn me in to the Jews? You're no kin of mine. You're nothing but a collaborator.'

Another work of propaganda, mediating Hamas's identity on Al-Aqsa TV, is *Fe'ran al-Fasad fi Ghazza* (The Mice of Corruption in Gaza, 2007). The short film uses direct symbolism and overtly communicates anti-Fatah propaganda. The opening scene shows a relief map of Gaza and the West Bank, with a lion crouching between them. The next scenes show a large group of mice on the West Bank, brandishing weapons taken from a box with a Star of David on it. Some of the mice are carrying Palestinian flags and a picture of their leader, a sly-looking mouse wearing sunglasses and a tie, with a cigar in his mouth. Their leader appears and begins throwing banknotes to a mass of unarmed mice. The next moment, the leader orders his soldiers to begin the invasion of Gaza. The Palestinian flag is replaced with a black skull-and-crossbones flag. Mournful music accompanies the scene showing the belligerent mice preparing to spread destruction by retrieving ammunition from a box with an American flag on it. The following scenes show scorched plants and broken city signs, followed by images of burning photos of humans scattered on the ground, a bonfire of religious books and the torching of buildings (one being the Islamic University). The militant mice tear off a woman's veil, symbolically take an axe to a box painted with the colours of the Palestinian flag and the word *shar'iyya* (legality) written on it. They then set fire to a mosque and kill a white dove.

Witnessing the destruction all around, and deciding that he has had enough, the lion roars and drives the mice out of Gaza. The mournful song is replaced by a battle hymn: 'May those who plant sedition leave this homeland, leave us, we want to live, we've had enough sorrows.' The last scene shows healing drops of rain and new plants sprouting from the scorched fields, while the lion stands next to a Palestinian flag. It can be assumed that the lion represents the Palestinian people, associated with the supporters of Hamas who have had enough of the corruption of the mice of Fatah, and what they regard as their selling out of the Palestinian national cause to foreign powers.

Shaykh al-Mujahedeen – Ahmad Yassin, *an Animation about the Founder of Hamas*

It was as recently as 2013 that the first 3D animated series on Hamas's leader was released. As its title *Shaykh al-Mujahedeen – Ahmad Yassin* (Sheikh of the Mujaheds – Ahmad Yassin) indicates, the animation recounts the life of Ahmad Yassin, founder and leader of the Hamas movement until his assassination in 2004. The thirty-episode series was produced by and exclusively presented on Al-Aqsa TV in 2013, and visually recalls the style of realistic 3D video games rather than animated shows. The scripts were written by Hazem al-Shaʿrawi (b. 1978), director of the Al-Aqsa channel. The production background of the series is largely reflected in the text: a heroic, propagandistic representation of the life of Hamas's founder coupled with an articulation of the nationalist-Islamic identity advocated by Hamas.

The series has two narratives. The first, which also serves as a frame for the main story, recounts the life of a family of five: a father, a mother, a grandmother and two children, a girl called Nusayba and her brother Moʿaz. Most scenes are set in their family home, a large house with pictures of the Dome

Figure 2.11 *Shaykh al-Mujahedeen – Ahmad Yassin* (Sheikh of the Mujaheds – Ahmad Yassin): based on a true-ish story. 2013 © Al-Aqsa TV.

of the Rock and other Palestinian locations hanging on the walls. The house is located in modern Gaza which is idealised as a peaceful and tidy place. The characters and the relationships between them represent an 'Islamic family model' whose members often express the love and admiration they have for each other, and where the children show respect towards their parents. With the exception of some teasing between the children, there appears to be no conflicts in the family.

The family members in the first narrative speak *fusha* Arabic, although some phrases are in colloquial Palestinian dialect. The dialogues reflect the clear Islamic identity of the text, as both adults and children use religious phrases such as *halal* (permissible), *hasanaat* (good deeds/reward for good deeds) and *Bismillah* (in the name of Allah). Religious identity is also stressed on the narrative and visual levels, with characters praying and women wearing veils even in their homes. The Islamic identity of the text largely reflects the Islamist views of Hamas. Unlike many Salafi-oriented Islamic animations from Saudi Arabia, *Shaykh al-Mujahedeen* features an instrumental theme tune played on a lute (*oud*). Similarly to the real-life supporters of Hamas, the main characters are bearded men, while secular characters are presented as clean-shaven or with a moustache at most.[67] The series presents Islam as advocating universal human values by associating concepts like justice ('*adl*), respect (*ihtiram*) and solidarity (*taʿatuf*) with Islamic principles. Besides its Islamist characteristics, the text also carries a general educational message aimed at children. For example, in one episode, the mother gives the children milk, explaining that it is good for them. In another scene, Nusayba is delighted after being told by her mother that she can only play on the computer after finishing her homework. In a similar scene, Moʿaz is angry with himself for not understanding a biology lesson and gladly accepts his mother's proposal of adding an extra half-hour of learning at the expense of playtime.

The second narrative revolves around the life of Ahmad Yassin, which is recounted by the father after Moʿaz asks him for help in choosing a famous person to write about as homework. The story covers Yassin's life from his childhood onwards. It offers an idealised portrait of a leader loved and respected by his people.

The text of the second narrative, through the character of Ahmad Yassin, also advocates a Palestinian-Islamic identity, largely compatible with the ideology of Hamas. In one instance, he quotes the Prophet Muhammad to prove that learning languages is important and approved by Allah. As with the frame narrative, the second narrative also mixes *fusha* Arabic and colloquial Palestinian. When shown as a child, Sheikh Yassin speaks colloquial Palestinian, while as an adult he starts to use *fusha* Arabic, mixed with colloquial Palestinian. Otherness is highlighted, with Egyptian characters using an Egyptian dialect, and British and Jewish characters both having a strong accent when speaking Arabic.

The text puts a special emphasis on Yassin's religious education. Yassin is presented as an exceptional child who is not only skilled in leisure activities like hunting birds, but also has a talent for learning English, and is admired by the British for his capabilities. He is shown to be a gifted speaker, giving talks in a local mosque at the age of nine. His moral qualities are highlighted by quotations. In Episode 1, when asked by their teacher about their future plans, instead of joining in with the other children who talk about their plans to become a racing car driver or to make a lot of money, Yassin answers, 'I would like to see good done to the people. I would like to help my mother with her pilgrimage [to Mecca] and make a pilgrimage for my father, and I would like to become a teacher and teach people how to be good.'

The later episodes of the series focus on Yassin's religious and political activism. The moral and political conclusions are often drawn in the family narrative, when the characters evaluate the events of the past. Episode 6 shows Yassin being imprisoned for a couple of days after his return from Egypt. The father explains the activity of the Muslim Brotherhood in Egypt: 'Their activities in the mosques were teaching about religion and the distribution of helpful tapes, teaching people the Qur'an and helping the poor.' Mo'az asks, 'Why do they dislike these activities, even though they are good deeds?' His father answers, 'The government was afraid that these men will succeed in influencing the people, and the people love them. And then they will elect them, so they will become presidents and ministers in their stead.' In Episode 13, the father elaborates further:

> The sons of Islamic movements are always struggling against the governments, as the governments are *zalim* [oppressors] ... The goal is not that

the Islamic Movement rule the countries and become ministers or presidents. The goal is to right the many wrongs that happen in the country . . . There are many *haram* [forbidden] spreading across the country, like pubs and dancing places.

Despite all the criticism against governments, the series does not mention the rival Fatah faction in a negative context, nor does it include visual marks on Palestinian leaders. It seems likely that at the time the series was produced, the rival factions were engaged in negotiations for a possible reconciliation.

The series is consistent in victimising the Palestinian people and justifying their struggles against the Israelis. The cartoon presents the *Nakba* (the Palestinian exodus of 1948), which occurred when Yassin was five, as a disaster, emphasised by the inclusion of real documentary photographs. The Israelis are denoted not as Jews (*Yahood*), but as Israelis (*Isra'iliyyun*), who, being the enemy, are demonised. In Episode 4, Nusayba draws a conclusion: 'This is what the Israelis are like. They always lie and kill people, but keep saying that they are vulnerable.' In Episode 13, the grandmother blames the Israelis for the strife between Palestinians. 'Without doubt, the occupiers use all the opportunities to incite internal strife [*fitna*] between the brothers, so they do not turn against them in resistance.' The series largely justifies attacks on Israelis as acts of self-defence. In Episode 21, a Palestinian man leaves his family after his son asks for chocolate and his daughter for a doll. The next scene shows an Israeli truck driver hitting Arab bystanders, the father among them, and saying: 'Tomorrow the children will grow and will want to regain the rights of their fathers. They shall all die. I shall drink their blood . . . the Arabs shall die.'

Stressing the identity of the text, the characters of the first narrative completely identify with Ahmad Yassin's ideas. Both Mo'az and Nusayba cheer when their father tells them about Yassin's successes and they are sad when he is defeated. They often refer to the resistance and Palestinian Islamists in the first person plural, indicating their moral support.

Humanist Approaches to Palestinian Identity in Foreign-funded Palestinian Animation

Foreign funding has a strong potential to provide Palestinian animation producers with the opportunity to move beyond local disputes and focus on a broader Palestinian identity. However, most probably due to the funders' priorities, the authors assert that the overall topics carry humanistic values or a universal identity, rather than advocating the Palestinian cause or stressing a Palestinian identity in particular.

One such case is *Khayal al-Haql* (The Scarecrow), released in 2013 by Zaitoon Animation & Games, a small company that operates out of the University College of Applied Science in Gaza, maintained by the education department of the ruling Hamas regime. They had previously released a children's educational animation *Why?*, showing a Palestinian child's perspective of the Separation Barrier in basic 2D computer-animated style. Despite the institutional background, the general content shows neutrality in domestic affairs. The budget of $147,000 that covered the training of the local animators and the production was funded by the World Bank, which did not claim authority over the text (BBC 2013). Director Khalil al-Mazen asserts that the film's message is humanitarian: 'The world is used to seeing Palestinian children surrounded by death, destruction and war, but this film focuses on their simple dreams' (AFP 2013). Usayd Maʿadi, designer and lighting specialist, agrees that the main aim of the feature is to communicate the 'brutality of occupation, which doesn't spare children'. Textually, *Khayal al-Haql* promotes a Palestinian identity through the use of local dialect and by showing local scenes. The plot of the forty-minute production tells the story of a nine-year-old Palestinian orphan called Rima. Before dying in a car crash, her parents left Rima a scarecrow that stood on the family's land near the border. One day, the scarecrow is taken away by an Israeli soldier, so Rima sets off with her schoolfriends on a mission to find it. According to the producer, the scarecrow represents the guardian of the Palestinian land.

Another example is *Fatenah*, an emotive story from 2009. The twenty-seven-minute story is based on a 2005 report by the World Health Organization (WHO) and Physcans for Human Rights entitled 'Breast Cancer in the Gaza Strip: The Struggle for Survival of Fatma Bargouth'. It became the first animated cartoon produced in Gaza to reach the big screen of international festivals. Sponsored by the authoring agencies of the 2005 report, it was produced by Dar Films, a small company that had made several documentaries before.[68] The film's producer Saʿeed Andoni and director Ahmad Habash used photos taken in the Gaza Strip for background to create a documentary-like atmosphere, and combined it with 3D characters.

Despite the fact that the story is rather localised by its use of scenes in Gaza referring to local life and employing the Gaza dialect (with the exception of the Israeli characters who speak either English or Hebrew), the authors claim a global identity for the text, in line with the agenda of the sponsors. According to Andoni, Fatenah could represent any woman from the Gaza Strip who seeks medical treatment not available in local healthcare facilities (Tabar 2009).

The story takes places in the al-Shateʾ Refugee Camp in Gaza in 2004, where Fatenah works as a seamstress in a local factory, and lives in sorry circumstances suffering regular power cuts and financial hardship. After feeling a pain in her breast, Fatenah seeks medical advice. Unfortunately, she is faced by the incompetence of local doctors: one of them suggests that she should loosen her bra, while another says her condition will probably go away once she marries. It takes six months for Palestinian doctors to take her concerns seriously and diagnose breast cancer. Fatenah registers for treatment in an Israeli hospital. Unfortunately, she is denied entry and becomes tied up in Israeli and Palestinian bureaucracy for three months. After finally reaching the Israeli hospital, the doctors inform her that the tumour has spread and she must undergo a mastectomy. This leads to Fatenah's death, visualised as a disappearance into a white abyss. Unlike the majority of productions revolving around the Palestinian issue, *Fatenah* is hardly political at all. While the narrative presents Israeli soldiers and border guards unfavourably, it portrays the doctors and staff at the Israeli hospital as sympathetic and willing to help her. At one point, the film seems to abandon its domestic neutrality by showing portraits of Yasser Arafat and Mahmoud Abbas on the wall, perhaps a less than subtle reference to the leaders who ran Gaza in 2004 and in the eyes of many Palestinians failed to improve the quality of life of the people.

The most successful animation to date internationally is *The Wanted 18* (2014). Directed by Amer Shomali and Canadian director Paul Cowan, the

Figure 2.12   *The Wanted 18*: the cows that joined the resistance. 2014 © Ahmad Habash and Paul Cowan.

seventy-five-minute documentary-animation hybrid combines clay motion, interviews, graphic illustrations and live-action footage. *The Wanted 18* was created in cooperation with the National Film Board of Canada and premiered at the 2014 Toronto International Film Festival before winning the Abu Dhabi Best Documentary in the Arab World prize. Targeting an international audience, the film was dubbed into English, while some of the interviews are in colloquial Arabic and subtitled in English.

The plot, based on a true story, takes us back to the first Intifada in the late 1980s, when Palestinians of Beit Sahour, a Christian-majority village close to Bethlehem, decided to boycott Israeli goods. As the sole source of milk is Tnuva, an Israeli company, the local revolutionary committee decides to buy eighteen cows from an Israeli kibbutz to produce their own milk. Featuring the story of four cows, Rivka, Ruth, Lola and Goldie, *The Wanted 18* is a documentary account of a community's self-organisation and solidarity during the Intifada. The animated part of the film is split into a comic-like storytelling and clay animation featuring the four cows who – as Israeli cows – are at first upset about being sold to Palestinians, then over time grow sympathetic to their new owners' cause.

Through talking-head style interviews, and archive and new footage, the film shows how the collective farm becomes a landmark and the cows acquire the status of local celebrities. As the Israelis discover the farm to be a local symbol of resistance as well as a hideaway for Shomali's uncle, an especially visionary political activist, they declare the eighteen cows to be 'a threat to the national security of the state of Israel'. Soon, the cows go underground and are shown hiding in private homes in amusing clay animation spots.

As in the majority of Palestinian films, *The Wanted 18* has no happy ending. Rather, it ends in bittersweet melancholia, showing the community's disappointment and sense of abandonment by their leaders in the wake of the Oslo Accords that failed to fulfil the people's hope that they would regain rights lost since 1948, and the tragic fate of the cows being forcefully sold to the butcher. As a small sign of hope, Lola's young calf escapes from the truck, and the film ends with live shots of Shomali wandering the rocky hills surrounding the village, searching for the calf that represents the hope of a future generation of resistance.

Conclusion

The animated cartoons of this chapter have been produced primarily by institutions and individuals with close links to national cultural and media industries whose creations were mainly distributed on television channels targeting local audiences. The productions from Egypt, Jordan, the UAE, Tunisia, Algeria and the Palestinian Territories discussed here all mediate identities that are primarily focused on a national community. Animation from Egypt, a country of well-established film and media industries, and boasting the largest domestic audience in the Arab world, tends to focus on the 'self', revealing explicit national identities. Meanwhile, productions from the other countries, though maintaining their focus on the 'own', simultaneously drew layers of identities in line with the identity politics of a specific regime. The heroes of Jordanian *Ben wa 'Esam* travel through time and space to meet scientists from all over the Arab world, highlighting Jordan's Arab identity. By regarding all of Algeria's neither Algerian nor Arab Muslim rulers of the past as legitimate and non-Muslims as illegitimate, *Al-Jaza'ir Tarikh wa Hadarah* presents the Algerian nation as integral to the Muslim *'ummah*. On the other hand, the Tunisian *Viva Carthago* imagines Tunisians as part of the Mediterranean civilisation, in line with the agenda of Bourghiba's historians and Euromed, who funded the project. In the case of Palestinan animations funded by transnational resources, Palestinian producers represent their community as a part of humanity and their cause as a humanist struggle.

On the visual level, in national animation local environments and characters are largely foregrounded, while the visual otherness of other Arab countries and characters from these countries is strongly accentuated. Countries not experiencing violent colonisation or occupation, such as Egypt, Jordan and the United Arab Emirates, tend to focus more on celebrating the 'self' without casting a negative light on the 'other', as does Tunisia. Conversely, the bitter colonial past of Algeria and the ongoing Palestinian struggle against occupation often result in a vilification of the 'other'.

Regarding visual styles, animators and authors have been inspired by American, European or Japanese visual traditions. Disney has been a primary inspiration for Egyptian authors, while French schools influenced Tunisian and Algerian animations. The UAE, a latecomer in animation production, drew not only from Disney, but also from Pixar, both highly influential. In contrast, Palestinian authors generally struggle with a lack of sufficient sources as well as a lack of opportunities to develop unique styles.

The use of local dialects ('*ammiyya*) in these productions is a symbol of national identity, while the 'otherness' of Arabs from other countries and non-Arabs alike is accentuated by their dialects and accents. However, the use of language differs according to each country's national approach to identity. While in the case of Egypt, the UAE and the Palestinian Territories we find that '*ammiyya* serves an indicator of national identity, this is not the case in the Jordanian *Ben wa 'Esam*, as authors preferred to use *fusha* in order to highlight the educational value of the series. In the case of *Al-Jaza'ir Tarikh wa Hadarah* we witness a mix of language, with *fusha* used for narrating Algeria's pre-twentieth-century history, as a reflection of its Arab and Muslim identity, while '*ammiyya* is spoken in twentieth-century scenes to formulate an Algerian national identity.

In fact, the narrative itself is the most important indicator of a national identity in the vast majority of cases. On the narrative level, the overall subject matter, cultural references and intertextuality depend on the particularities of the production background and the country of origin. This chapter has also revealed how some productions go beyond advocating national identities and engage in mediating political messages and even propaganda.

Notes

1. As the Frenkel brothers are no longer alive, it proved impossible to check the accuracy of the anecdotal elements in the family's history. Therefore, I have only quoted information on which there was agreement in the lecture notes of Dr Rashida al-Shafe'i and Mohammad Ghazala, and in the dissertation of Ahmed el-Sherbeny.
2. *Al-Ahram*, 16 March 1936, p. 3. Quoted in the lecture notes of Dr Rashida al-Shafe'i, and also in Ahmed el-Sherbeny's dissertation.
3. *Al-Ahram*, 31 July 1936. Quoted in the lecture notes of Dr Rashida al-Shafe'i, and also in Ahmed el-Sherbeny's dissertation.
4. Although its origin is unknown, the lecture notes of Dr Rashida al-Shafe'i, Ahmed el-Sherbeny and Mohammad Ghazala have verified the anecdote relating to the name of Mish Mish Effendi.
5. *Nashid al-Amal* (The Song of Hope) is a 1937 movie directed by Ahmed Badrakhan, featuring stars such as Umm Kolthoum and Zaki Toleimat.
6. Betty Boop is an American animated character created by Max Fleischer in 1930. She began her career as a caricature of singer Helen Kane. Betty Boop is regarded as the first animated sex symbol.
7. Featuring live characters in animated productions was a tradition already used in the *Bosko* cartoons and in M. J. Winkler's *Felix the Cat in Hollywood*, a 1923 short cartoon featuring Felix the Cat. In the episode, Felix goes to Hollywood and meets Charlie Chaplin, Douglas Fairbanks, William S. Hart, Will Hays, Snub Pollard and Ben Turpin in the first animated cartoon to feature caricatures of Hollywood celebrities.
8. These productions were created using Dufaycolor, an early French and British additive colour photographic film process for motion pictures.
9. Gabriel Nahhas was born in 1906 in Alexandria, Egypt, into a Lebanese Christian family. He was one of the founders of Studio Nahhas in Cairo and the owner of Nahas Films, the production/distribution company known throughout the Arab world. After his death in 1963, the Egyptian government nationalised Studio Nahas. Between 1932 and 1963, he produced around sixty films, including *Baba Aris*, the first Arab colour film.
10. Al-Ahram Studio was founded by two Greek businessmen, Evangelos Avramusis and Peris Plenes, in 1944. The studio worked with several Egyptian directors, most notably Togo Mizrahi. Many films made by the studio were distributed in Greece.

11. Lecture notes of Dr Rashida al-Shafe'i, Ahmad el-Sherbeny and Mohammad Ghazala.
12. Ibid.
13. Norman McLaren (1914 –87) was a Canadian animator and director who worked for the National Film Board of Canada. He was a pioneer in a number of areas of both animation and filmmaking, including drawn-on film animation, pixilation and graphical sound. He was awarded the Best Documentary Oscar for *Neighbours* in 1952. In 1969, his *Pas de deux* earned him the BAFTA Award for Best Animated Film.
14. Lecture notes of Dr Rashida al-Shafe'i, Ahmad el-Sherbeny and Mohammad Ghazala.
15. Their ranks included Mohamed Haseeb (1937–2001), Noshi Iskandar (1938–2009) and Zakariyya Ajlan from the training section; Maher Nassar and Farouq 'Arafa from the photographic section; and Rada Gibran and Dlawar Hosni from the decoration section.
16. In 1963, Moheb invited three German professionals, one specialising in cinema tricks, the other two in animation, to share their skills with the Egyptian team.
17. The first commercial produced by Moheb was *Ahmar Shfayf Qasma* (Red Lips Parting). In 1962 his department produced a number of commercials.
18. I was given information on the life of Mona Abu al-Nasr from her son, Sharif Gamal, during a personal interview (Cairo, 8 September 2012).
19. Personal interview with Sharif Gamal (Cairo, 8 September 2012).
20. At the time, Egyptian Television's cartoon department was mainly producing title sequences and other animations for a wide range of television spots.
21. Personal interview with Sharif Gamal (Cairo, 8 September 2012).
22. Mohamed Mounir (b. 1954) is an Egyptian singer and actor. He incorporates various genres into his music, including classical Arab music, Nubian music, blues, jazz and reggae.
23. On soap operas, see Abu-Lughod (1993).
24. Season 1, episode 3.
25. According to Sharif Gamal, Cairo Cartoon organised study trips for scenario writers in order to ensure that an authentic image of each foreign country would be presented.
26. Personal interview with Tarek Rashed (Cairo, 8 September 2012).
27. Competition for animators was especially stiff in the month before Ramadan,

as most TV companies signed contracts with producers to create content that would debut at the beginning of of Ramadan. This information was confirmed by all my interviewees.

28. Personal interviews with Tarek Rashed (Cairo, 8 September 2012), 'Abbas ibn 'Abbas (Cairo, 10 September 2012) and Mohamed Elmazen (Cairo, 6 September 2012).

29. As happened to Coincide, the producer of the renowned animated sitcom *Bsant wa Dyasty*. Sameh Mustafa, the company's owner, told me in a personal interview that the company had been facing financial problems since Nile Life ceased purchasing their animation productions (Cairo, 16 September 2012).

30. Both Tarek Rashed of Tarek Rashed Studios and Omar Maghary of Matrix stated that roughly 70 per cent of their contracts were directed to foreign markets, while only 30 per cent remained in Egypt.

31. Mohammed Sa'eed Harib is a UAE national born in 1978. He studied at North Eastern University in Boston between 1995 and 2001, after which he joined DMC's marketing department in 2003. He was later appointed Art Director for the Technology and Media Free Zone Authority.

32. Lammtara was established in September 2005, with funding of around 3 million Dhs provided by the Mohamed bin Rashid Establishment for Young Business Leaders.

33. Season 3, episode 7.

34. Season 4, episode 3.

35. Season 3, episode 8.

36. On 22 February 2011, Muammar al-Qaddafi gave a speech vowing to hunt down protesters '*Shibr-Shibr, Bayt-Bayt, Zanga-Zanga*' (inch by inch, house by house, alley by alley). A few days later, a satirical remix was released on YouTube, and quickly became popular among the Libyan opposition.

37. The Hashemite Kingdom of Transjordan became an independent sovereign state in 1946. Two years later, during the 1948 Arab-Israeli war, Abdullah I took the title of king and changed the name of the country to The Hashemite Kingdom of Jordan.

38. The Islamic Action Front (*Jabhat al-'Amal al-Islamiyy*) is a Jordanian political party, founded in 1992. Three years after the Jordanian-Israeli peace treaty, it boycotted parliamentary elections.

39. Although the Arab name 'Esam is not the equivalent of Izzy, I am following the producers' official translation.

40. In 2004, Jordanian-born Abu Musab al-Zarqawi (b. 1966) became the leader

of al-Qaeda in Iraq. Releasing amateur videos online, al-Zarqawi established his media image as a 'cool', Rambo-like jihadist.
41. Personal interview with Mongi Sancho (Tunis, 16 March 2013).
42. Ibid.
43. The titles and dates are from an unpublished list of titles from the Association Tunisienne de l'Animation.
44. The titles and dates are from an unpublished list of titles from the Association Tunisienne de l'Animation.
45. The titles and dates are from an unpublished list of titles from the Association Tunisienne de l'Animation.
46. Interview with Mohamed Habib 'Attia (originally published in *La Presse*), http://www.tunizien.net/62909-tunisie--entretien-avec-mohamed-habib-attia-producteur-executif-de-la-serie-de-dessins-animes-viva-carthago.html
47. Executive Decree No. 94–42 of 29 January 1994.
48. 'The teaching of history is a mandatory and fundamental subject in the national education system.' Article 62 of the Law of 5 April 1999. School attendance is mandatory for children aged six to sixteen.
49. From September 1966, history was taught in Classical Arabic.
50. List kindly provided by the Association Tunisienne de l'Animation.
51. Telephone interview with Seddik Tayeb Cherif, director of Studio El Bouraq (15 March 2013).
52. One case in point is *Zim et Zam* (Zim and Zam), an animation series released by Matoub Masinissa in 2006, which was actually the first 3D animated short film in Algeria.
53. Telephone interview with Seddik Tayeb Cherif, director of Studio El Bouraq (15 March 2013).
54. Ibid.
55. The series had the following seasons: *Il était une fois . . . l'Homme* (1978), *Il était une fois . . . l'Espace* (1982), *Il était une fois . . . la Vie* (1986), *Il était une fois . . . les Amériques* (1991), *Il était une fois . . . les Découvreurs* (1994), *Il était une fois . . . les Explorateurs* (1997), *Il était une fois . . . notre Terre* (2008).
56. Episode 5.
57. Episode 10.
58. Abu 'Abdullah al-Husayn ibn Ahmad ibn Zakariyya al-Shi'i (d. 911) was an Ismaili Shia missionary whose ideas greatly influenced the Fatimid dynasty (909–1171).
59. Episode 18.

60. Episode 28.
61. As mentioned, 'jihad' has strongly nationalistic undertones in Algerian political discourse.
62. Episode 50.
63. When Islamists assassinated artists and intellectuals in the early 1990s, they often accused them of being *Hizb Franca* (The Party of France). Later, political opponents frequently accused each other of being 'collaborators' as a form of character assassination.
64. This is shown by the fact that various people who worked in the field stopped producing animations and the companies' websites are no longer available.
65. Sketch in Motion: http://www.sketchinmotion.com/project-view/74
66. Gilad Shalit is a former soldier in the Israel Defense Forces (IDF) who, on 25 June 2006, was captured by Hamas militants in a cross-border raid near the Israeli border at Gaza.
67. While supporters of the Muslim Brotherhood do not have strict codes for beard styles, Salafis often leave their beards long while shaving their moustaches.
68. *Fatenah*, a two-year-project, was awarded a $60,000 budget by the WHO.

3

Arab Animated Sitcoms: Vehicles for the Mediation of Critical Notions of National Identities

Introduction

Since the mid-2000s, animated sitcoms have become one of the most widespread genres of animated cartoons in the Arab world. In less than a decade, the sitcom animation craze has swept the Middle East, with more than thirty titles released by authors from different countries. Aimed at all ages, the shows are usually produced by local companies or creative individuals. They debut on state-owned or private satellite channels that mainly target local general audiences, such as Sama Dubai, Roya TV (Jordan), Al Sharqiya (Iraq), Hannibal TV (Tunisia) and Al-Watan (Kuwait). Many animations, especially those with no stable financial background or creative capital, ended after a single season; a significant number, however, were successful enough to win long-term contracts with advertising partners, whose logos appeared in the productions.

Some of these shows even grew into flagship productions, launched during the most valuable prime time slots during the months of Ramadan when families gather for dinner (*iftar*) and watch television together (Armbrust 2006). As Abu-Lughod noted, Ramadan is the favoured time for broadcasting many popular dramatic serials, which year by year become a national and cultural frame of reference (2008: 6–7). In this regard, the premiere of sitcom animations at Ramadan alone indicates that animation as such is no longer regarded as merely a child-friendly, second-class format by Arab producers and media personnel.

Generally speaking, the characters in Arab sitcom animated cartoons tend to be visually, behaviourally and linguistically stereotyped figures imbued with national characteristics although speaking a local dialect, while the sitcom is set in a local environment and refers to local events. The cartoons also target not only children but adults too, since they often contain messages relating to social and even political issues. Given the production background, the distribution, and the overall concept of Arab sitcom animated cartoons, these series often advocate identities bound up with the nation as an 'imagined community'. Nevertheless, it is striking to see that the social criticism that is characteristic of globally distributed sitcoms such as *The Simpsons* and *South Park* is to some extent also present in the Arab versions of the genre. This shows that animation is able to accommodate critical visions of the nation, and even mediate alternative notions that diverge from the official visions of particular national identities.

While the adaptation of sitcoms has become common practice around the world, it has turned out to be a challenging exercise in the milieu of the religious conservatism and restricted political freedom of the Middle East. Arab animated sitcoms therefore represent an interesting hybrid, striking a balance between the local, the regional and the global. Despite being modelled on basic ideas of successful Western sitcom programmes, the shows have a distinctly Arab and national flavour through modes of comedy that cater to the tastes of local audiences.

The Development of Mature Animation and the Animated Sitcom Genre

Since the inception of the animation genre in the 1930s, animated spots in cinema were popular among audiences of all ages. Later, with the overwhelming success of Walt Disney's *Snow White and the Seven Dwarfs* in 1938, the trend was to make children's animations, while adult themes were neglected (Inge 2004). This was undoubtedly the most dominant trend in the subsequent development of filmed and televisual animation (Larson 2003: 55–73). Animated programming has been an important element of American television since the first channels were established in the 1950s. The first animation shown in a prime time slot was *The Flintstones* by Hanna-Barbera Productions in 1960. Encouraged by the success of the animated sitcom, prime time slots were opened for cartoons such as *Matty's Funday Funnies*, *Bugs Bunny*, *Calvin and the Colonel*. When none of these programmes became successful, they disappeared from prime time slots and had second lives in slots when children would normally be watching. The failure of cartoons to win large adult audiences discouraged further investment in the genre and led to the perception that the animated cartoon was essentially a children's format. Only in the late 1980s did animations reclaim mature audiences in prime time (Booker 2006).

The Simpsons began in 1989. As the first animated variant of the family sitcom genre, it became the most successful animated series in American television history. Being traditionally a live-action genre, sitcoms automatically garnered more respect as a format than the animated cartoon, which by then had gained the reputation as being only for children. What made *The Simpsons* more adult than *The Flintstones* were the pop culture references and the socio-political commentary (Gray 2006). Many critics described *The Simpsons* as a postmodern creation due to its hyper-reflexivity and self-awareness (Collins 1992: 335–6). *The Simpsons* has been linked to generic codes of realism, notions of cultural validity and assumptions of target audiences. Due to its sensitive mixture, it has been successfully merchandised to children and adults alike (Ozersky 1991).

The success of *The Simpsons* paved the way for dozens of animated sitcoms and mature animations, among them *South Park* (1997–), *Family Guy* (1999–) and *American Dad* (2005–), which became popular among both American and international audiences. The worldwide popularity of American animated sitcoms proved to be inspirational for Arab writers. In the early 2000s, an 'Arabisation' process of the animated sitcom genre began, with the aim of adapting a global genre to the local environment.

Political Criticism and Censorship in the Arab World

Censorship varies widely in the Arab world. The countries of the Levant are in general more culturally liberal than Saudi Arabia and the entire Gulf region. Political satire has long been an element of modern Egyptian culture, starting from the time of British rule in the 1920s and 1930s, with satirists ridiculing the colonial masters (Kishtainy 1985). It is a tradition that survived after the establishment of Egyptian television in the early 1960s. Social and political issues with a critical bearing on puritanism, the patriarchal system, had been treated in a humorous way in Egyptian films (Armbrust 2000: 292–327). Regarding the Mubarak era, there was a tendency among television writers and directors to position themselves as critics of the regime and of particular policies. Even though some of them were part of the establishment, they nonetheless sought to be the 'voice of the people' (Abu-Lughod 2008: 13). Genres such as soap operas went even further, provoking debates on sensitive social issues (Abu-Lughod 1995).

In more conservative Arab countries, satire and criticism were not tolerated until a few decades ago. Press, radio and, later, terrestrial television programming were all under strict government censorship. Change only came after the proliferation of satellite channels in the 1990s. Realising that televised media had slipped out of their hands, the grip of local censors weakened and traditional hierarchies were challenged by comedies in Oman, Kuwait and elsewhere in the Arab world. A new trend crystallised with the appearance of *Tash ma Tash* (No Big Deal, 1992–2010). The Saudi sitcom indirectly challenged authoritarian governance by addressing controversial issues in the public sphere. It boldly attacked fundamentalist teaching in schools and the segregation of women, criticising hypocritical religious devoutness as well as state corruption, police brutality, bureaucracy, the last remaining vestiges of patronage-based tribalism and the regulation that prohibits Saudi women to travel without a male guardian (*mahram*) (Jensen 2012).

Arab Animated Sitcoms as Platforms for Critical Approaches to National Identities

Animated sitcoms fit the category of what Wells defined as 'political animation', a genre that is well suited to making moral, ethical, political and even religious statements (Wells 2002: 68). Animated sitcoms challenge culture by using allusive, responsive or disruptive strategies, with plotlines usually focusing on the fictional or the absurd (Gournelos 2009). Despite their critical attitude, it is apparent that Arab animated sitcoms broadcast on mainstream channels do not necessarily undertake a head-on confrontation with existing hierarchies (Sayfo 2015). The creators of Arab animated cartoons – including sitcoms – remain highly dependent on particular media hierarchies structured by political, economic and even personal power relations. Authors largely rely on channels to air their products and, the latter being costly enterprises, also on sponsors – either government or private – to cover production costs. Animations have a better chance of exacting 'concessions' from media and political institutions if they are operating within the existing hegemonic systems. This type of strategic consideration necessarily leads to self-censorship well before animating work even begins (Sayfo 2015).

Still, given their format, animated sitcoms have relative freedom compared to live series and comedies by virtue of their assumed innocence that enables them to transcend taboo issues. According to Wells, animation 'offers a greater opportunity for film-makers to be more imaginative and less conservative' (1998: 6). Wells also notes that the 'very language of animation seems to carry with it an inherent innocence which has served to disguise and dilute the potency of some of its more daring imagery'. Surely this is an opportunity for parody on which animated sitcoms capitalise.

Animation was used for comical reasons in the Arab world for the first time in 1993, when the animation department of Future Television, a free-to-air Lebanese station founded by former prime minister Rafic Hariri, released *Kalil wa Dimn* (Kalil and Dimn), an adaptation of an old folk tale, with anthropomorphic characters tackling political and social issues. The daily sketches were produced at the station's animation department by animator George Khoury and his team. In 1995 the show was succeeded by *Ta'aleeq al-Yaoum* (Comments of the Day), a political cartoon series broadcast after the evening news, in which the main character, a newsreader, read fake news items and made scornful comments. In 2001, *Rusuum Mutaharrira* (Liberated Drawings) aired. This show focused on a different theme and was directed by a single animator each week (Ghaibeh and Khoury 2017).

While such Lebanese shows were explicitly political, animation in general still struggles with credibility. 'For them [decision makers at television channels] animation is still a childish format, which could not be taken seriously', said Sameh Mustafa, Egyptian producer of *Bsant wa Dyasty* (Bsant and Dyasty).[1] Because of this presumption, he argued, allegories, hidden references and parallels with real life are often overlooked by censors. Still, there are four main kinds of content that are potentially censored. First, any sexual content and illustration of the female body. Second, even though religious authorities are rarely in charge of censorship at most channels, they watch out for religious references or religious criticism made in animations. Third, institutions in other Arab countries that are criticised by a particular episode of an animation may feel misrepresented. The fourth factor largely depends on the personal preferences of censors.

Production and distribution that limit humour and criticism also constrain challenges to official discourses over identity. The general framework of approaches to identity is largely dependent on the politics of the particular country, which also define the limits or provide opportunities for criticism.

When analysing the production background of Arab sitcom animations, it is striking to see the proportion of young professionals involved. Pioneering creators of Arab animated sitcoms such as Mohammed Saʿeed Harib (*Freej*), Mohammed Haidar (*Shaabiat Al Cartoon*), Riad Ghariani (*Tunis 2050*) and others are young Arab intellectuals who have received a Western education or are at least familiar with Western cultural productions. Most of them have professed that American animations such as *The Simpsons*, *South Park* and *Family Guy* inspired them to create animations adapted to their native cultural context. The critical potential of the sitcom animation genre is an important factor for these young Arab producers in choosing this particular genre to express their ideas and notions of identity.

Boldness certainly has its limits. The ability of American sitcom animations to reflect satirically on current issues lies in their production process. The series are aired on a seasonal basis that usually lasts three months, and the production process of the entire series is not always completed before the airing of the first episode; producers are thus able to react swiftly to current social and political events. In contrast, Arab animated sitcoms are largely produced during the year to debut on the first day of Ramadan, with one episode aired every night until the end of the Ramadan month. Thus, the ability of Arab animated sitcoms to reflect on current events is limited compared to their American counterparts. Their topics are restricted to events dominating public discourse during the six months preceding Ramadan. Reflecting on settled discourses can reduce the satirical impact and provide a relatively safe means of avoiding harsh reactions. Animated sitcoms, then, may not only contest but also legitimise power (Sayfo 2015).

Exploring Identities of Arab Sitcom Animations

Jordan

The brainchild of Jordanian political cartoonist Emad Hajjaj, *Abu Mahjoub* debuted in the Amman-based *Al-Ra'y* newspaper at the time of the second parliamentary elections in 1993. The character of Abu Mahjoub quickly became popular. Walking by posters of the candidates while making satirical remarks, the character reflected his creator's aim: to 'raise public awareness, deliver a message or simply tell a story in the most striking and effective manner' (Al-Masri 2016: 47).

Abu Mahjoub is a slender, middle-aged man, with a long chin and a crooked moustache. He generally wears a cheap pinstripe suit and – his most important accessory – the traditional red-and-white headdress (*kufiyah*) which is a symbolic reference to his national identity, and indicates that he represents the average Jordanian man. While according to Hajjaj, Abu Mahjoub was inspired by his own father,[2] he reads more like a stereotypical and comical representation of a lower-middle-class Jordanian male, who is lazy, cynical and, according to Jordanian critics, sexually frustrated. The character, then, serves as a mouthpiece for the daily struggles, and political and social frustrations widely shared in society (Al-Mahadin 2003). Indeed, even his name, which translates as 'Father of Mahjoub' or 'Father of the hidden', alludes to Hajjaj's aim to reveal the hidden practices of a society (Al-Masri 2016). *Abu Mahjoub* is barely political, as the focus of the stories is predominantly on general social practices rather than specific political events. Unlike the majority of Hajjaj's political cartoons intended for a transnational Arab audience, and hence in *fusha* Arabic, the *Abu Mahjoub* strips are written in colloquial Jordanian dialect and ultimately target a national readership (Mango 2004).

Abu Mahjoub is often surrounded by his family, mainly his wife, Umm Mahjoub, an overweight, cranky woman and a 'typical mother', as Hajjaj put it to me in a telephone interview.[3] Like her husband in his *kufiyah*, Umm Mahjoub is always wearing her headscarf. One other important character, present in the vast majority of the cartoons, is Abu Mohamed, who serves as a foil to reveal the inadequacies, shortcomings, weaknesses, strengths and constructed consciousness of the protagonist (Al-Mahadin 2003). By the end of the 1990s *Abu Mahjoub* appeared in various Jordanian political newspapers and had become a local brand, gaining wide popularity among the Jordanian middle class for – as Jordanian news agency Ammon declared – 'his way of conveying the pulse of ordinary people in a simple language without any makeup or filtering' (Al-Masri 2016).

In 1999, Hajjaj came up with the idea to put the still images into motion. The first flash-animated spots of *Abu Mahjoub* were released in 2001 and were distributed online. Given the small scale of the production, the storyline of each one-minute spot was based on drawn cartoons. Facing the challenges of animation production, Hajjaj hired scriptwriters to develop stories. During Ramadan 2003, Abu Mahjoub's iconic greeting, '*Hala 'ammi*' (Welcome, my uncle) was used in the title song, as the thirty stories of *Abu Mahjoub*, each lasting forty-five to sixty seconds, became the very first homegrown animated cartoon appearing on Jordanian TV and a forerunner of Arab animated sitcoms.

The plots are largely built around short dialogues and a handful of scenes at most. Similarly to the cartoons, these early *Abu Mahjoub* spots are defined by strong social criticism revolving around issues of general concern such as the rising cost of living, rampant corruption, unemployment or inappropri-

Figure 3.1 *Abu Mahjoub*: an average man from Jordan. 2004 © Emad Hajjaj.

ate social practices like gossip, unmerited patronage or envy. One episode shows several important social events, like high-profile meetings and prayers, being disturbed by a pop song used as the ringtone of a mobile phone, with the last scene showing a phone ringing in Abu Mahjoub's pocket when he is lowering a body into the grave at a funeral: a clear criticism of the increasing prevalence of mobile phones in the early 2000s in Jordan. Another episode highlights the social problems of old marriage traditions that have adapted poorly to modern life. The story kicks off with Abu Mahjoub dragging his son out of a nightclub, as they have been invited to the house of a potential bride to negotiate marriage conditions. However, after hearing the potential father-in-law's unrealistically high financial demands, Abu Mahjoub and his son escape back to the nightclub together, which is still more affordable in the harsh economic circumstances and not related to old social traditions. A third episode takes the fissures between local Jordanians' and emigrants' changed identities into account. The one-scene episode shows a dialogue between Abu Mahjoub and his son, who has just returned from a long stay in the United States. While the son wears earrings (extremely uncommon in Arab societies) and a baseball cap, and speaks Arabic with an American accent, he self-confidently lectures his father on religion and explains how he frequently visited a mosque in Chicago and makes his wife wear a niqab (a veil covering the face).

After Hajjaj and his crew had released a second season of *Abu Mahjoub* during Ramadan 2004, the new management at the Jordanian TV channel cancelled the contract. The decision came at a time when Hajjaj was attracting increasing scandal as a result of drawing ministers and even the king himself. Though no legal action followed, Hajjaj became a persona non-grata, and *Abu Mahjoub* was exiled to newspapers for seven years (Mango 2004).

Benefiting from the liberalising media policies of the Jordanian government, in January 2011 Roya TV, a private channel, was launched by the Al-Sayegh Group, a Jordanian industrial conglomerate (Sakr 2013b). Roya TV quickly rose to become a popular platform for homegrown sitcom animations, like *Shoofee ʿAynak* (See It With Your Eyes) and *Nahafaat ʿAilatna* (Funny Stories of Our Family), both created by the Sketch in Motion studio and featuring the popular Jordanian comic character of Sumʿa. During Ramadan 2011, *Abu Mahjoub* also returned to the screen with thirty spots of four minutes each broadcast between skits and stand-up comedy as part of a comedy hour. The visuals were redesigned in 3D by a small Egyptian animation studio, then for the next season were redesigned again into an aesthetically more cartoon-like 2D style by a Jordanian studio. While the episodes grew longer, and the stories became more nuanced, they retained their focus on social issues.

Because of the non-governmental ownership of Roya TV, the new *Abu Mahjoub* contained more daring, although still not explicit, political commentary. In one episode Abu Mahjoub and Abu Mohamed participate in a lifestyle course where they are taught that they should laugh as a way of preserving good mental health. As a result they end up reading a newspaper and laughing at domestic news that is meant to be serious. Another episode, in a reference to the Arab Spring and the ensuing shift in Jordanian politics, features Abu Mahjoub, Abu Mohamed and Abu Rubhi, standing in two lines in a room together with a group of men dressed in police uniform. They are participating in a lecture the aim of which is to teach policemen how to deal with the 'citizen' (*muwatin*), a species that was discovered in the 'spring' and should be respected and taken care of. Later, the policemen treat with exaggerated politeness a trembling citizen who enters the room, but when he falls over, the police carry on dancing in their heavy boots, accidentally kicking him. The episode is an account of the Arab citizen's deep mistrust of the authorities and the common assumption that, regardless of the political intention, things will eventually turn out badly for the average citizen.[4]

Despite its political content, *Abu Mahjoub* remained within the boundaries of safe social criticism. Doing so, it even gained the approval of the government, as in 2015 the Ministry of Environment commissioned a special episode to raise environmental awareness.

The United Arab Emirates

Dubai Media Incorporated (DMI), the official media organisation of the government of Dubai, was established in 2003 as a government-owned company comprising a number of print, radio and TV channels. Sama Dubai replaced a general business channel in 2005. It was meant to be a primary platform for local cultural events and a wide variety of locally produced programmes. As already explored in the case of *Freej*, Sama Dubai has been an important platform for homegrown production, and as such, for mediating local identities. However, there are other sitcom animated cartoons, also presented on Sama Dubai, which present Emirati realities and identity in a way that is less in line with the government's policies of heritage revival as is the case with *Freej*.

One example of such Emirati sitcoms is *Khousa Bousa* (Khousa Bousa),[5] a 3D animation series produced by Neyla al-Sahy. The first season of fifteen episodes debuted during Ramadan 2009 on Sama Dubai. Production was then halted until it made a return on Abu Dhabi Channel in 2013. While the scripts were written by Emiratis, the animation process for the first season was outsourced to the Egyptian Tarek Rashed Studio. Then, in 2013, as a result of the political uncertainties in Egypt and the producers' disappointment in the visual quality of the animation, they signed with Indian Busy Bee studios for the coming seasons (Al-Quds al-'Arabi 2013). *Khousa Bousa* is a satirical series dealing with locally relevant issues, such as the relationship between children and their parents, the high costs of getting married, the negative effects of social networking sites and the relationship between Emirati families and their housemaids. However, the plots focus not on Emiratis alone, but also on non-national residents of the UAE, through the character of Nafisa, an Egyptian woman, and Umm Anas, a Syrian schoolteacher, among others. The otherness of non-Emirati Arabs is indicated by dialect and through the women wearing dresses in styles associated with other countries. Socio-economic differences are also highlighted by dialogues in which Egyptians and Syrians are often shown as concerned about their finances. However, the episodes cannot regarded as mere celebrations of Emiratiness, as they also involve criticism of Emiratis. Episode 5 of the second season starts with Fatima, the Sudanese maid, going on holiday. The grandmother, Hamama, decides to find a temporary replacement with the help of a relative who runs an agency. At the agency, the maids are lined up in a way reminiscent of a slave market; they carry signs showing their nationality and prices. Hamama brings home a Filipina, who upsets the family when she threatens to call a human rights organisation. She horrifies them even more when she suggests that Sheikha, a young female member of the family, should have a boyfriend, something unheard of in the conservative Emirati society. So Hamama exchanges the Filipina maid for a Muslim Indonesian one, who gossips with the neighbour's servant and ends up in a fierce argument about wages. At the end of the episode, the problem is solved by the return of Fatima, who is first praised by Hamama then quickly sent to make dinner. Episode 11 of the second season revolves around a similar issue, showing how foreign workers, fed up with unjust treatment, leave the country, leaving spoiled Emiratis desperate.

During the 2016 season *Khousa Bousa*'s representation of the 'other' was met with ire when Egyptian scriptwriter Amr Samir Atef criticised the series on social media for misrepresenting Egyptians as shabby beggars. Another concern was the character of Nafisa, shown to be a superficial person caring only about her looks. Similarly outraged was Egyptian blogger Wael Abbas, who even accused the cartoon of being 'racist' for its portrayal of Egyptians as 'hooligans and beggars'. Due to their poor financial situation, Egyptians were also shown as eating cheap, bad-quality food and wearing old-fashioned clothes (Al-Mirsal 2016).

Another example of adapted sitcom animations is *Shaabiat Al Cartoon* (Animation Neighbourhood). Similarly to Lammtara, the producer of *Freej*, Fanar Production, the company behind *Shaabiat Al Cartoon*, was also established as a result of the Dubai government's policy of supporting the creative industries.[6] Like *Freej*, *Shaabiat Al Cartoon* debuted in 2006 with thirty twenty-minute episodes, with each new season beginning at Ramadan. The concept itself dates back to 2004, when it started out as a mobile phone animation.[7] Conceived by caricaturist Mohammed Haidar, *Shaabiat Al Cartoon* has been sponsored by the Emirati telecommunications company Etisalat, largely owned by the UAE government.[8] One can therefore assume that the producers are not willing to risk a head-on confrontation with local authorities by engaging in political criticism.

Together with *Freej*, *Shaabiat Al Cartoon* was a major source of inspiration for many later productions.[9] Mohammed Haidar insisted that his main goal was to produce a successful comedy cartoon rather than to preserve the Emirati identity (Al-Qassemi 2009). An approach of this type results in a more exposed criticism when the 'own' is represented. At the same time, the producers state on their webpage that '[e]very Fanar Project is based on capturing the spirit of Emirati culture, traditions and lifestyles across the multi-cultural population living in the UAE and the region'.[10]

ARAB ANIMATED SITCOMS | 117

Figure 3.2 *Shaabiat Al Cartoon* (Animation Neighbourhood). 2006 © Fanar Production.

Shaabiat Al Cartoon revolves around the life of various individuals and families living in an Emirati suburb. It was one of the first animations to directly address local social affairs and to portray the multinational mosaic of Emirati society by including twenty-four characters of local and non-Emirati background (Al-Bayan 2008). Unlike *Freej*, *Shaabiat Al Cartoon* does not show Emirati society as being integrated, but accentuates the differences between the various social groups. Diversity is highlighted through appearance, clothing and accents. One of the central characters is Shambee, a man of ʿ*ajam* (Iranian) background, who – unlike Umm ʿAllawi in *Freej* – struggles to fit into Emirati society. In one episode, Shambee feels outcast by his friends because of his ʿ*ajam*-sounding family name, and so he changes it to a (supposedly) better-sounding Arab Bedouin name. However, after failing to embody Bedouin identity and proving to be a terrible Bedouin poet, his plan comes to nothing.

Another central character is Bou Mahyer, a Bedouin by birth, who is often confused by the modernity of Dubai. Through his character, many of the stories focus on problems brought on by modernisation such as rising prices, prejudice, tribal allegiances, marriage, social relations and even polygamy.

These diverse situational characters come together to create what Nichola

Dobson calls a 'constructed reality' in a sense that it selects characters and locations and mixes them up in order to create comical situations (Dobson 2003: 86). The animation also employs what Matheson defines as hyper-irony, a type of humour that prompts the audience not only to recognise the stereotypes that society has created, but also to laugh at themselves (Matheson 2001). In this regard, *Shaabiat Al Cartoon* participates in the imagination and re-imagination of an Emirati identity by making the audience identify with the diverse social constructs presented in the animation.

Even though the episodes contain criticism of certain aspects of Emirati society, producers of both *Khousa Bousa* and *Shaabiat Al Cartoon* remain well within the limits of tolerated criticism that enabled them to establish their position as parts of the Emirati popular culture and allowed them to sign deals with renowned local companies.

Egypt

The privatisation of Egyptian media and media industries in the 2000s led to an increase in the number of production companies. Sakr observed how the local business elite largely benefited from the privatisation as 'personal networks were deployed to safeguard monopolies for the benefit of business and the Mubarak regime' (Sakr 2008: 269) Rather than relinquishing its monopoly on terrestrial broadcasting, the government allowed both local and foreign broadcasters to operate by satellite from a designated free zone linked to two government investments: a production studio complex based in Cairo and the launch of Nilesat, Egypt's own broadcasting satellite in 1998 (Sakr 2001: 110; 2007a: 195).

The example of *Bakkar* has shown how the animated format was used as a celebration of Egyptian identity. However, there are a number of Egyptian productions that cannot be viewed as pure celebrations of Egyptian-ness as they articulate criticism towards social and even political phenomena. One example is *'Aelat al-Ustaz 'Ameen* (The Family of Mr Ameen), a 2008 production made by Cairo Cartoon, the same company that produced *Bakkar*. The series, made up of thirty-one fifteen-minute episodes, was released after the death of Mona Abu al-Nasr, when her son Sharif Gamal took over the management of the company. It revolves around the life of an Egyptian family from Cairo and their Saudi Arabian neighbours, and was shown not only on Egyptian television, but also on Saudi MBC1. Because of such market considerations, *'Aelat al-Ustaz 'Ameen* shows the difference between Saudis and Egyptians mainly through dialect but also through behaviour – for example, the Saudi parents are presented as calmer people than the Egyptians – without raising one identity over the other. However, as Sharif Gamal explained to me, the family of Ustaz 'Ameen was conceived in such a way as to enable Egyptians to identify with it.[11]

One highly successful Egyptian sitcom animation is *Bsant wa Dyasty*, a satirical 3D series that debuted on Nile Life in 2007 and continued with new seasons until 2012, a year of political turmoil in Egypt that resulted in a crisis in Egyptian media production. The animation work was produced by Coincide Animation Production, owned by Sameh Mustafa, who also wrote the series. *Bsant wa Dyasty* is neither an adaptation nor a remake of previous works, even though the main characters were inspired by an untitled cartoon published in *Nuna*, an Egyptian children's magazine.

The animation shows the life of a man and his wife living in a small village in Upper Egypt and their encounters with modern technology. The voices of the main characters are provided by the well-known actors Salah

Figure 3.3 *Bsant wa Dyasty* (Bsant and Dyasty). 2007 © Coincide Animation Production.

'Abdullah (Bsant) and Hanan Turk (Dyasty), both speaking a mimicked Upper Egyptian dialect. The series features countless references to current issues and even political events in Egypt. The episodes often cover topics such as mobile phones and other everyday themes, but in many cases, they have a political content and even touch upon sensitive domestic issues. In one episode, Bsant becomes a Member of Parliament and passes laws that enable him to gain a monopoly over the production of confectionery. He then increases prices to maximise profit. This episode was a barely veiled allusion to Ahmad 'Ezz, a businessman with close ties to the Mubarak regime, who became a steel magnate and drove up steel prices, leading to a rise in property prices. 'Ezz was sentenced to seven years' imprisonment in 2011 after the fall of Mubarak. Other episodes were inspired by international events. One episode recounted a football match between the village of Bsant and a neighbouring village called Arnobia (*arnab* means 'rabbit' in Arabic). As emotions run wild, the game ends in violent clashes between the supporters – who are portrayed as short-tempered and dim-witted, in an echo of the riots that took place at the Algerian-Egyptian game in 2009 (BBC 2009b). Despite touching on sensitive issues, no episodes were censored by Egyptian TV. Even though the village of Bsant was designed as a microcosm of Egypt, differences are highlighted vis-à-vis not other villages, but other countries, as there are a number of references to the domestic issues of other Arab nations such as the internal clashes between factions in Palestine and in Sudan.[12]

Super Henedy is an Egyptian animation that premiered in 2008. Sharif Gamal's show is a blend of detective stories, sitcoms and Egyptian comedies. The stories revolve around the character of Mohammad Henedy, known as Super Henedy, a brilliant detective. The Egyptian comedian Mohammad Henedy appeared in a variety of comedies that were popular among older audiences and was also known to children after being the voice actor of characters in both Disney's *The Lion King* and Pixar's *Monsters, Inc*. The series thus targets mature and children's audiences alike. In view of Mohammad Henedy's regional popularity, as well as for financial reasons, the series was first aired on Dubai TV.[13] The series reflects social and other current issues in a rather explicit way, similar to Egyptian live comedies. The stories are all written around the character of Super Henedy, who solves problems ranging from bird flu to the loss of his friend's hair.

Most episodes are set in Cairo, with direct references to the street names and popular locales. In some episodes Super Henedy travels to other Arab countries, and Egyptian identity is also highlighted by presenting the contrast in dialect, clothing, appearance and landscapes. One episode, '*Ziyarat Super Henedy ilal-Soudan*' (Super Henedy's Visit to Sudan), in which Super Henedy describes the Sudanese as 'a backward people', was criticised by Sudanese journalists for portraying negative stereotypes (Al-Arabiya 2008). In general, though, *Super Henedy* is less engaged in social criticism than the vast majority of sitcoms, as it is more an animated version of classic police comedies, where the focus is on funny characters and adventures rather than on representations of real life.

Iraq

After the fall of Saddam Hussein in April 2003, Iraq's media environment transformed from a centralised propaganda machine into a diverse landscape. The new Iraqi broadcasting environment, however, includes very few neutral outlets, with the vast majority of channels promoting particular sectarian and political identities, representing the political interests of the funding sources (Amos 2010). Regarding their funding, Kim divided Iraqi broadcasting into three categories: private, partisan and state-run. In this categorisation, private broadcasting outlets compete for wider audiences and commercial profits. Partisan channels mediate their patron's political or ideological messages. Meanwhile, state-run channels rely on the national or provincial governments' financial support, and are hence influenced by the government (Kim 2011).

Al Sharqiya was the first private media company in Iraq. It was founded in 2004 by former Baathist businessman Sa'd Bazzaz, and presented a mix of original entertainment programmes and news programming (Amos 2010). Al Sharqiya quickly rose to become a critic of the Shia-dominated government. In 2006, its critical attitude led to government accusations of discriminating against the country's Shia population and inciting sectarian violence (Isakhan 2009). After the forced closure of Al Sharqiya's Baghdad offices, Bazzaz moved the headquarters to Dubai. Since then, Al Sharqiya has become politically more direct: in the 2010 elections, the channel's coverage reflected a clear support of the Sunni coalition headed by Iyad Allawi (Al Mir'at 2010).

From the very beginning, the channel has served as a primary platform for drama and comedy productions written and produced by Iraqis in an Iraqi dialect.

Al-'Ataak is an Iraqi animation series of thirty fifteen-minute episodes directed by Muhannad Abu-Khumra and which aired on Al Sharqiya TV in 2011. The series was produced by Etana Productions, Abu-Khumra's company, which, like Al Sharqiya TV, is based in Dubai. The series largely deals with problems of economic hardship, social inequality, the rising cost of living and other problems that, according to the producers, preoccupied the population in pre-invasion Iraq (Al Sharqiya 2011). In order to stress the Iraqi identity, it was dubbed in an Iraqi, or more specifically, a Baghdadi, dialect. The plot of *Al-'Ataak* centres on the struggles of a poor Iraqi man called Gumu'ah al-'Ataak who falls in love with Hanadi, a woman from a wealthy family. The lovers are forbidden to marry due to the social distance between them: 'Ataak does not have a regular job, while his father is a night watchman and his mother a cleaner at a local school, where they live in a janitor's apartment. After 'Ataak's many failed attempts to make money, the problem is resolved in the final episode in a rather unusual way: his beloved's family loses their wealth, and the young couple can finally marry.

After the success of *Al-'Ataak*, Abu-Khumra released a number of similarly themed series, one of the most significant among them being *Al-Rayes*

Figure 3.4 *Al-'Ataak*: a tale of everyday struggle in Baghdad. 2011 © Etana Production.

(The President, 2013). The plot tells the story of an elderly man selling *lablabi*, a typical Iraqi food made of chickpeas, from his cart. He is called Al-Rayes by the locals not only because of his wisdom, but also because he has seen many presidents come and go. The series portrays a corrupt, ruined Baghdad that is a dangerous place to live and is run by arrogant authorities. It thus largely voices the concerns and identities of Sunni Iraqis feeling excluded by the Shia-dominated government of Nuri al-Maliki. The narrative does not include any reference to the sect of the characters, but presents them in a way that all Iraqi people can relate to.[14]

Both *Al-'Ataak* and *Al-Rayes* use similar humour and express political and social criticism quite explicitly when addressing the fissures in Iraqi society. However, they still avoid stereotypes when it comes to portraying people with diverse sectarian backgrounds, a rather sensitive issue in present-day Iraq.

Kuwait

Like the vast majority of Gulf societies, Kuwait has a diverse population, consisting of urban Arabs and Bedouins, with 36 per cent Shia and 64 per cent Sunni Muslims. Local identities are rooted in tribal and political affiliations, and family bonds.

The present rulers of the country, the Al-Sabah family, rose to power in the mid-eighteenth century. The country gained its independence in 1961, after centuries of Ottoman Turkish and British rule. After the regional turmoil of the Iraq-Iran war from 1980 to 1988, Kuwait faced an invasion by the Iraqi army in August 1990; the resulting Iraqi presence lasted until February 1991. The war with Iraq became a fundamental element in the construction of national identity and the definition of Kuwaitiness (Wheeler 2000). In 1992, the satellite broadcasting service Kuwait TV 1 was launched, and became an important platform for mediating national identity. In 2006, the Kuwaiti parliament enacted a press and publication law, eased restrictions on newspaper licences and limited the government's rights to close down media outlets. Simultaneously, the Audio and Visual Act was passed, legalising private television channels in the country.

As the memory of the Iraqi invasion faded, local political fissures reemerged. Divisions along identity, ideological and personal lines as well as fissures within the ruling family were mirrored in the privately owned press and electronic media. The Kuwaiti ruling family had mastered the art of alliance building. The fact that the parliament is composed of liberals, Muslim Brotherhood, Salafis, Shia, tribal representatives and independents, representing various social and political identities, opened the gates to 'divide and rule' policies (Selvik 2011). While all political factions have a different approach to Kuwaiti identity, traditional social links and affiliations, such as sect and tribe, for example, largely maintain a sense of Kuwaitiness.

The spread of satellite channels in the Arab world, including in Kuwait, and the distribution of foreign channels by satellites such as Arabsat and Nilesat led to Kuwaiti audiences being introduced to foreign television programmes and formats, one of which was *South Park*.[15] Kuwaiti director and producer Nawaf Salem al-Shammari was one of the many Arab fans of the show.[16] Al-Shammari founded Farooha Media Productions, and in 2000 released the first season of *Qutʿa 13* (Block 13), a Kuwaiti adaptation of *South Park* for Kuwaiti Al-Watan TV. Largely targeting the domestic Kuwaiti market using the global format, *Block 13* survived for three seasons. Its visual and audio markers – most of them naturalistic and therefore highly localised – stamp *Block 13* with Kuwaitiness, a hybrid identity grafted onto an original and innovative text.

Block 13 retained the basic structure of *South Park*, but offered variations in terms of the leading characters, the backgrounds and the storylines. The plot revolves around the adventures of four schoolchildren in Kuwait City. Instead of Cartman, Kyle, Stan and Kenny, the Arab version features ʿAbboud, ʿAzzouz, Hammoud and Salloum, all of whom retained some of the original characters' traits, but were redesigned to fit into the Kuwaiti environment. Cartman's blue hat was replaced with a *taqiya*, while Kenny wears an Arab *kufiyah* instead of a parka, which also muffles his voice. Other characteristics were also adapted: for example, Salloum's family is as poor as Kenny's and he, too, is often killed in the episodes.

Unlike *South Park*, which was intended for a mature audience, *Block 13* was written to suit younger viewers too. The series was stripped of culturally sensitive issues such as sexual references and crude language. On the other hand, *Block 13* builds on ethnic stereotypes, mainly by using dialects or by imitating foreign languages, and it also contains many allusions to regional popular culture. In this regard, *Block 13* presented Kuwaitiness vis-à-vis foreigners living in the country. Like the majority of Arab sitcom animations, *Block 13* reflects on social issues such as racism, family relations and generation gaps, but does not engage in negotiating them, settling instead for humour based on high-pitched voices, unrealistic characters or representations of national stereotypes. In the case of some Syrian male characters, for example, we see moustached male figures represented as they were portrayed on popular Syrian television dramas set in the nineteenth century.

In contrast, the animated satire *Youmiyyat Bou Qatada wa Bou Nabeel* (Everyday Stories of Bou Qatada and Bou Nabeel) contained unveiled overt political commentary. The show is based on the political cartoons of Mohammad Thallab that have appeared in the daily newspaper *Al-Watan* since 2005.[17] *Al-Watan* was a leftist newspaper until it was sold to ʿAli al-Khalifa, former Minister of Oil and member of the ruling Al-Sabah family, during the Iraqi occupation. ʿAli al-Khalifa made his son, Khalifa ʿAli al-Khalifa, the editor-in-chief. That time, the paper prized itself on being a medium willing to host opinions and criticism of all political platforms. The rapid shift of the media balance towards television, coupled with the political turmoil in 2006, led to the establishment of Al-Watan TV, a satellite television company also known as the Kuwait Media Group.[18]

In 2006, an animated adaptation of *Youmiyyat Bou Qatada wa Bou Nabeel* was released. The series of twenty-eight episodes, each thirteen minutes long, was directed by Faysal al-Ibrahim. Although animation work was outsourced to the Egyptian Tarek Rashed Studio, the voices were recorded locally. *Youmiyyat Bou Qatada wa Bou Nabeel*, still debuting new seasons for Ramadan, is one of the most political animated sitcoms. It directly tackles current issues of local public discourse and holds up a satirical, warped mirror to different socio-political groups in Kuwaiti society. Of course, the criticism and approaches to identity issues in *Youmiyyat Bou Qatada wa Bou Nabeel* must be set against the background of the ownership structure of Al-Watan TV.

The show revolves around three main characters: Bou Qatada, Bou Nabeel and Bou Meshʿal. The characters resemble those in the original printed cartoon version that portrays stereotyped personalities of the Kuwaiti political scene. The character of Bou Qatada is a direct portrayal of Kuwaiti Islamists. He sports a Salafi-style beard and is obsessed with observing the *sharia* (Islamic law) and making it the sole source of legislation in Kuwait. He is a great critic of liberal values and materialism. One of the recurring jokes is a bag of weapons stored in Bou Qatada's closet in preparation for a possible *jihad*. Many of the episodes focus on his zealotry, which is shared by his friend Bou 'Omara, a Salafi of Egyptian origin. In one episode, *Fath al-Andalus* (The Conquest of Andalusia), the two decide to reconquer and Islamise Spain. Arming themselves with swords, they travel to Morocco and then cross the Strait of Gibraltar in a boat. In the end, they are arrested by the Spanish police for harassing sunbathers on the beach. Bou Qatada's wife, Umm Qatada, is presented as a woman with a great deal of love and respect for her husband and who secretly wishes that he were more emotional and romantic. This is a direct criticism of Salafis who – according to the liberal creators of the show – are preoccupied with grandiose attempts to restore their notions of Islam, but in the meantime neglect daily life, including their families.

Bou Nabeel, the son of Bou Qatada, represents the liberal businessman, often accused by his father of worshipping the United States. The materialism and loss of *turath* in Kuwaiti society is criticised through the character of Bou Nabeel and his family. The family is characterised by unequal power relations. Terrified of his wife's strong will, Bou Qatada mostly obeys Umm Qatada, who, sharing his enchantment with modernism, often demands money to buy luxury goods. Bou Nabeel is presented as the spoiled son, speaking a

Figure 3.5 *Youmiyyat Bou Qatada wa Bou Nabeel* (Everyday Stories of Bou Qatada and Bou Nabeel): a political take on Kuwaiti society. 2007 © Faysal al-Ibrahim.

strange mix of English and Kuwaiti Arabic dialect as a sign of the loss of tradition and the negative influence of American/Western culture.

Bou Mesh'al, the third main character, is a traditional man who demonstrates great respect for Bedouin values, even though he is from Rumaithya, an urban neighbourhood inhabited by an *'ajam* community. He imitates a Bedouin accent randomly interspersed with an *'ajam* accent. The character embodies the social phenomenon of the loss of *'ajam* identity for the sake of assimilation to Kuwaiti society. In one episode, Bou Mesh'al decides to create and register a tribe of his own and to become the leader of his tribe. After making new connections and getting to know people, he decides to become involved in politics, but is arrested for corruption. At the end of the episode, Bou Nabeel suggests that Bou Mesh'al should seek the help of a politician who is a member of his new tribe, in a reference to the importance of old tribal affiliations and identities in contemporary Kuwaiti politics.[19]

In order to accentuate his Bedouin identity, Bou Mesh'al makes his wife, Umm Mesh'al, wear a niqab, covering her face, rather than a hijab (a headscarf). Umm Mesh'al speaks with a strong, over-exaggerated *'ajam* accent.

Much of the humour in the series is based on the clashes between the widely differing worldviews of the main characters and their families. Despite being critical of Islamic radicalism, the creators show a respect for Islamic values, and thus do not challenge Islamic identities.

While most Arab animated sitcoms are wary of criticising other Arab countries and only allude to issues with other countries through symbols, *Youmiyyat Bou Qatada wa Bou Nabeel* is relatively bold in its criticism. One possible source of this is the growing sense of Kuwaitiness after the Iraqi invasion and during the subsequent period of war (Ghabra 1997: 367). In one episode, *'Iraq al-Shaqiqa* (Brotherly Iraq), the creators mock the diplomatic discourse of the Kuwait government that pretends to have left the grievances of the invasion behind. As the protagonists cross the Iraqi border on their way to Basra, they are shocked by the rubbish littering the streets and are targeted by snipers. Going to a restaurant, an Iraqi waiter accuses them of stealing the country's wealth. Next, they meet two 'brotherly' Iraqis speaking such an unintelligible dialect that subtitles are necessary. At the end of the episode, the Kuwaitis are kidnapped by Islamists, but are eventually set free after their kidnappers realise that no one likes Kuwaitis enough to pay a ransom for them.

Another episode of *Youmiyyat Bou Qatada wa Bou Nabeel* even sparked diplomatic tension between Kuwait and Morocco. The two main characters visit the Moroccan city of Agadir where they meet two young women. The women invite them into their home and their mother offers the men coffee into which she has mixed a magic potion that will cast a spell on them to get them to marry her daughters. The episode drew criticism from Moroccan officials, who complained that the episode depicted their country as a land of sorcery, dancing and moral laxity. Because of the ownership structure of Al-Watan, both the TV channel and the Kuwaiti government were forced to apologise (Al-Ashraf 2010).

With the inclusion of characters representing various approaches to Kuwaiti identity, *Youmiyyat Bou Qatada wa Bou Nabeel* participates in a negotiation of Kuwaitiness. At the same time, it also presents various aspects of Kuwaiti society as integral elements of the country. It stresses the Kuwaiti identity even more with the presentation of characters with a non-Kuwaiti background, and by highlighting differences both on the visual and the linguistic levels. By presenting the protagonists travelling abroad, it shows the differences between Kuwait and other Arab countries, with the aim of creating a sense of Kuwaitiness in the audience.

Saudi Arabia

The Middle East Broadcasting Centre (MBC), a television enterprise founded in 1991 and privately owned by a group of businessmen and shareholders including Walid al-Ibrahim, the brother-in-law of King Fahd (1982–2005), has long been viewed as a means for the Saudi state to increase its regional influence as well as to support the political ambitions of certain members of Saudi Arabia's ruling elite (Sakr 2001: 42–3). In 2002, the headquarters were moved to Dubai and two years later MBC began to transform itself into a network of specialised channels (Sakr 2007a: 130). The sharp decline of Saudi oil income in the late 1990s caused a drop in financial support that led to the channel's reorientation to entertainment in the hope of mobilising advertising revenue (Sakr 2007: 169). Given the ownership of MBC, the channel continued to be characterised by self-censorship. Its exclusive productions are therefore largely neutral or supportive of the social, political and religious identities advocated by the Saudi state.

In 2006, *Youmiyyat Mnahy* (Everyday Stories of Mnahy) appeared on MBC. The 2D animated version of the popular Saudi comedian Fayez al-Maleki was directed by Mazen Tah. The twenty-episode comedy revolves around Mnahy, the protagonist, who fights the stereotypes of the West towards Arabs in a comical way. A year later, MBC aired *Muzna wa Fami* (Muzna and Fami), a twenty-episode series directed by 'Ali al-A'raj presenting funny stories about Saudi society and its relationship with modern technology. The show is set in the year 2100, and features a family whose life, technologically speaking, is stuck in 2007.

Taish 'Eyal (*Family Business*), a series that debuted on MBC in 2012, is an animated adaptation of *Tash ma Tash*. The original concept was a locally produced sitcom that premiered on Saudi TV Channel 1 in 1992. The series was produced with the approval of the Saudi Ministry of Information; later, in 2006, it was moved to MBC. It was the first Saudi comedyto delve into a subtle critique of local traditions and even of the religious establishment, issues that had previously been beyond criticism. *Tash ma Tash* also demanded political reforms and called for the demolishing of systems of patronage (Raphaeli 2005). It was the first television production addressing issues of this kind that could be viewed as a challenge to the beneficiaries of the hierarchies being criticised.

While the authorship of the animated version, *Taish 'Eyal*, is Saudi, the animation work itself was outsourced to India. Everything from the characters to the locations is similar to the original. Some of the actors, such as Fahd al-Hayan, Naser al-Qasby and 'Abdullah al-Sadhan, who had voice roles in *Tash ma Tash*, also lent their voices to the characters of the new series.

Although *Taish 'Eyal* was intended to fill the gap *Tash ma Tash* had left after its cancellation, the animation did not deliver. *Tash ma Tash* addressed various sensitive issues in a critical manner, while *Taish 'Eyal* is a conservative comedy, with most of the jokes building on the characters, and the plots themselves containing moral lessons for the viewers. Altogether, the narrative does not challenge dominant discourses on Saudi identity, but, instead, mediates the official approach, blending an Islamic identity with a national Saudi one. Still, given the generic characteristics of *Taish 'Eyal*, it could be regarded as a sitcom. However, unlike the sitcom animations of other Arab countries, *Taish 'Eyal* presents local society as homogeneous, with the exception of foreign characters whose otherness is clearly marked bothvisually and linguistically. The episode *Al-Tariq ila Makkah* (The Road to Mecca) narrates the family's pilgrimage. The episode paints an idealised picture of Islam and the pilgrimage, with sentimental undertones. The episode also shows how the Saudi family forges a friendship with a Korean family. While differences in language and appearance are clearly distinguishable, the families are presented as equals under the banner of Islam. Another episode, *Al-Shagghala* (The Female Worker) is a critique of the exploitation of domestic workers, as it shows the family's treatment of a newly hired Indonesian maid. Waited upon by the maid, the children become lazy and ignorant, upsetting her immensely. In the episode, the Friday sermon (*khutba*) can be heard from loudspeakers in the background, describing how the Prophet Muhammad treated his servants with justice. Unable to bear the pressure, the maid returns to her homeland, leaving the family remorseful. In general, *Taish 'Eyal* does not articulate an alternative national identity and instead turns to humour for venting emotions 'safely'. Nonetheless it blends official notions with mild criticism of social affairs and behaviour.

Al-Masageel (2011–13) is a 2D animation series that is a Jordanian-Saudi co-production. While the original idea for the series came from the Jordanian Sketch in Motion company, it was produced by Scenario Creative Production, a company linked to Saudi MBC 1. The authorship of the series of thirty fifteen-minute episodes is shared by both partners: the animation, the storyboard and the directing were the responsibility of the Jordanians, while the characters' voices were recorded in Saudi Arabia.

The series is a parody of popular Bedouin soap operas, mediating 'markers of tribal identity and memory' (Prager 2014). *Al-Masageel* was a pioneer in the animated portrayal of the cultural heritage of the Bedouin people tied not to a particular country, but to an entire region. Meanwhile, the visual characteristics indicate a Saudi identity, with female characters wearing colourful clothes in line with Saudi Bedouin costumes.[20]

The story revolves around a Middle Eastern Bedouin tribe called al-Masageel and the modern world around them. With the exception of Kabour, the Indian member of the tribe whose exact background is left vague, the other members speak a Bedouin dialect. During my visit to their Amman studio, Sketch in Motion director Zaidoun Karadsheh drew my attention to

Figure 3.6 *Al-Masageel*: a Bedouin tribe's encounter with modernity. 2011 © MBC.

the particular dialects spoken by the characters of *Al-Masageel*. As he pointed out, all of them have Saudi Bedouin accents, with the exception of two characters: Sahera, the wise woman who practises witchcraft, and Hanshal, a thief, both of whom are a source of humorous plots. While the members of the tribe were dubbed by renowned Saudi actors and actresses, Sahera's voice was rendered by Jordanian actress Reem Saʿada, and Hanshal was dubbed by the Jordanian actor Muʿtasim al-Fahmawi, both imitating a Jordanian Bedouin accent in order to meet the approval of the Saudi critics and public.

The main characters are the tribe's sheikh, his servant Galmad, Muʿtazz, the sheikh's daughter who is desperate to be married, the sheik's son who is fascinated with American hip-hop culture and three warriors of the tribe portrayed as modern strongmen, all fans of American action movies and computer games.

The plots typically take place in the tribes' camp in the desert. A critical attitude towards the concept of modernity is alluded to by the tents in the background, all equipped with satellite dishes. One of the episodes, 'The *iBa3er*', recounts the fate of a new innovation, a huge robot mule. The word itself has many connotations. *Baeer* means 'mule' in Arabic. The '*i*' refers to various Apple products, highly popular among Arab teens and young adults alike. The numeral 3 stands for the way a particular Arab consonant (ʿ) is written when Latin letters are used for online chatting and text messages.

In the episode, the sheikh of the tribe invests in the iBa3er hoping that it will improve the tribe's reputation. However, his son and other boys steal the robot as part of their attempt to challenge young joyriders in the desert – a direct reference to the social phenomenon of joyriding in Saudi Arabia (Menoret 2014). Unfortunately, at it turns out, the prototype had some errors, so the iBa3er crashes.

Al-Masageel contains a fair number of references not only to Arab, but also to Western popular culture. These include allusions to eBay, YouTube, *Superman* and movies such as *Titanic*. As a relocalisation of an adaptation, there are also references to Disney's *Aladdin*: when Galmad finds a magic lantern, the Jinn appearing before him bears an uncanny resemblance to the genie in *Aladdin*, a cutting criticism of the Disneyfication of Arab culture.

The series also contains a few references to current issues, like the criticism of the lavish lifestyles of oil state societies. In one of the episodes, oil is discovered in the home of the al-Masageel tribe, allowing the tribe to live in luxury for a time. When the oil wells run dry, life returns to what it used to be.

The show also clearly references classical Bedouin tales. In one episode, a mammoth frozen in ice is discovered near the tribe's home. After masses of tourists and reporters invade the area, the tribe's sheikh decides to cook the mammoth to show the guests his hospitality. This episode refers to the traditional story of a generous Bedouin, the proud owner of a rare horse, which he refuses to sell to anyone. One day, the sultan sends his servant to buy the horse. The Bedouin greets the illustrious guest with a lavish feast. In the end he reveals that, as a generous host, he has slain and roasted his horse to honour his guest.

Tunisia

The previous chapter has shown how the notion of national unity, and therefore a common national identity, was central to Zine el-Abidine Ben Ali's authoritarian regime and any questioning or demonstration of the contrary was frowned upon (Sadiki 2002). This policy had formed the backbone of Tunisian media. However, in November 2003, Ben Ali announced the decision to open up the radio and television market to the private sector. In 2005, Hannibal TV, a private television channel owned by local businessman Larbi

Nasra, began broadcasting. The liberalising policies came as a response with the aim of winning back audiences that had turned to other sources following the proliferation of Arab satellite channels. The media reform was thus essentially 'a top-down process that was meant to restructure and upgrade some of the foundations of Ben Ali's authoritarian rule and in many ways the reform has achieved its objectives' (Haugbølle and Cavatorta 2012).

First broadcast on Hannibal TV and directed by Sami Faour, *Tunis 2050* is a Tunisian animation created by Riad Ghariani and his team at CGS in 2009, which continued with three seasons of fifteen seventeen-minute episodes that aired during the month of Ramadan in 2010, 2011 and 2013 and on Elhiwar Ettounsi during Ramadan 2020. Regarding its funding, *Tunis 2050* differed from Egyptian and Gulf animations. Since they lacked governmental or institutional supporters, the producers of *Tunis 2050* had to find alternative funding sources (Byrne 2011). Costs were largely covered by companies whose logos appear in the title sequence and also in the series in the form of large advertisements in the animated cityscape.

Inspired by *The Jetsons* and *Futurama*, the plot of *Tunis 2050* is set in a Tunis of the future, where subways are suspended in the air above Bab Bhar, and the district of Al-Menzah has become an ultramodern city. The main characters are all members of a nuclear family: 'Abdelhamid, the father,

Figure 3.7 *Tunis 2050*: discussing the present through talking about the future. 2009 © CGS.

Ms Yasmin, the mother, and their three children, Nihel, Skander and Slim. Although the plots take place in the future, *Tunis 2050* exhibits generic features of science fiction such as a thinking robot, futuristic vehicles and hypermodern buildings. By introducing different characters, *Tunis 2050* analyses and, at the same time, critically defines 'Tunisian-ness'. With the inclusion of French phrases in dialogues (a characteristic of a Western education, and of the Tunisian liberal middle class) and fewer references to religious and pan-Arab discourses, the show articulates a liberal national identity.

Tunis 2050 did not ignore the historical moment of the 2011 fall of the Ben Ali regime. The title of the first episode of the third season in 2012 was a celebration of the revolution, with a song about freedom and people waving not only the Tunisian flag, but also banners of all the North African Arab countries. The first two episodes of the season also addressed the challenges faced by Tunisians in the new elections. The season also includes a character from one of the Gulf States. His origin is highlighted with a stereotypical accent and typical white clothes. In the story, the rich foreigner supports the political ambitions of Lubna, his blonde lover, by offering a free sports car to everyone who votes for her.[21] The inclusion of this non-Tunisian character is a clear reference to what is considered as Gulf intervention in Tunisian domestic politics after Ben Ali's fall in supporting the Islamist Al-Nahda Party, and also as a symbol of Tunisian identity vis-à-vis other Arab identities.[22] By locating the plot in the future and with its use of humour, *Tunis 2050* comments on actual political and social events in a safe way and can be relatively bold in addressing sensitive issues.

Conclusion

Sitcom animation, a Western genre, was hybridised by Arab authors to accommodate the particularities and sensitivities of the Arab world. Authors have tried to find a balance between adapting generic characteristics of the genre such as critical attitudes, while remaining within the limits of allowed criticism in their countries. As the case studies have shown, despite cultural similarities between the Arab countries, the Arab world does exhibit stark differences in how political systems affect media and production industries. Regarding censorship, there are significant differences in the approaches of media outlets, depending on political environment and ownership structures.

In addition, approaches to political issues, including notions of national identities, differ from one country to the next.

Arab sitcom animated cartoons share a number of textual characteristics with the 'national' animated cartoons discussed in Chapter 2. Similarly to those productions, sitcom animated cartoons also target national audiences, use local dialects, present scenes and characters with local hues, and are filled with local references on the level of the narrative. Given the generic characteristics, however, sitcom animated cartoons are more critical, as they confront local audiences with an exaggerated version of their realities and also challenge official notions of identity by articulating 'alternative' national identities. Humour enables a certain measure of criticism in sitcom animated cartoons. Since animation is often regarded as a 'childish' format it provides an appropriate space for critical attitudes. However, as Arab sitcom animations operate within existing political and media hierarchies, authors rarely venture to engage in head-on confrontations with official notions of identities. Still, the assumed innocence of the animated format and humour offers an opportunity to challenge official discourses on national identities, albeit to a small degree.

The presentation of societies in their diversity, the representation of minority groups and the showcasing of social and ethnic diversities are all means of challenging the official notion of national identities.

By representing different segments of local societies, both on the ethnic and the cultural levels, a number of Arab sitcom animations challenge official notions of national identities that often present the people as united and homogeneous. In these cases, producers engage in political discourses, while carefully avoiding issues that could spark censorship. The presentation of diverse social and even political groups from this perspective does not mean the trading of one national identity for another (Islamic, pan-Arab, etc.). Rather, it can be seen as the presentation of the 'national' as a mosaic that covers more than one community or group of people. By presenting Arabs from other states and by highlighting the differences between local and foreign Arabs – both visually and linguistically– these heterogeneous portrayals of the national stress national identities even more.

Thus, despite being modelled on successful Western sitcom programmes, the shows discussed in this chapter have both an Arab and a national flavour through distinct modes of comedy that cater to the tastes of local audiences. Arab sitcom animated cartoons can therefore be regarded as a hybrid format, fusing Western characteristics with regional and national particularities.

Notes

1. Personal interviews with Sameh Mustafa, producer of *Bsant wa Dyasty* (Cairo, 6 September 2012); personal interview with Tarek Rashed (Cairo, 8 September 2012); personal interview with Riad Ghariani (Tunis, 23 March 2013).
2. Telephone interview with Emad Hajjaj, 12 August 2017.
3. Ibid.
4. Ibid.
5. Khousa Bousa is an old Emirati game that was once popular among young girls. The players sing a traditional song and point on each of their fingers in turn until the end of the song.
6. Fanar Production was established in 2008 by Adnan Omar al-Obthani, managing director, and Haidar Mohamed, co-founder and general manager.
7. See the official webpage of Fanar Production: http://www.fanarproduction.com/en/10/projects/
8. Emirates Telecommunications Corporation (Etisalat) was founded in 1976 as a joint-stock company between International Aeradio Limited, a British company, and local partners. After a change in ownership structure in 1983, the UAE government held a 60 per cent share in the company, while the remaining 40 per cent was publicly traded.
9. The 2D visual style of *Shaabiat Al Cartoon* was later adopted by works such as *al-Masageel* and other animations.
10. See http://www.fanarproduction.com/en/4/about-us/
11. Personal interview with Sharif Gamal (Cairo, 12 September 2012).
12. Season 2, episode 7.
13. Personal interview with Sharif Gamal (Cairo, 12 September 2012).
14. The series does not include references to the Kurds, who tend to differentiate themselves from the Arabs on an ethnic basis.
15. The American animated cartoon show originally debuted on Comedy Central in 1997. Created by Trey Parker and Matt Stone, it soon became a fixture in a market dominated by high-quality animations produced by Disney and Pixar. Revolving around schoolchildren from a fictional town in Colorado, the sitcom became immensely popular not only in the United States, but in many other countries. Notorious for its dark, surreal humour, crude lan-

guage and adult-references, *South Park* was labelled an animated satire by critics.
16. Kuwaiti Nawaf Salem al-Shammari is a Kuwaiti director and producer, who produced many television serials and plays.
17. *Al-Watan* is published by the Al-Watan publishing house. The editor-in-chief is Sheikh Khalifa 'Ali al-Khalifa al-Sabah, a member of the Kuwaiti royal family.
18. The Kuwait Media Group Company was founded in 2006 and is based in Safat, Kuwait.
19. Season 1, episode 2.
20. Jordanian Bedouin clothes are traditionally black.
21. Season 4, episode 5.
22. Personal interview with Riad Ghariani (Tunis, 23 March 2013).

4

Approaches to Pan-Arab Identities

Introduction

The origins of pan-Arabism as an ideological movement with the goal of constructing a political and social identity is closely tied to the Al-Nahda movement of the late nineteenth century. Pan-Arab nationalism started as a cultural phenomenon particularly advocated by individuals and groups from Greater Syria. Later, in the early twentieth century, it evolved into a more overtly political movement (Tibi 1997: 61–6, 116). The majority of pan-Arab thinkers share the views of Sati' al-Husri (1882–1968), who defined the 'Arab nation' as a cultural-ethnic nation whose members are united by a common language and a shared culture (Charif 2000: 204). The linguistic unity of elite culture across the Arabic-speaking world lies at the heart of Pan-Arabism. *Fusha* Arabic constitutes a lingua franca reaching beyond geographical barriers. Moreover, it plays an essential part in the historical Arab self-perception as the first people responsible for the spread of Islam.

Pan-Arabism rose to a major political force in the decades after World War II, as the majority of thinkers viewed modern state borders as artificial creations of Western colonial powers, hence their declared goal was to demolish them. Established in 1947 by two Syrians, Michel 'Aflaq, an Orthodox Christian, and Salahuddin Bitar, a Sunni Muslim, the transnational Baath Party advocated 'Unity, Freedom and Socialism', referring to the unity of

Arab countries, freedom from colonial rule, and social justice (Kaylani 1972). The pan-Arab ideological trend placed Arab identity before traditional identities such as tribal affiliation, kinship ties and sectarian affiliation, and declared that the Arab world is a cultural unity bound by language and shared history.

These ideas of Pan-Arabism were put into practice during the presidency of Egypt's leader Gemal 'Abdel Nasser (1956–70) when Egypt and Syria were united under the banner of the United Arab Republic (UAR) in 1958. The UAR was dissolved three years later, and the defeat of the united forces of Egypt, Jordan and Syria in the Six-Day War of 1967 led to a gradual disillusionment with pan-Arab ideologies. The death of Nasser in 1970 marked the end of Arab unity. However, anti-colonialist and Arab nationalist rhetoric survived and continued to be a self-legitimising factor for the regimes of Baathist Iraq (1968–2003) and Baathist Syria (1963–).

Though pan-Arab nationalism failedpolitically, a sense of cultural and linguistic unity in the region remained and is reflected in the media market. Chalaby argued that 'the process of media globalization involves the formation of a second international layer that fits in between the national and global levels: the geo-cultural region' (Chalaby 2005: 4). As Sakr observed, the population of the Arab world makes up a community large enough to be a viable market for Arabic productions (Sakr 2004: 78). Coupled with the proliferation of satellite technologies in the 1990s, the transnational flow of cultural and media productions was facilitated even further. The coincidence of these two factors enabled authors to address the Arab world as a geocultural/geolinguistic region.

A significant number of Arab cultural and media productions therefore continued to target an all-Arab/Arabic-speaking audience. Cultural and media productions promoting an Arab identity not tied to national states involve the mediation of a 'transnational imagined community' (Aksoy and Robbins 2000; 2003). Alluding to a shared past, these productions tend to present the Arab world as a homogeneous group of people, glossing over the cultural variety found in the Arab world in order to create pan-Arab identities extending well beyond the national borders. These cultural and media productions often carry conflicting notions of Arab identities – depending on the production background – both within and beyond the national borders. One case in point is Syrian historical television drama, largely produced by elites close to the Baathist regime, mediating Syrian ideas of Arabism to all Arab audiences (Salamandra 2005; Dick 2005). Likewise, wealthy Gulf States have grown into new media powerhouses and launched pan-Arab satellite channels in order to support their broader political and economic interests, and claiming a voice in defining 'Arabness'.

While early pan-Arabism was decidedly secular, the Pan-Arab regimes of Iraq and Syria responded to social and political realities by adopting notions of Islam into their discourses. Baathist political leaderships established ambiguous but robust partnerships with religious figures in order to maintain legitimacy, and used religion as a mobilisation tool from time to time. Regimes of the Gulf countries, too, have built loose alliances, carefully avoiding confrontation between political and religious narratives. This approach also informed cultural and media productions which were generally careful not to hurt religious sensibilities, and showed a tendency in representing Islam not as a religion but rather as part of the Arab culture.

This chapter will analyse animated cartoons produced by the media industries of Arab countries as well as by transnational organisations that have a declared pan-Arab political agenda. It will start with the animations produced by the cultural and media industries of two other regimes with a declared pan-Arab agenda: Baathist Iraq (1968–2003) and Baathist Syria (1963–). Even though there are several transnational political organisations in the Arab world, only one of them is involved in animated cartoon production. I will therefore explore the identity of animated cartoons produced by the Gulf Cooperation Council's (GCC) Joint Programme Production Institution (JPPI), a Kuwaiti-based transnational organisation with the declared goal of advocating a shared Gulf Arab identity, distributed primarily on state-owned channels of the member states. Since pan-Arab children's television channels are increasingly dynamic actors in animated cartoon production, this chapter will also examine the animated cartoons produced by satellite channels, with a special focus on Qatari Al Jazeera Children's Channel (JCC, renamed Jeem TV in 2013) in order to understand their approaches to Arab identity.

Mediating a Pan-Arab Identity in Baathist Iraq

The Development of Film and Animation Industries in Iraq

While the early stages of Iraqi cinema date back to 1909 when a limited number of cinematic productions were released, it was not until the 1940s that a handful of private companies produced black-and-white movies. Early Iraqi cinema largely used technological equipment imported from the British colonial rulers by local secularist elites. The overwhelming majority of the films produced before 1950 were non-political melodramatic romances set in rural milieus. The early period of Iraqi cinema ended with the 1958 military coup that toppled the British-installed King Faisal. The Free Officers, led by General ʿAbd al-Karim Qasim, the first president of independent Iraq (1958–63), nationalised the cinema industry and subordinated it to the movement's new Arab nationalist ideals. Attempts to promote local production began in the regime's first year, and Baghdad television showed plays by Iraqi writers, folk dancing and documentaries on Iraq (Bashkin 2011). In 1959, the Iraqi Film and Theatre Organisation (*al-Muʾassasa al-ʿAmma lil-Sinima wal-Masrah*) was created with the declared aim of supervising cinema productions. The number of films produced remained low during the following decades.[1]

State control of the film industry even intensified after the Baath Party seized power in 1968. In early 1969, the pan-Arab nationalist regime enacted the Publications Law that declared the media to be the 'fourth branch' of governance (*al-sulta al-rabiʿa*). Yet, although they were officially declared to be 'independent', all media became mere branches of the central power (Bengio 1998: 8).

Teaching history became a primary tool of political influence and indoctrination, and it was characterised by two discourses. The first targeted the educated classes through books, articles and public debates, while the second was designed to appeal to the wider public, often using visual genres such as festivals, statues, stamps and, of course, films (Bengio 1998: 169). One example was the grandiose cinematic production *Al-Qadisiyya* (Qadisiyya, 1981). The film was screened in every cinema in the country as a celebration of the victory of the great Arab leader Saʾd Ibn Abi Waqqas over the troops of the Persian king Yazdigird in CE 636. Needless to say, reviving such historical themes was a central part of preparing public opinion for the war against Iran which lasted from September 1980 to August 1988 (Bengio 1998: 172–3).

Modern Iraq had been home to various ethnic groups (Arabs, Kurds, Assyrians, Turkmens and so on) and religious communities (Sunni Muslims, Shia Muslims and Christians), and the country was also divided along tribal lines. The aim of Saddam Hussein, himself a Sunni Muslim from the central Iraqi town of Tikrit, was to give Iraq a secularist pan-Arab identity. For Saddam, consolidating power included subtle agreements with local elites, building cross-sectarian client systems by elevating members of different groups to power and also through repression. Empowered with oil money, Saddam also strove to provide general welfare and to spread propaganda in order to create an 'Iraqi nation', an imagined community characterised by tradition and unity. Reviving the memory of ancient Babylon had been one of the cornerstones for defining Iraqiness since the early years of the Iraqi Baath Party. Artists were encouraged to show the historical greatness of Mesopotamia in order to create a common historical tradition that could be shared by all Iraqis, irrespective of their sectarian background (Bengio 1998: 92). This tradition was not only continued but also reinforced under Saddam Hussein's rule, as he often drew inspiration from the models of Mesopotamian rulers of the distant past to whom he likened himself (Bengio 1998: 69). Baathist historical and political discourse also proclaimed the Sumerians, the Babylonians and, for all practical purposes, all Semitic peoples to be Arabs. It perceived the emergence of early civilisations and the rise of monotheistic religions as a single continuum in which Arabs formed the links between cultures and creeds (Bengio 1998: 168).

The early days of Iraqi animation date back to 1968 when UNESCO delegate Norman Emberson Hoy travelled to Baghdad and set up a team of professionals in local media and film industries to produce animation trials. The project resulted in short cartoon inserts prepared for a live-action film, *The Feather and the Knife* (Hoy 1969).

The first Iraqi animated cartoon was an eleven-minute production, *al-Kurat al-Qadam al-Amreekiyya* (American Football), which was shown at the Palestinian Film Festival in Baghdad in 1972. The film was directed by Victor Haddad and animated by Bassam Faraj. It claims a pan-Arab identity

Figure 4.1 *Al-Kurat al-Qadam al-Amreekiyya* (American Football): the united Arab team beats America. 1972 © Bassam Faraj.

as it features an All-Arab football team competing with an American team and repeatedly shows a crowd waving the flags of Palestine, Syria, Iraq and Egypt. Each time the American team scores a goal, the numerals of the year of an Arab defeat such as 48 (referring to the establishment of Israel) and 67 (the Israeli victory over the united Arab armies) is shown on the scoreboard. As Bassam Faraj explained in a personal interview, the core idea was to show Palestinians getting back at pro-Zionist powers, which, according to the official discourse, were associated with the United States.[2] The game ends with the victory of the Arab team. The film – being the single animated production at the festival – won the award for best animated production.

In 1974, Faraj travelled to Hungary to study journalism, where he became an opponent of the Baathist regime. He remains in Hungarian exile. After working with Hungarian animation studios, he established his own company together with his compatriot Thamer al-Zaidi in 1989. Dana Film Studio later became a main partner in the productions of the GCC's JPPI and other Gulf productions (Jaseen 2006).

After seizing power in 1979, Saddam Hussein quickly realised the importance of media and propaganda in consolidating his power and devoted many efforts to create a well-established media infrastructure in Iraq (Shafik 2007b: 23). In 1980, as part of the propaganda that accompanied the Iran–Iraq war, Iraqi TV's Children's Department released a number of short spots, each three to four minutes long, presented in the time slot dedicated to children. Heavily influenced by *Tom and Jerry*, the low-frame celluloid films show the supreme leader of the Iranian Islamic revolution as a pitiful character either clucking like a chicken or speaking in an exaggerated, overly enunciated Persian accent. An episode called *Awham Khomeini* (Delusions of Khomeini) showed the Iranian leader scared by an Iraqi missile and trying to escape on the back of an Iranian missile. Falling into the sea and eaten by a shark, the spirit of Satan leaves his body through his mouth. In *Khomeini wal-Misbah al-Sehriyy* (Khomeini and the Magic Torch) Khomeini finds Aladdin's magic lamp in a cave, then asks the genie – who is referred to as 'Efreet (devil) – to destroy Iraq. To his misfortune, 'Efreet returns defeated by the glorious Iraqi army and takes revenge on Khomeini by beating him up.

Al-'Amirah wal-Nahr

As there were no private productions at the time, in 1980 the Revolutionary Council decided to establish the semi-private company Babylon (*Sharikat Babil lil-Intaj al-Sinima'iyy wal-Tilfiziyooniyy*) in order to stimulate film production (Shafik 2007b: 33). The story of Iraqi animation runs parallel to the story of Babylon, as in the early 1980s it offered scholarships for young artists to study animation in several European countries.[3]

The highest-profile Iraqi animation was *Al-'Amirah wal-Nahr* (The Princess and the River) which remained the sole feature-length animation venture of the Saddam era, released in 1982. The $1 million dollar budget movie was funded by Iraqi Television's Arab Centre for Animation, founded by Iraqi director Faissal al-Yasseri, with the support of the Iraqi Ministry of Culture, in the same year. The film was produced by Babylon, whereas the scripts were written by Australian scenario writer John Palmer. As no animation studios were available in Iraq, animation work was outsourced to East Germany. The voices of the main characters were dubbed by popular Iraqi actors such as Sa'd 'Ardas, Khalil al-Refa'iyy and Lena al-Bati'. The animated movie was dubbed not into the Iraqi dialect but into *fusha* Arabic, to stress the pan-Arab nationalist nature of the Iraqi cultural production.

While the film includes countless references to national (Iraqi) identity and targets a domestic audience, it includes markers of Arab identity such as the setting of the story in Sumer. The allegory of Sumer can be understood as a reference to Arabs fighting each other rather than focusing on larger enemies, one of the frequent themes of Iraqi Baathist discourse.

The story of *Al-'Amirah wal-Nahr* is in fact an adaptation of an old Mesopotamian tale and takes place in the ancient Mesopotamian city of Lagash. The plot begins in the royal castle of Lagash, with the king speaking his parting words to his three daughters before he passes away. According to ancestral tradition, the future ruler must pass three tests in order to gain the throne: she has to swim across the river without waking the dragon that resides at the bottom; she has to cross the desert of death; and finally she has to enter the golden forest and take the golden apple from a tree guarded by a giant snake and a bird. All three ventures are especially risky as Nanna, the Moon God, only helps the one who is pure of heart. Ur-mina, the oldest princess, embarks on the quest first. Attempting to circumvent the rules, she orders the army to protect her. However, the dragon of the river is woken and pulls her under. The second princess, Ur-nina, takes her pet lion with her. She swims across the river, crosses the desert, reaches the tree and steals the apple. However, when swimming back across the river, she also wakes up the dragon, which kills her. Sunani, the third princess, overcomes her grief over the loss of her sisters, and knowing that the fate of the kingdom lies in her hands, she too embarks on the quest for the throne. Accompanied by a loyal peasant, she reaches the tree. However, she is attacked by one of the evil generals who threatens to wake up the snake if she does not consent to marry him. Luckily, the peasant saves the princess by killing the general as well as the snake, the bird and even the dragon of the river. In the end, Sunani becomes queen of the Land of the Two Rivers.

On the surface, *Al-'Amirah wal-Nahr* differs little from the usual folk tales and myths about kings and princesses. However, the sub-plot and the overall rhetoric make the movie more of a propaganda piece. According to the frame story, Sumer is at war with the neighbouring kingdom of Aqqad (which is described as 'brotherly' in the movie's rhetoric), and there is a

Figure 4.2 *Al-'Amirah wal-Nahr* (The Princess and the River): an old tale in the service of Saddam Hussein. 1982 © Babylon.

general hostility between the twelve kingdoms of the Land of the Two Rivers. Before his death, the king of Lagash declares that the unification of the hostile kingdoms should be the primary task of his successor, whoever it may be. Some of the scenes are set in the city of Aqqad and feature its young and handsome king, Naram, who is goaded by his evil advisors to attack Lagash. It also shows that a greater and evil empire (Nafar) and its wicked ruler ('Eiran) are behind the plot of dividing the Sumerians, who should be one people. In order to stress the need for unity among the Sumerians, slogans such as 'We are all Sumerians!' are often repeated, similarly to the condemnation of Sumerians fighting against each other rather than uniting against 'Eiran, whose name alone leaves little doubt that he is a reference to Saddam Hussein's great enemy of the time, Iran.

At the end of the story, the kings of Sumer and the people of the kingdoms come together to celebrate Sunani. Standing in front of a cheering crowd, the queen turns to the people: 'I beseech you all to renounce your quarrels and to work on restoring the unity of the Land of the Two Rivers, and reviving our old glory'. Sunani continues by declaring that unity is only the beginning and that the great battle is to be fought against the common enemy.

This message is, obviously, a multilayered one. The quarrelling kingdoms of Sumer can be regarded as metaphors both for Iraqi political factions and social groups, and for the rivalry between Arab countries. In a 2012 interview on Iraqi al-Ittijah TV, Faissal al-Yasseri himself acknowledged that the film contains overt references to the so called Revolution of 17 July 1968.

Regarding its visuals, the film failed to articulate a unique style, most probably because the animators were Western artists. In this respect, *Al-'Amirah wal-Nahr* echoes the period's popular American and French style in portraying an ancient Middle Eastern environment. Similarly to European as well as Disney productions, the characters are represented in accordance with their roles in the story. Good characters, like the old king and Sunani, are presented as physically pleasing to the eye with round faces and big dark eyes, while the evil 'Eiran and others are shown to have angular faces, a hawkish nose, tiny eyes and long black beards.

Faissal al-Yasseri set out to produce television series mediating an Iraqi-centred pan-Arab identity aimed at both national and regional audiences. The first was *'Oudat al-Misbah al-Sehriyy* (The Return of the Magic Lantern) in 1984, a series of thirteen seventeen-minute episodes combining live photographic and video backgrounds of Baghdad's historical sites with animated characters. Inspired by *The Arabian Nights*, the series tells the story of a modern Baghdadi boy who finds a magic lantern. The genie, who is represented as a boy the same age as the protagonist, tells stories of the past, while in exchange the boy shows the genie around modern Baghdad, where, as a creature from the past, he is surprised by the advanced technology. The last episode ended with the genie and the boy finding a magic carpet in the Baghdad Museum. The next series, called *Al-Rehlah al-'Ajeebah ilal-Madee* (The Miraculous Journey to the Past) picked up in 1985 where the previous series had left off, telling the adventures of the boy and the genie travelling through time and space to visit famous people and witness important events from the Arab past.

Later, al-Yasseri decided to return to the topic of ancient Mesopotamia, creating *Malhamat Gilgamesh* (The Epic of Gilgamesh) in 1986, a ten-episode series on ancient mythology; this was followed a year later by *Babel al-Jadeedah* (The New Babel) and in 1988 by a science-fiction series about a search for alternative energy in outer space (Bendazzi 2015: 377). By choosing history and folk tales, animation producers of Baathist Iraq played a safe game, hence consolidating their positions in the media industries. Doing so, they facilitated the articulation of political narratives of pan-Arabism without directly engaging in such discourse themselves. Meanwhile, Islamic references in these productions were rare. When they did exist, they were largely restricted to the presentation of historical Islamic architecture as monuments of a glorious past, in line with the *qawmi* (nationalist) narratives of their time that fused Baathist ideology embedded in Islamic heritage, while emphasising a secularist idea of development.

The war against Iran (1980–8) dried up the financial sources for further animation productions in Iraq as the country became indebted to its neighbours and international banks (Farouk-Sluglett 2001: 265–6). The situation turned even worse after the invasion of Kuwait, when, in August 1990, the United Nations imposed broad sanctions on Iraq. As cinema equipment, stock and chemicals for film laboratories were also forbidden as part of the sanctions, the cinema industry went into decline.

Though the Iraqi animation industry has not recovered since, historical and folkloric narratives of the Baathist pan-Arabism regime have survived the regime's collapse. In 2013, a decade after Saddam Hussein's fall, independent Iraqi-German filmmaker Furat al-Jamil released *Baghdad Night* with the support of Ruya Foundation.[4] The noir-style ten-minute 3D rendition of Baghdad tells the story of the ghoul Saʿluwa, a famous character in Iraqi folklore. The plot takes us to the old Qambar ʿAli district of Baghdad and begins with what seems to be an ordinary day for an Iraqi taxi driver. He picks up a beautiful young woman on a street corner at dusk, and, at her request, takes her to an old graveyard. In lieu of a fare, the woman gives the taxi driver a small golden bell. Compelled to transport her again and again, the driver is seduced by Saʿluwa over three nights, until, disregarding her repeated warnings, he cannot resist his curiosity and follows her into the graveyard just to discover her real identity (Shields 2017). By retelling Saʿluwa's story in animation and placing it in today's Baghdad, Furat al-Jamil creates a sense of continued history that expresses a hope, voiced by the character of Saʿluwa, that good times will return to the city torn by war and political fragmentation.

Mediating a Pan-Arab Identity in Baathist Syria

Media Policies in post-independence Syria

The decade after Syria gained independence in 1946 was marked by political instability. Syrian television began broadcasting in 1960, at the time when Syria was united with Egypt under the banner of the United Arab Republic. A year later, in 1961, Syria split from Egypt to re-establish itself as the Syrian Arab Republic, allowing local media to be independent of Egyptian influence. The state monopoly over cultural production was completed with the Baath Party's accession to power in 1963.

The new pan-Arab nationalist regime attempted to control every aspect of cultural life (Boëx 2011). A new law, passed in 1963, monopolised all media – except a few radio stations broadcasting from abroad – which left Syrians without access to information about political matters other than that coming from media controlled by local authorities and the state.[5] The regime set three main objectives for the media: first, to spread awareness of the goals of the Baathist Revolution; second, to disseminate socialist and nationalist ideas to Syrians; and, third, to gain support from domestic and international public opinion as well as from Syrian émigrés.

Film production, distribution and first film screenings became the privilege of the state-controlled Al-Mu'assasa al-'Amma lil-Sinema (National Film Organisation, NFO). While placing filmmaking into the nationalist discourse, unlike many similar institutions of other authoritarian Arab countries, the NFO did not practise direct censorship and did not officially ban particular cinematic or television productions. However, authorities rarely hesitated to give filmmakers hints, and, in some cases, they also shelved finished productions if the producers did not comply with their demands (Salti 2006). The NFO also offered scholarships abroad and attractive career opportunities for young people in the industry, facilitating the creation of an elite of loyalist filmmakers whose expressions of mild political criticism would be tolerated.

In March 1971, Prime Minister Hafez al-Assad became president after consolidating his support in the Baathist leadership. Assad, a member of the minority Alawite community, announced a non-sectarian, inclusive, pan-Arab political agenda in order to win the support of other minorities, while, at the same time, making serious efforts to reach an agreement with influential Sunni elites (Seale 1995: 169–84). He also formed alliances with members of the Sunni religious scholars (*ulema*) (Pierret 2013).

Assad's non-sectarian agenda became a core of the local media that was ruled by relatively liberal policies. This cultural burgeoning lasted until the end of the decade, when the rise of an armed Islamist opposition and the economic difficulties of the 1980s put an end to it.

Despite the turmoil of the early 1980s and the fact that supporting animation was a low priority of the NFO, some young individuals laid the foundation for national animation production. Filmmaker Mwaffaq Katt released his first short celluloid production *Juha fil-Mahkameh* (Juha at the Court) in 1985, which was followed by around forty more *Juha* stories in the coming years. The Juha, a 'wise fool' character of popular jokes, was a safe choice, as it was widely known and regarded as part of the national and regional folklore as well as a source of innocent comedy. A more political production of Katt's, *Hikaya Mismariyya* (A Story of Nails), followed in 1991. Combining pen drawing with celluloid, the four-minute animation is a universal anti-war statement. It begins with two tall nails quarrelling as they stand on the opposite edges of a hole. As the bickering becomes tense, the two nails rally their armies of small nails, who engage in fighting until the hole is filled with their dead bodies. When the battle is over, the two tall nails return to the scene, jump on the bodies of those who fought on their behalf and kiss each other.

Samir Jabr was another influential Syrian animator. His breakout film was *Isharat al-Murur* (The Traffic Signal) in 1987, a short educational celluloid animation for children about pedestrian road safety. Jabr and Katt were among those who lobbied the director-general of Syrian Television until the establishment of an animation department was approved in 1985 (Van de Peer 2017: 112). In the same year a partnership with Neilson Hordell Ltd in London was formed for the import and export of animated content for television. Despite the promising start, the NFO's interest in animation remained reluctant for more than half a decade.

Following a period of tight control as part of the crackdown on the opposition in the early 1980s, the Syrian state loosened its hold over film production by the late 1980s and early 1990s. Wedeen argues that this liberalisation was a response to the elimination of organised opposition as well as to the persistent attempts of individual artists, playwrights, directors, poets, cartoonists and other media personalities to produce works that could offer an alternative to the regime's self-proclaimed ideals of omnipotence and indispensability (Wedeen 1999: 90–1). Exchanges between Syrian and Western artists, for example, now became more common. Investment Law 10, passed in 1991, also encouraged private-sector entrepreneurs to create television programmes for commercial entertainment. Though economic policies allowed a degree of privatisation in production companies, those companies tended to be owned by individuals with strong links to the regime, and although many Syrian television series were produced by private production companies, television stations remained under strict government control (Salamandra 2004: 116). It is not surprising then that the most successful private entrepreneurs were those with strong ties to the regime and with experience in the television industry.

One prominent individual who worked on the liberalisation of the Syrian media industries was ʿAbdel-Nabiyy Hijazi (1938–2013) who served as general director at the Hayʾa al-Idhaʿa wal-Tilfiziyoon (Organisation of Radio and Television) between 1988 and 1996.[6] Very soon afterwards, the Hijazi family became the backbone of Syrian animation production.

The Establishment of a Syrian Animation Industry in the 1990s

In the early 1980s, Syrian Television set up a department for dubbing (Hijazi 2012). It dubbed not only films and series, but also a number of foreign animated cartoons into *fusha* Arabic, and the state channel then presented them to local audiences. One prominent sound engineer in the dubbing department was Mannaaʿ Hijazi, ʿAbdel-Nabiyy Hijazi's son.[7] Mannaaʿ Hijazi profited from his experience in dubbing and his good working relations with well-known Syrian actors who lent their voice for the productions. After the government introduced more liberal policies, Hijazi established his own company, Venus for Art Production (also referred to as al-Zahra, 'The Flower'), in 1992.[8] Within a few years, Venus became not only a mediator between Western animation producers and Arab television channels, but also a major gatekeeper that decided which animations were suitable for

Arab children and adapted foreign products to local and regional audiences. They purchased Disney and Hanna-Barbera animations and Japanese anime, dubbed them into *fusha* Arabic and sold the products or the broadcasting rights to television stations around the Arab world. Venus not only dubbed but also 'Arabised' animations by giving the characters Arab names, such as Capitain Majid.

The introduction of satellite technology to the Arab world in the mid-1990s offered Venus even more opportunities. Less than a decade after its establishment, Venus owned the rights of more than 5,000 dubbed episodes of a wide range of Japanese and American animations. This gave the company the idea of establishing its own children's channel, Spacetoon TV, in 2000.[9] Initially based in Damascus, in 2007 the channel moved its headquarters to Dubai. It mainly aired animations dubbed by Venus, later starting to produce its own shows via its animation company, Tiger Production, founded in 2001 by Mannaaʿ Hijazi (Hijazi 2012).

The liberal economic policies also gave other private companies the opportunity to participate in the production and animation business. Star Animation for Artistic Production was established in 1995 in Damascus, although it only acquired its licence from the Chamber of Film and Animation Industries two years later, in 1997.[10] After releasing a number of feature-length productions, in 2004 Star Animation was rebranded as EmariToons and relocated to the UAE.

As most prominent animation companies maintained strong professional ties with official Syrian media and even government institutions, children's media in general, and animation in particular, became an integral part of the local cultural industry. In 2004, Al-Muʾassasa al-ʿAmma lil-Sinima (General Organisation for Cinema) established a special section for children's cinema with the declared goal of participating in the production of one feature-length animated production every year. In the same year, the Mudiriyyat al-Intaj al-Tilfiziyooniyy (Directorate of Television Production) purchased modern equipment and invited a Canadian expert as an advisor on setting up the foundation to produce the first Syrian animated series, *Jazeerat al-Mughamarat* (Island of Adventures), written by Ahmad Maʿrouf and directed by Mwaffaq Katt (Hijazi 2012).

The NFO continued its soft censorship, resulting in productions that remained in line with the official discourse. The increasingly easy access to 3D animation software, however, enabled authors like Akram Agha to produce low-profile, politically loaded productions, which were sidelined by the NFO and the mainstream animation scene. Akram Agha released *Intibah* (Attention), a mix of pen-drawn and computer-generated 3D animation in 2005. The surrealist three-minute piece shows images of children who are turned into bullets by a machine, and guns pouring blood. In 2008, Agha produced *Hidha' al-Jenral* (The General's Boot), a seventeen-minute 3D animation whose story revolves around a pair of heavy boots – a symbol of authoritarian oppression. Though no word was spoken either in *Intibah* or in *Hidha' al-Jenral,* the inclusion of Middle Eastern cityscapes and oriental tones in both productions blended the universal message of peace with an Arab flavour.

As support from the NFO remained largely reluctant, a number of Syrian animators sought international cooperation and foreign customers. Soon, many established links with emerging Gulf production companies and visionary TV channels to enter the pan-Arab children's media market. One of those pioneers was Sulafa Hijazi, who started her career dubbing foreign animation at Venus in 1997 before becoming a founder member of the Spacetoon TV team where she worked from 1999 to 2001. Soon, she established contacts in the Gulf and established a profile in the production of pan-Arab edutainment cartoons. Her first production was *Dumtom Salemeen* (You Stay Safe), a series of sixty-five episodes of five minutes each, produced for the GCC's JPPI in 2002. Through the comical adventures of a Gulf family, the episodes address a variety of environmental issues of concern in the Arab region, such as water and energy consumption, pollution and agricultural development. Two years later, Hijazi was commissioned by the JPPI to create animated spots for *Madeenat al-Ma'loomaat* (Data City), a edutainment series of fifty-two episodes of twenty-seven minutes each, showing a fictional Arab city that blends modernity and traditional culture by mixing live action with animation. When the JCC channel was launched in 2007, Hijazi released *Bayti al-'Arabi* (My Arab House) a production of fifty-two half-hour episodes bringing together real-life footage, cartoons, 2D, 3D and puppets. As a general concept, the show features interiors of Arab homes, focusing on common visual traits from various Arab countries, and hence creating a sense of cultural unity among the viewers from different countries.

In 2010, Sulafa Hijazi set up her studio, blue.dar that signed with the JPPI to produce *Malsoun.org*, an edutainment series combined with an online platform. The animation comprised sixty episodes of five minutes each, centred on the character of Malsoun, a beloved parrot from *Iftah Ya Simsim* (Open Sesame!), the Arabic version of *Sesame Street*. In each episode, the two protagonists, a girl and her little brother, ask a question about geography, biology, history, the arts or another topic, then press a button on their digital watch that alerts Malsoun, who arrives by teleport from the world of the internet to answer their question or to take them on a journey. Visually, Hijazi continued to develop her visual style by designing typical Arab characters, which she had started a few years earlier when working on her high-profile feature project *Tuyur al-Yasmeen* (The Jasmine Birds).

Tuyur al-Yasmeen

Made in 2009, the sixty-nine-minute *Tuyur al-Yasmeen* was the last Syrian feature-length animation production made before the country descended into civil war two years later. Produced by Tiger Production and funded by the Ministry of Culture's General Establishment for Cinema. In our interview, Hijazi stressed the story's universal values.[11]

Unlike the majority of Syrian animations, the plot of *Tuyur al-Yasmeen* is not set in a specifically Arab or Middle Eastern environment. However, the title links the film, and the bird community of the animation, to Syria, as Damascus is often referred to as the City of Jasmine (*Madinat al-Yasmeen*) in Syrian literature. The characters speak *fusha* Arabic and the story is set in a fictional natural environment whose localism is not marked by buildings and characters, but by Arabo-Islamic symbolism. The trees have hand-shaped leaves, resembling the amulets known as *khamsa*, and the rocks of the mountains form patterns resembling Islamic mosaics. Even though the main characters are birds, they still have some Arab characteristics, such as large eyes and thick eyebrows, and are dressed in clothes that evoke traditional garb, such as the *ghallabiyya*.

The protagonist is a small bird called Ghaith. His father was a healer, moving from one bird community to another, gathering herbs and helping

Figure 4.3 *Tuyur al-Yasmeen* (The Jasmine Birds): evoking Arabo-Islamic symbolism in animation. 2009 © Tiger Production.

the sick. On his way back home from one of these journeys, he dies in an accident. Ghaith decides to continue his father's work, and begins roaming the forests with his friend Hetton. An epidemic breaks out in the community of the jasmine birds and their fate now lies in the hands of Ghaith who struggles to find the rare herbs that will heal them. Ghaith falls in love with Hetton, and together they visit the communities his father once helped. He comes to realise that his father will never be truly dead because he will always be remembered for his good deeds.

Tuyur al-Yasmeen is unique among Syrian animations with its moderate political criticism. The leader of the Jasmine bird community has enjoyed his position since childhood, and while the community itself is made up of only seven citizens, they are ruled by 700 ministers. The story also includes a fictional species of bird which gathers to deal with the devastation wreaked on a community by disease and distrust, but ends up arguing without reaching any decisions. Both are clear references to, and criticism of, the bureaucracy experienced by Middle Eastern and North African Arabs. Expressing social criticism, the plot also features a fictional species of fish. Despite their tiny size and vegetarianism, the fish are presented as dangerous, as they gather around their victims and drive them mad by quarrelling, a reference to the often vicious arguments in the Arab world.

What makes *Tuyur al-Yasmeen* stand out from other Baathist animations is the obvious intention to develop a distinctive visual style that is a hybrid of Disney and Arab illustration traditions. In our interview, Sulafa Hijazi explained how her aim was to draw the birds (with a focus on the character of Ghaith) in an Arab style. She also explained how she was inspired by Disney characters when developing the production that she claims carries an Arab identity both in style and in symbolism.[12] *Tuyur al-Yasmeen* remains both Sulafa Hijazi and Syria's most ambitious and critically acclaimed production, having won several awards inn international festivals in the United States, Russia, India, Egypt, Iran and the Netherlands.

Al-Jarrah

Al-Jarrah (The Jug), produced by Star Animation in 2001, is an animated adaptation of an old folk tale, directed by Ammar al-Sharbaji and written by Ahmad Natouf. It is one of the most moralistic Syrian animations, with a clear-cut moral lesson and schematic characters. Although the production does not directly address political and social issues, the narrative fits perfectly into Baathist propaganda. The characters speak *fusha* Arabic to stress the film's Arab identity. The visual markers of both the characters and the backgrounds indicate a Middle Eastern environment, hence presenting the national or sub-regional as being of regional (geolinguistic) validity.

The protagonist is a man called 'Amin ('truthful') who buys a farm from a man called Saleh ('righteous') and goes to live there with his wife and children. As the family begins to renovate the buildings, they find a jug full of gold. After arguing with his family, 'Amin decides that returning the jug to its previous owner is a matter of honour ('*amana*). By chance, their greedy neighbour 'Enad ('obstinacy') spots them finding the jug and decides to steal the gold. The next day, 'Amin and his children are carrying the jug to Saleh's house. While they are crossing a bridge, it collapses. 'Amin saves his children, but the jug falls into the river. 'Enad fishes the treasure out of the water and hides it in a cave. After finding out what her husband did, 'Enad's wife refuses the ill-gotten goods. Meanwhile, 'Amin's sorrow over the loss of the '*amana* is underscored with an emotional soundtrack. Torn between the duties of loyalty to her evil husband and her own morality, 'Enad's wife leaves a map that helps 'Amin find the treasure and return it to Saleh. Saleh refuses to take the treasure, so the two turn to the local sheikh for advice. The old man promises to answer them the next morning and hides the jug in his house, not noticing that 'Enad is watching him. The next morning 'Enad knocks on the sheikh's door dressed as a beggar and searches for the treasure after the sheikh has left the room to fetch him some food. 'Amin, his son Hasan and Saleh arrive to hear the sheikh's advice and realise that the treasure has disappeared. 'Enad sneaks out, but the others catch him trying to hide the treasure. The happy ending sees 'Amin and Saleh deciding to keep part of the treasure and give the rest away to the poor.

Baathist 'revolutionary' ideals appear directly in the narrative, in the form of phrases common in Syrian primary school textbooks.[13] In the scenes showing 'Amin's family working on their farm, songs praising work are featured, with lines such as 'Let's begin rebuilding by rejuvenating the old!' and 'We plant in order to harvest, looking up high, striving to elevate ourselves!' Meanwhile, Islam – in line with the Baathist discourse – is presented not explicitly as a religion but as a part of the culture, integrated into the visuals and text. The wives of both Saleh and 'Enad wear the hijab, and when making her moral statement about stealing the treasure, 'Enad's wife labels it as '*mal haram*', evoking the Islamic concept of '*haram*' in the sense of 'forbidden by God'.[14] At one point, she tells her husband that he will 'burn in the fire of hell' for what he did. In addition, the sheikh is presented as an authority on moral issues, with Saleh and his son asking him for advice.

The style of the series reflects efforts to follow Disney's hyper-realism, and the portrayals of good and evil characters follow suit, adding little to the production's pan-Arab identity. The narrative also resembles Disney animations in many respects. Short spots, independent of the main storyline, tell funny stories of animals such as squirrels, rats, hens and a rooster, while 'Enad has surrealistic dreams of giant ice creams flying in space, reminiscent of Disney dream interludes.

The characters are presented as either good or evil. While 'Amin's family, Saleh and the sheikh are presented as likeable people through both visual markers and voice, 'Enad has greenish skin, evil eyes and sharp, unpleasant features. 'Amin's family is happy and balanced, while 'Enad is constantly arguing with his wife and his donkey.

Figure 4.4 *Al-Jarrah* (The Jug): a moralistic tale of old Syria. 2001 © Star Animation.

Through the use of *fusha* Arabic and a presentation of Middle Eastern characters and milieus, as well as the mediation of morals appreciated by Arabs regardless of their country of origin or religion – such as honesty, trustworthiness, diligence and respect – *Al-Jarrah* articulates an Arab identity without any particular national characteristics.

Khait al-Hayat

The production of *Khait al-Hayat* (Yarn of Life) is an example of the collaboration between the public and private sector in Baathist Syria's media production. Made in 2007, the feature-length film was produced by Tiger Production and sponsored by the Ministry of Culture's General Establishment for Cinema. It was directed by Razam Hijazi – ʿAbdel-Nabiyy Hijazi's eldest daughter – and the script was written by Diana Fares.

The narrative is set in a medieval Middle Eastern Muslim environment with no direct reference to any particular place or time. However, the scenes and the visualisation of the characters indicate that the story takes place at the time when the Abbasid caliphate was invaded by the Mongols. The film is dubbed into *fusha* Arabic, while the visual style and narrative clearly show the influence of American animated cartoons, most notably *The Prince of Egypt* by Dreamworks (1998).

Like *Tuyur al-Yasmeen*, *Khait al-Hayat* is a localised adaptation of a story with a universal moral validity. The plot revolves around an Arab boy called 'Ala', whose ethnic origin remains vague. Since his father passed away, 'Ala' has lived with his mother in a small village, where she tries to make ends meet by embroidering clothes. Seeing his mother's struggles day by day, 'Ala' lives in constant sadness, and dreams about growing up and making her life easier. Bullied by the other children, he befriends wise speaking animals. One day his bird and turtle friends take him on a magic journey where he meets the Elder of Time, a kind-hearted old woman who gives him a magical yarn of life: whenever he pulls at the thread, he can travel forward in time to a future point in his life. After pulling the thread, 'Ala' becomes a strong young man, capable of taking care of his mother. Later, he marries and has a son. Whenever he faces difficulties, 'Ala' turns to the yarn to solve the problem. However, as time goes on, he has to face the sadness of seeing his loved ones pass away. Finally, the day comes when his son has to join the army to fight the country's enemies. Frightened by the possibility of losing his son, 'Ala' despairs as to whether he should use the yarn or not. In the end, he decides he will, although not to go forward in time, but instead to return to his childhood and face the old hardships that now seem more bearable than the problems of adulthood. In the end, the film conveys the moral message that life's troubles cannot be escaped.

Despite its universal moral and its narrative that cannot be linked to a particular country or culture, *Khait al-Hayat* carries a definite pan-Arab identity, given the use of *fusha* Arabic and its Middle Eastern characters and environment lacking any national characteristics. However, in this case, the presentation of a pan-Arab identity is less direct than in the other animated cartoons discussed in this chapter. Language and visual representations are the only indicators of identity here, whereas the narrative itself lacks any references to the Middle East or Arabs.

Khait al-Hayat portrays poverty and hardship as a God-given fact, and rather than try to change these aspects of life, they are to be accepted and borne with dignity. Such messages were particularly poignant in 2007, the year the film was released. That was also the year of Bashar al-Assad's first re-election, and a time when liberalisation politics were already in effect but were not improving the lives of people who were not closely linked to the regime. Due to Iraq's political instability, the number of Iraqi refugees in Syria exceeded 1.2 million, resulting in a general rise in property and rent prices and putting economic pressure on average Syrians (Al-Khalidi et al. 2007). By glorifying simple life and advocating universal values, *Khait al-Hayat* addresses Syrians and other Arabs facing hardship equally.

Characteristics and Identities of Syrian Animated Cartoons

As cultural productions, Syrian animated cartoons are inseparable from the Baathist cultural and media industries. Given that it was the local media and political milieu that provided policies, the institutional background and, in some cases, financial support, Syrian animated cartoons share special characteristics that set them apart from the animations of other Arab countries. Like a number of Syrian television productions, animated cartoons were dubbed into *fusha* Arabic, most probably to accentuate the all-Arab validity of the productions. Visually, they present Arab characters, environments and symbols. However, their appropriation of Arabness is largely identified with Middle Eastern culture in both scenery and symbols.

Due to the characteristics of local cultural and media industries as well as the personal preferences of the producers, they often carry universal moral messages and never challenge official discourses directly. The films often include Islamic references both on the visual and the verbal levels, which can most likely be ascribed to the fact that most of the prominent participants in the Syrian animation industry – such as the Hijazis – are moderate Sunni Muslims. Islamic morals are generally presented not as religious, but as universal human values.

As the majority of Syrian animations are not series but feature-length productions, Disney animations had a strong influence on the texts and narratives. With regard to the visual style, anime as well as Disney has had an undeniable impact on several Syrian animations. More recent productions are visibly trying to follow the road paved by Disney works. Given the lack of resources and limited institutional support of animation, Syrian animated cartoons have failed to develop an established or unique style. Within this context, Hijazi's works in general and *The Jasmine Birds* in particular can be considered a milestone in the history of modern animation in Syria.

Unfortunately, the political turmoil of 2011 froze the budding animation scene. In early 2012 members of the Hijazi family were imprisoned for alleged revolutionary activities, which led Sulafa Hijazi to leave the country (Van de Peer 2013). Having moved to Germany, she launched *The Memory Box*, an animation workshop funded by the German Foreign Office to help refugee children overcome trauma, and from her Frankfurt exile she frequently publishes anti-war cartoons and graphics. Mwaffaq Katt was also among those who fled; he is still busy in a secret location, drawing cartoons critical of the Syrian regime.

Mediating Gulf Arab Identity in the Productions of the Gulf Cooperation Council

The Establishment of the JPPI

After the end of colonialism in the Middle East, there were several attempts to create a political unity based on common culture and identity among different countries.

The Gulf was no exception to this trend. Since the early 1970s, different initiatives for cooperation were proposed by the heads of state of the Gulf countries. The oil embargo of the OPEC countries in response to American involvement in the 1973 Arab-Israeli war highlighted the possible benefits of Gulf countries coordinating their policies (Rizvi 1982). In 1976, the then prime minister and crown prince of Kuwait, Sheikh Jabir al-Sabah, called for 'the establishment of a Gulf union, with the object of realising cooperation in all economic, political, educational and informational spheres, to serve the interests of the region' (Gulf Information and Research Centre 1983: 15). This was followed by the proposal of Sultan Qaboos bin Said of Oman in November for a gathering of the foreign ministers of the Arab Gulf countries to negotiate on security issues. The Soviet invasion of Afghanistan in December 1978 and the outbreak of the Iran–Iraq war in 1980 pushed the Gulf States to broaden their cooperation.

In order to achieve their political goals, the prominent leaders of the Arab Gulf countries rarely missed the opportunity to stress their common Arab, Gulf and Islamic identities. Later, slogans relating to this common identity found their way into the charter of the GCC, a political and economic organisation established in 1981. As the charter stresses, the member states are 'fully aware of the ties of special relations, common characteristics and similar systems founded on the creed of Islam which bind them' (Charter of the Gulf Cooperation Council 1981). Despite the common characteristics, establishing such a community based on the proposed commonalities was challenging. As most Gulf countries were relatively new formations, national identities were not well established, and the majority of Gulf societies remained characterised by identities connected to tribal, sectarian and other traditional affiliations. Therefore, early cooperation between Gulf countries focused on small steps in order to demonstrate goodwill and pave the way for further cooperation. Media cooperation – as a platform for safe diplomacy – among Gulf States preceded the formation of political organisations. This cooperation began with periodic meetings between the Ministers of Information of the Gulf countries, including Iraq. Starting in the late 1970s, eight joint media institutions were established, with the goal of unifying media policies. One of these was the Joint Program Production Institution (JPPI), established in Abu Dhabi on 4 January 1976, under Law Decree No. 71/1976 by the ministers of information of Bahrain, Kuwait, Oman, Qatar, Saudi Arabia and the UAE. The permanent headquarters was set up in Kuwait. Since its founding, the organisation has always had a Kuwaiti director, while each member country delegates a member to the board. Identity formation has been a goal from the beginning, as stated in its charter. Another goal was to focus on the production of television and radio programmes for the national channels of the member states, through the 'revival of the Arab and Islamic history and highlighting the ideals of the Islamic religion' and the 'revival of the Gulf heritage, specifically traditions by recording them in documentary films'.[15] As the objective of reviving 'Islamic history' suggests, the identity promoted by the JPPI is an Islamic one as well as a pan-Arab one. However, given that the identity of the GCC is largely determined by Arab and Gulf culture rather than Islam, media productions, including animated cartoons, produced by the JPPI are more concerned with mediating an Arab identity than merely a religious one.

APPROACHES TO PAN-ARAB IDENTITIES | 163

Mediating a Gulf Arab Identity in the Animations of the JPPI

The JPPI has produced a number of television programmes, including dramas, documentaries and, of course, animations. Its animation production is characterised by a large number of projects, including feature-length productions and series. However, the number of pilots or unfinished productions is also high.

Given the production background, one might assume that JPPI productions would promote an Arab Gulf identity. However, an identity of this type can be multi-layered, blending Islamic, Arab, Gulf and specific national identities, depending on the background of a particular production. All animated cartoons produced under the banner of the JPPI are dubbed into *fusha* Arabic as a marker of shared identity. While this linguistic choice is obviously a marker of a pan-Arab rather than an exclusively Gulf identity, it is also an effective means of avoiding the mediation of national characteristics. Regarding visual identity, the authors often intend to construct a Gulf environment and Gulf characters without including actual buildings that would be a direct reference to particular states.

The first animated productions signed by the JPPI were one- and two-minute films teaching Arabic letters and numbers presented in *Iftah Ya Simsim*, the Arab adaptation of *Sesame Street* that premiered in Kuwait in 1979 and ran until 1990 in different Arab countries. On the visual level, Gulf identity was stressed in the very first episode by a spot teaching the letter *waw* that featured a man in white clothing, evoking the common style of dress of men in the Gulf.

These characteristics were also maintained in the case of *Za'toor*, an animated series of fifteen ten-minute episodes released in 1995. Despite the Kuwaiti dominance of the production, the identity is indicated in the title credits, *Musalsal al-Kartoun al-Khaleejiyy* (Gulf Cartoon Series). The adventures of the protagonist, Za'toor the donkey, and his human friends are set in a rural environment that can easily be associated with any of the Gulf countries, including southern Iraq. The main characters are children of different skin shades, presented as good friends, without any kind of cultural or social differences between them being shown. Further, the physical appearance and clothing of the characters cannot be restricted to any particular Gulf country.

Figure 4.5 *Za'toor*: a donkey for all people of the Gulf. 1995 © GCC JPPI.

One case in point is the character of a policeman wearing a blue-and-white uniform, which bears no resemblance to the uniforms worn by any of the police forces in Gulf countries. Through its use of *fusha* Arabic, *Za'toor* mediates an Arab identity in which Arabness is largely associated with a Gulf environment. Here, religion is only used as a frame and presented as part of the culture, indicated by mosques and women veiled according to Gulf customs. This approach shares many similarities with the national animated cartoons discussed in Chapter 2 and the productions mediating alternative national identities covered in Chapter 3.

The pan-Arab identity is stressed even more in the case of *Sunna' al-Hadarah* (Civilisation Makers), an edutainment series of fifty ten-minute episodes released in 2005, directed by Husayn al-Namr and, later, by Ahmad al-Tourjuman. Produced by the Kuwaiti company Imprint, the series was a genuinely pan-Arab project, involving a number of different nationalities, such as Saudi executive producer Hashem Muhammad al-Shakhs, Egyptian sound engineer Ibrahim Dasouqi and Syrian writer Osama al-Roumaniyy. On the textual level, the series avoids the inclusion of national characteristics. The frame narrative takes place in the present and revolves around a boy named Badr who lives in a town called Madinat al-Fawakih (City of Fruits). In each episode, Badr is taken back in time to meet famous Arab scientists and inventors from Andalusia, North Africa, the Middle East and the Gulf.

The focus on Arab, rather than Muslim, individuals stresses the Arab identity. The theme song includes an oft-repeated phrase, 'Arabs are the makers of civilisation!', using presentations of a glorious past to create a pan-Arabic identity in the present.

Arab identity is also stressed in *Ibn al-Ghaba* (Son of the Forest), a feature-length production from 2006 directed by Thamer al-Zaidi. As in the case of *Zaʿtoor*, while the majority of participants were from the Gulf (Kuwait in particular), production was largely outsourced to the Hungarian Dana Studio which – at least in the case of *Zaʿtoor* – results in a visual style similar to that of many animation productions of socialist Hungary (Al-Sharq Al-Awsat 2004). Although the opening credits define the production as *al-Film al-Kartooniyy al-Khaleejiyy al-ʿArabiyy* (The Arab Gulf Animated Cartoon), references to an Arab environment appear at the very beginning through the presentation of a medieval Arab coastal city, without any indication as to its identity. However, the lack of references can largely be explained by the plot, which is based on the Robinson Crusoe-like story of Ibn Tufayl's *Hajj Ibn Yaqzan* (The History of Hajj Ibn Yaqzan).[16] As the narrative takes place on a deserted island, the lack of references to Arab countries or individuals can hardly be taken as a statement on identity. The production was also presented on JCC as a part of the preservation of the Arab literary heritage (Al Jazeera 2006).

Among the productions that avoid the inclusion of any particular national characteristics, we find *Ahmad wa Kanʿaan* (Ahmad and Kanʿaan), a 3D series of twenty episodes of five minutes each, released in 2009. Most episodes revolve around moralistic issues, presenting Kanʿaan as a fat, simple-minded and selfish boy, who is given moral lessons by his friend Ahmad, who is slim and clever. While the producer Habib Hussein and the director Faysal al-Ibrahim are from Kuwait, as are the companies involved, Ustudio and Cable Vision, Kuwaiti identity is not highlighted (al-Bannay 2009). In contrast, Gulf identities are highlighted not only with cityscapes and characters wearing Gulf costumes, but also with more direct references such as the opening scene in one of the episodes, which takes place in the classroom of the two protagonists and shows the teacher explaining the establishment of the GCC.

As the JPPI generally acted as a funder of animated cartoons produced by different authors and animators, the visual style of the productions varies. Because of the large number of Hungarian artists involved, *Zaʿtoor* bears a resemblance to certain Eastern European productions. The different episodes of *Sunnaʿ al-Hadarah* have varying styles, given that the authors changed from time to time.

In JPPI productions, Islam is largely presented as being essential and integral to Arab culture, while the emphasis is on presenting a pan-Arab identity that is occasionally associated with Arab Gulf culture.

Pan-Arab Children's Channels as Players in Animation Production

The Boom of Arab Children's Channels since the Early 2000s

Arab satellite channels targeting both general and child audiences have recently become as important to producers and customers of animated cartoons as general and entertainment channels are.

Until the 1990s, terrestrial television broadcasting was controlled by national governments and reached audiences within the national borders. The introduction of satellite technology ended government monopolies and led to the proliferation of Arab satellite channels. Since the 1990s, not only governments, but also political parties, religious institutions, individuals, business enterprises and cultural foundations, have been able to create and launch their own channels, as well as broadcast on existing ones, and can reach beyond national borders.

Despite the large number of players, the Arab free-to-air (FTA) market is dominated by a small number of channels. These channels are owned by exclusive groups from the Gulf: MBC, Rotana, the Abu Dhabi Media, Dubai Media Inc. and Al Jazeera. However, in some regions such as Egypt and Lebanon, local channels dominate (Dubai Press Club 2010: 47). Launching television stations remains a capital-intensive enterprise and is therefore dominated by political and economic elites. The same is the case regarding the production of exclusive animated cartoons.

Launching satellite stations has also come to serve broader (national) political strategies, as media powerhouses such as Saudi Arabia, the UAE and Lebanon struggle to reach audiences and advertisers beyond their national borders (Sakr 2007a: 1–15). Given the lack of a clear separation between the structures of economic and political forces in the Arab world, the interests often seem to be inseparable.

The spread of pan-Arab channels led to the emergence of a new kind of pan-Arab public space dominated by actors from the Gulf. Transnational Arab broadcasting played a significant role in creating both a regional pan-Arab identity and a regional media market. By advancing a form of cultural globalisation, well-funded, Gulf-owned transnational media outlets have the potential to provide a platform for mediating their own approaches to political and religious identities.

Having reached out to adults, Arab broadcasters naturally wanted to do the same to younger audiences as well. The pioneer in this field was ART, a Cairo-based company founded by Saudi businessman Saleh Kamel in 1993. As Egyptian authorities did not want to lose their primacy in media to a Saudi-owned company, a government-owned channel, Nile Family and Kids Channel, was launched in 1998.[17] However, Arab children as potential consumers were first discovered in the late 1990s by advanced Western companies, which established regionally adapted versions of their existing channels. In 1996, Nickelodeon Arabia was launched, followed by Disney Channel Middle East (DCME) in 1997. In its first year, DCME offered a variety of children's animations in both English and Arabic, and, a year later, all programmes became available in Arabic. Both Nickelodeon and DCME were available only in homes subscribing to cable services that include these channels among their packages.[18] In 2001, E-junior, a third pay-TV channel, was launched. Created by E-Vision, an Emirati cable provider, E-Junior was exclusively available to E-Vision customers and aired only English cartoons dubbed into Arabic. More recently, in 2010, Cartoon Network launched its free-to-air Arab channel (Bladd 2010).

The first significant Arab-owned dedicated FTA TV channel was Spacetoon TV, launched in 2000 by a Syrian private company that enjoyed good relations with the state. Rather than creating original content, the channel aired mainly US cartoons which it had dubbed into Arabic alongside other cartoons made by smaller American and Japanese companies.

The largest growth in the Arab demand for homegrown animation was in the early and mid-2000s, when major Arab broadcasting companies entered the market (Sayfo 2017a). In 2004, the Saudi-owned MBC launched MBC3, a free-to-air children's channel. It broadcasts dubbed animated series as well as Western live-action children's shows. A year later, JCC, the first pan-Arab edutainment channel, was launched as a collaborative project between Al Jazeera Network and the Qatar Foundation for Education.

The success of Arab children's channels and increasingly easy access to both technology and content encouraged further players to enter the market. Government-sponsored channels such as Saudi Ajyal (2009) and Jordanian Karamesh TV (2009) were launched. Both broadcast imported animations and home-made programmes, the latter often with nationalistic undertones. At the same time, religious forces also discovered the importance of satellite channels in reaching out to young audiences. In 2004, the Salafi-oriented Almajd TV Network, owned by Saudi businessman ʿAbdulrahman al-Shmemri, launched Al-Majd Kids Channel, showing live-action shows, children reciting passages from the Qurʾan and short educational animation spots, among other things. Another Saudi channel, Semsem, was launched in 2010. Toyour al-Jannah TV (2008) was founded by a Palestinian-Jordanian, Khaled Miqdar. Based in Amman, but broadcasting from Bahrain, the channel broadcasts religious songs (*anasheed*; sing. *nasheed*) for Muslim children. At the same time, Shia channels appeared on the scene too. Hadi TV, owned by the British-Pakistani Hadi Foundation, was launched in 2009, and was soon followed by the Iranian-backed Hodhod TV (2010) and Taha TV (2010). Aimed at Christians of the Arab Middle East, SAT-7 Kids (2007), a Christian gospel channel and a member of the SAT-7 satellite television network, began operating. The boom in children's channels led to further thematisation in content. Pre-school channels such as Al-Majd's Basma were launched in 2008, while Al Jazeera's Baraem began broadcasting a year later (Sayfo 2014).

Although there have been major improvements in the Arab children's TV industry, not all channel proved to be viable. Some with a weaker financial background dropped out. Even bigger players were forced to cease broadcasting, such as Nickelodeon Arabia, relaunched in 2008, which closed down in September 2011 due to the bankruptcy of its Emirati owner, who sold the franchise back to Europe.[19]

Identities of Animations Produced by Satellite Channels

Similarly to other Arab channels, children's channels also have their own agendas. Kunkel and Watkins noted how non-commercial sources of funding tend to be directed towards more informational and educational programmes, while profit-oriented channels focus more on entertaining content (Kunkel and Watkins 1987). It is quite obvious that the content of profit-oriented Arabic children's channels such as Disney Channel Middle East, Cartoon Network Arabic and Spacetoon TV largely provide entertainment and avoid engagement in sensitive issues of identity. In contrast, channels funded by affluent governmental insitutions (such as Karamesh TV and JCC) or religious institutions (Al-Majd, Hodhod TV) carry more informational, educational and even propagandistic content, with the intention of mediating identities that fit the agendas of their sponsors.

As the satellite channels target Arab audiences across national borders, they tend to promote pan-Arab regional identities. However, some of them are controlled by national governments, and therefore stress local identities. Others emphasise an Islamic identity (see Chapter 5). Therefore, when analysing the identities promoted by animated cartoons of particular television channels, it is also essential to investigate the channel's background.

As feature-length animation films and high-quality animated series are expensive to create, the largest producers of exclusive animated content are affluent channels such as JCC and MBC3. Therefore, the identity issues of the majority of Arab children's channels can be largely traced to short productions such as video clips. As it would be rather challenging to fill airtime with exclusive content, satellite channels often only serve as customers of already existing productions. The choice of which animated content to buy can be influenced by a wide range of considerations such as price, plans for market expansion and personal preferences. However, generally speaking, products chosen for purchase rarely challenge the official identity agenda of particular channels. Most purchased content either coincides with the political and religious agendas and identities of the channels, or is neutral in those terms.

Al Jazeera Children's Channel

JCC was launched in 2005, addressing a target audience of children aged seven to fifteen. Its $50 million annual budget is one of the largest among children's channels of the Arab world. However, JCC's financial arrangements differ from those of the Al Jazeera parent channels (ITP 2005). JCC was created as a private shareholding company by the Al Jazeera Network and the Qatar Foundation for Education, Science and Community Development, with 10 per cent and 90 per cent shares respectively. The headquarters are in Education City in Qatar.[20]

When it was established, JCC announced that it had a public service mission to educate Arab children (Baatout and Chaise 2005). Sheikh Hamad bin Thamer al-Thani, board chairman of the Al Jazeera group, said the channel would be 'an alternative' to the 'violent and inappropriate material' that children are exposed to every day.[21] JCC also announced its intention to produce 40 per cent of its programmes, including live magazine programmes and discussions, while the remaining 60 per cent would be purchased from a variety of studios and channels around the world. JCC's first steps were supervised by Lagardère International Images, a French company experienced in making educational programmes. Due to this strategic relationship, a certain amount of French animated content appeared in the programmes of JCC. In 2013, JCC was rebranded as Jeem TV in order to save it from the regional loss of popularity the parent channel faced following the Arab uprisings (Sakr and Steemers 2017).

The identity politics of JCC can be understood within the framework of Al Jazeera's politics in general. Batora has shown that 'for small and medium-sized states, public diplomacy represents an opportunity to gain influence and shape [the] international agenda in ways that go beyond their limited hard power resources' (Bátora 2006). Qatar used two main strategies, public diplomacy and nation branding, in order to gain more recognition in the Arab and international arenas (Peterson 2006: 745). As a result, Al Jazeera has been seen as a tool for both the survival and the promotion of public diplomacy.[22] It plays a major role in creating a pan-Arabic identity among its audience, both by spreading *fusha* Arabic and by covering Arab affairs. These priorities can also be observed in the case of JCC and, more recently, Jeem TV, mostly through dedicated pan-Arab programmes, such as *Qala al-Rawi* (The Storyteller Says) and *Bayti al-'Arabi* (My Arabian House), which often include propagandistic pan-Arab content.[23] At the same time, the international Qatari society enables the participation of children from all Arab countries, giving programmes a pan-Arab feel.

Despite the ambitious start, Qatari managers disrupted the development of the exclusive content-producing capacity by laying off around 150 staff members in 2011 and 2012 (Steemers and Sakr 2015). Therefore, neither JCC nor Jeem TV has the capacity to produce sufficient animated series of good quality on their own. They have thus entered into both occasional and continuous cooperation with production and animation companies from Arab and Muslim countries. Since they fund and broadcast these productions, JCC and Jeem TV can be regarded as authors who maintain authority over the text.

Animated cartoons produced by JCC and Jeem TV largely avoid the presentation of particular Arab national identities. Even if some productions include scenes from specific countries, the markers of otherness are reduced. A pan-Arab identity is largely advocated by the use of *fusha* Arabic and the inclusion of characters that can be associated with any Arab country. Remediating themes from Arab literature and history, and using them in the construction of a Pan-Arab identity is a common feature of these animations.

Saladin: the Animated Series

Saladin: the Animated Series (2009) is the first JCC production that was ambitious regarding budget and quality. The estimated $10 million production is made up of thirteen episodes of twenty-six minutes, animated in advanced 3D technology aimed at ten- to fifteen-year-olds. The production began in 2004 as a co-production between Multimedia Development Corporation (MDeC) and JCC. MDeC is a multimedia company incorporated under the Companies Act of Malaysia, owned and funded by the Malaysian government. According to Kamil Othman, the vice-president of MDeC's creative department, the idea behind the Saladin animation was to 'show to the world that Malaysian talents can tackle any subject, even if the origins are not Malaysian' (Patrick 2006). Describing the concept, JCC's then executive general manager Mahmoud Bouneb stated, 'We wanted to have a fictional figure that our children can identify with. We did not want to have just a history lesson on screen, but to present a heroic figure from the Arab world's history' (Al-Harthy 2010). In line with the definition of authorship in animation as proposed in Chapter 1, the Malaysian background of the production does not affect its identity, as creative authority regarding the narrative was maintained by the Qataris.

The choice of Saladin's character alone is as a statement of Arab identity, given the fact that the historical person of Kurdish origin behind the animated character, Salah al-Din Yusuf ibn 'Ayyoub (c. 1138–93) was consequently ignored when he was Arabised many times in twentieth-century Arab popular culture (Sayfo 2017b).

The Saladin presented in *Saladin: the Animated Series* has been stripped of all political analogies. The stories take place in a fictional period of the eighteen-year-old Saladin's life. The stories can hardly be called historically accurate; rather, they resemble similar plots in Disney cartoons, as the protagonist, together with his loyal friends, embarks on various adventures. The official website of the animation describes Saladin as 'the ultimate hero – courageous in the face of danger, never willing to admit defeat and funny when he needs to be', adding that '[i]n a world of danger, there's only one man you'll want in your corner – SALADIN'.[24] However, the authors' very choice of the character of Saladin suggests their intention to present an Arab/Muslim hero in order to stress an Arab/Muslim identity.

The Arab and Islamic identity of the text of *Saladin: the Animated Series* is largely reduced to Middle Eastern characters, environments and townscapes alongside the occasional religious phrase in conversations. As a possible symbol of the series' pan-Arab identity, Saladin and his friends travel around what would be today's Syria, Jordan and Iraq, passing through villages and cities that differ little from one another, encountering Arab characters who share a common physical appearance, wear more or less identical costumes and speak *fusha* Arabic. Set in a fictional twelfth century, the narrative does not include references to modern Arab states or regions, but refers only to territories ruled by Arabs and those occupied by the Crusaders.

Refraining from any engagement in religious discourses, the series promotes a moderate version of Islam by giving Saladin an emancipated female friend. The series has a message of tolerance, as one of Saladin's loyal friends

Figure 4.6 *Saladin: the Animated Series*: a historical hero in a Disneyesque adventure. 2009 © MDeC and AJCC.

and companions is a former Frankish solider named Duncan. The otherness of Duncan and the other non-Arab characters is highlighted with visual markers such as blond hair and fair skin. On the linguistic level, however, the non-Arab characters do not speak with an accent. Good and bad are not linked to ethnic or religious affiliation, as the enemies of the protagonists are both Arab bandits and Crusaders led by Reginald, their evil commander. It is important to note that the Crusaders are not referred to as the Arabic term *salibiyyun* (sing. *salibiyy*), a loaded expression evoking the bellicose discourse of the 'war on terror' of George W. Bush. When talking about their European enemies, the characters use the word *Firanga* (Franks), a relatively neutral term.

Despite its Arab identity, the series avoids showing direct continuity with previous pan-Arab or Islamist discourses. When referring to their own community, the characters use a neutral terminology. One case in point is Episode 7, which involves the character of Qassem, Saladin's grandfather, who is suspected of collaborating with Reginald by selling him a map of the secret wells in the desert to help the Crusaders' invasion. When a captured Crusader informs Saladin of his grandfather's plan, he angrily declares: '*Jaddee la yumkinu an yakhuna qawmahu abadan!*' (My grandfather would never betray his people!). At the end of the episode it emerges that Qassem was not a traitor, but was actually working for the Sultan's secret service in order to deceive Reginald.

Choosing the neutral term *qawm* (people) instead of terms used in nationalist and Islamist discourses, like nation (*'ummah*), fatherland (*watan*), people (*sha'b*), the producers avoid directly engaging in such discourses about identity.

Badr, the First Arab Anime

In 2016, the Al Jazeera-owned Bein Media Group purchased Miramax, an American entertainment company with a decade-long experience in quality animation production, providing Jeem TV with an opportunity to release high-quality original content. *Badr*, the first Arab anime series, debuted during Ramadan 2017. Given Miramax's input, the show's overall quality could rival the popular Japanese and American shows. By creating an anime, the creators played it safe given the unchallenged regional popularity of the format since the late 1970s.

The story tells the adventures of Badr, a young boy who lives in al-Dana, a small pearl-diving town on the Gulf peninsula in the pre-oil era. The hero, empowered by extraordinary abilities thanks to magic pearls from a bracelet he inherited from his ancestors, goes on a search for his father, a seaman who disappeared in mysterious circumstances during a snorkelling trip. Badr,

Figure 4.7   *Badr*: the first Arab anime. 2017 © Jeem TV.

together with his friends and the townspeople, fights back against Hamash, an ancient, evil seaman with supernatural abilities who intends to get his hands on all the magic pearls in order to gain complete power over the region. As the story unfolds, family secrets come to light and Badr faces evil spirits who threaten his family and community.

The creators of *Badr* claim a pan-Arab identity for the series. The goal was primarily to maintain an 'Arab cultural identity', and to instil values that would contribute to 'the upbringing of a promising young generation' ('Ali 2015). Indeed, the series is dubbed in *fusha* Arabic, which, together with the representations of a typical Gulf environment and characters wearing traditional Gulf attire that lack national or sub-regional characteristics, indicate a Gulf/Arab identity, as was also the case with the majority of JPPI animations. However, beneath the surface Badr hints at a Qatari identity. A redesigned map of the Gulf, shown at the end of the title, locates al-Dana in modern Qatar, and also highlights other fictional cities in the place of today's modern towns: Thuban (Abu Dhabi), Kaytous (Muscat), Nizam (Kuwait), Sinn al-Qurs (Dammam), 'Uqdah (Busher) and al-Moudiq al-Ahmar (the Strait of Hormuz). The Qatari identity of Badr is not highlighted any further besides an occasional reference made by supporting characters to the protagonist as '*muhareb al-jazeera*' (the warrior of the island) that could mean either Qatar or the Arabian peninsula as a whole. Meanwhile, the struggle of the people of al-Dana against Hamash is an obvious allegory to tiny Qatar's experience of being stuck between powerful Saudi Arabia and Iran.

Besides the presentation of female characters in traditional headscarves, the show does not include any references to an Islamic identity. Meanwhile, the people of al-Dana are referred to as '*sha'b*', a neutral term free from nationalist or religious overtones. While *Badr* may on occasion hint at a regional Qatari identity, all in all, the show advocates for a more general Gulf identity, mostly by avoiding direct references.

Conclusion

Mediations of pan-Arab identities are set within the framework of broader politics, and these notions can differ widely depending on the preferences of authors and the general production background as well as the political and/or historical context of the countries involved. Baathist Iraq's *Al-'Amirah wal-Nahr* largely articulates a national (Iraqi) identity, with the inclusion of some pan-Arab identity markers such as the use of *fusha* Arabic, and an allegory in the narrative relevant to both the national and the Pan-Arab level. However, given the fact that animated cartoon production in Baathist Iraq did not last long, it would be too bold to draw far-reaching conclusions on the identities of Iraqi pan-Arab animation production. Regarding the productions and animations from both Baathist Syria and the Gulf, there is an obvious tendency to 'regionalise the sub-regional' in the sense of presenting sub-regional identity markers as being of pan-Arab validity. However, given the production background, the Syrian and Gulf approaches are different. While Syrian animated cartoons tend to associate 'Arabness' with the Middle Eastern/Levantine physical and cultural environment, townscapes and attire, the animations produced by the GCC's JPPI prefer references to Gulf environments. Arabness within the geopolitical area is a contested idea whereas in productions for a transnational audience, there is no specific representation.

In contrast, animated cartoons produced by pan-Arab satellite channels targeting a transnational Arab audience from the Levant and the Gulf as well as Arab diasporas in Europe, generally avoid the presentation of scenes and characters that could be associated with specific countries or even sub-regions. Even if they do so, they treat these particularities as mosaics of a larger Arab culture and downplay differences to other Arab countries. However, pan-Arab satellite channels such as JCC are a recent and growing phenomenon.

Despite the different approaches to pan-Arab identities, there are a number of characteristics shared by Syrian Baathist, the GCC's JPPI and pan-Arab channel animation. A high number of productions were involved in promoting the notion of a shared Arab identity through the mediation of a shared past and culture as well as the general trend of remediating narratives from Islamic and Arab history and literature. Doing so, they celebrate the glorious past as a foundation of current pan-Arabic identities. Even if the narratives are original, they largely avoid references to specific features that would evoke associations with a specific country. They all use *fusha* Arabic as a marker of a preference for a general Arab identity instead of particular national identities. This approach is also highlighted visually, as pan-Arab productions mostly present characters and an environment that can be accepted as 'own' to all Arabs, regardless of their country. The narratives are either set in an unspecified Middle Eastern environment (*Za'toor, Al-Jarrah, Khait al-Hayat*) or involve plots with multiple scenes, located in various Arab countries highlighted as the 'own' both in the narrative and on the visual level (*Al-'Amirah wal-Nahr, Sunna' al-Hadarah, Saladin: the Animated Series*). The same holds true for the characters, who are either presented without indicating their actual nationality (*Za'toor, Al-Jarrah, Khait al-Hayat*), or as Arabs from different countries, while avoiding a focus on differences regarding physiognomy, costume, or culture (*Sunna' al-Hadarah, Ahmad wa Kan'aan, Saladin: the Animated Series*). At the same time, differences of this kind are often highlighted in relation to non-Arab characters, as a possible indicator of the intent to create a sense of 'otherness'. On the visual level, style alone has little to do with a pan-Arab identity as authors drew their inspiration from a wide range of sources and, with the exception of Sulafa Hijazi, none succeeded in developing a unique style.

While Islamic identities are not always stressed, Islam is usually presented as part of Arab culture. Islamic buildings such as mosques and minarets are shown. Several productions feature Islamic phrases used in daily life without engaging in discourses about religion, a trait shared by all Syrian productions, the only exception being *Tuyur al-Yasmeen*, a narrative set in the animal world.

Notes

1. Between 1969 and 1983, the Iraqi film industries produced only sixteen feature films (Shafik 2007b, pp. 31–3).
2. Personal interview with Bassam Faraj (Budapest, 10 October 2015).
3. Personal interview with 'Abbas ibn 'Abbas (Cairo, 10 September 2012).
4. The Ruya Foundation is an Iraqi-registered, non-profit NGO founded in 2012 with the aim of aiding and enriching culture in Iraq.
5. Law 4, ratified on 13 March 1963.
6. Telephone interview with Sulafa Hijazi (13 December 2013).
7. Mannaa' Hijazi was born in 1966. Members of the Hijazi family are involved in many fields of the Syrian animation industry (for example directing and artwork).
8. The company has used both names.

9. See Spacetoon TV's official website at spacetoon.com
10. Star Animation for Artistic Production was a subsidiary of the Daaboul Industrial Group, established in 1976 as a small company that manufactured aluminium.
11. Telephone interview with Sulafa Hijazi (13 December 2013).
12. Personal interview with Sulafa Hijazi (Copenhagen, 12 June 2014).
13. Propagating the nationalist ideology of the party is a core element of the Syrian National Curriculum, as stipulated in Article 21 of the Syrian Constitution.
14. Though in Christianity the concept of 'haram' does not exist, Arab Christians, like Muslims, also use the concept of 'mal haram' with reference to 'ill-gotten gains', i.e. money that has been earned through illegal or immoral activities.
15. The official home page of the GCC's JPPI is at https://www.gccjppi.com.kw/AboutUsEn.aspx?PageID=2
16. Ibn Tufayl was a philosopher and physician in early-twelfth-century Andalusia (see Chapter 5).
17. ART ceased broadcasting in the late 1990s.
18. DCME was exclusively available on the Orbit network, but later became available on Showtime Arabia too, after the merger of the two companies in 2009.
19. Nickelodeon Arabia was under the umbrella of the Emirati Arabian Television Network (ATN), the TV broadcasting arm of Arab Media Group that also incorporates MTV Arabia.
20. The Qatar Foundation, chaired by Sheikha Moza Bint Nasser al-Missned, one of Sheikh Hamad's wives, has invested heavily in education opportunities in the Emirates. The flagship initiative is Education City, a state-of-the-art campus complex launched in 2003.
21. 'Aljazeera launches children's channel', 20 September 2005, https://www.aljazeera.com/news/2005/9/20/aljazeera-launches-childrens-channel
22. For an analysis of Al Jazeera's public diplomacy strategy as a non-state actor, cf. Powers and Gilboa (2007) and Wildermuth (2005).
23. *Qala al-Rawi* (The Storyteller Says) is a programme about traditional Middle Eastern storytelling; *Bayti al-'Arabi* (My Arabian House) is an edutainment programme that gives information about Arab countries.
24. See http://www.saladin.tv

5

Advocating Islamic Identities in Arab Animation

Introduction

Islamic animation might sound controversial because of the long-held assumption that Islam forbids the representation of figural images in general, and the depiction of Prophet Muhammad in particular. Such widespread belief was significantly fuelled by the furore that broke out in many Muslim countries and diasporas following the September 2005 publication of a series of caricatures in the Danish newspaper *Jyllands-Posten*. Steven Spielberg's 1998 epic musical Biblical animation, *The Prince of Egypt*, was also received controversially in the Muslim world: it was banned in Egypt as well as in several non-Arab countries with a Muslim majority such as Malaysia (BBC 1999) and the Maldives for its portrayal of Joseph, who is also one of the prophets of Islam and should therefore not be depicted.[1] Despite such polemic, the visual arts of the Islamic world are rich in figurative illustrations from the thirteenth century to modern times, for example in the form of manuscript illustrations (Gruber 2009). Islamic animation is one of the most flourishing types of animation in the Arab world, and is often regarded by its producers as a vehicle to counter Disney's cultural imperialism. Advocating Islamic, non-nation-bounded identities, Arabic Islamic animations also reach beyond the borders of the Arab world and find their way to distant Muslim markets, and thus act as a vehicle for cultural imperialism itself.

There are different ways in which an animated cartoon can be considered Islamic, largely depending on whether Islam is defined as a culture or as a religion. In their book on Arab comic strips, Douglas and Malti-Douglas noted that comics can be Islamic in two ways: firstly, when 'moral guidance is presented in Islamic terms or with Islamic legitimization' (like applying Islamic terminology to non-religious issues) and secondly, when 'specifically Islamic topics are treated, whether religious discussions, historical evocations, or even the presentation of material from the sacred texts themselves from the *hadith* (teachings of the Prophet) to the Qur'an' (Douglas and Malti-Douglas 1994: 83–4). This definition is applicable to Arab animation, but I would add that 'historical evocations' can also be found in animated cartoons advocating national and pan-Arab identities. As the lines between national and Islamic identities are often blurred, I define an animation as 'Islamic' if there is a clear preference for an Islamic identity over an ethnic and/or national one. I also complement the definition proposed by Douglas and Malti-Douglas with the fact that, similarly to cartoon strips, a number of animations are Islamic in their titles and undertake a self-imposed mission to spread the Islamic faith and its values in a way that would affect the identities of their audience.

Given the number of countries and production companies involved, Islamic animation by now also includes a number of sub-genres as a result of the hybridisation of a Western format and local cultural characteristics. The most basic sub-genre of Islamic animation is most probably represented by low-cost animated video clips of (*anasheed*; sing. *nasheed*), religious songs with no instrumental accompaniment, and short educational spots teaching children about the practices of Islam. Such productions are largely aired on Islamic television channels dedicated to both general and children's audiences, as part of religious education. The introduction of CGI technologies in the 1990s and, later, of 3D enabled Arab producers to make their own animations. Low-budget Islamic animated productions are largely made by smaller companies, freelancers and animators affiliated to particular channels. *Anasheed* clips and Islamic education spots also offer niche markets for start-up production companies and animation studios, which lack the resources to produce feature-length productions or even their own series (Sayfo 2017a). As these clips are relatively easy to produce, they are an appropriate means of negotiating sectarian identities within Islam. Shia Muslim channels such as

HodHod TV and Hadi TV often present *anasheed* and spots on Shia imams and religious festivals, while Salafi channels present their puritan interpretation of Islam in similar spots.

In this chapter, I largely focus on series and feature-length productions. I distinguish three prominent approaches of Islamic animated cartoons, all of which are connected to the cultural and religious environment of particular countries and/or sub-regions. The first is Saudi-style Islamic animation, an approach that I link to the orthodox cultural-religious environment of Saudi Arabia and the Gulf. The second is Egyptian-style Islamic animation that reflects the political and religious environment of Egypt, while the third is a blend of Western and Muslim identities, produced by Arab Muslims living in the American diaspora, which I call 'Diaspora-Islamic animation'.

Portraying Islam as an Exclusive Truth: Saudi Productions

The Formation of Saudi-style Islamic Animation

Authors of Islamic animations from Saudi Arabia and the Gulf generally refer to their productions as *al-Kartoun al-Islamiyy* (Islamic animation). Their approach is grounded in Islamic identity, revolving around Islamic topics heavily influenced by the Wahhabi religious traditions of Saudi Arabia. Although the vast majority of these animations have indeed been produced by institutions in Saudi Arabia and the Gulf countries, there are several productions, if lower in number, from Middle Eastern Arab countries, which share generic characteristics with Saudi productions.

Saudi-style Islamic animation emerged in the mid-1990s, mostly through the activity of religious individuals who admired the professionalism of Walt Disney and chose animation as a vehicle for advocating their own Islamic identities for Muslim audiences. In this regard, the paradox of the simultaneous admiration and rejection of Western cultural productions can be observed. Despite the fact that Wahhabi Islam, which is the official doctrine of Saudi Arabia, is especially hostile towards figurative illustrations, there were relatively few obstacles to the production of animated cartoons in Saudi Arabia and the Gulf. By the 1990s a vivid culture of children's magazines in Saudi Arabia and the Gulf that was largely based on the comic strips of local artists had emerged (Douglas and Malti-Douglas 1994: 150–74). Further, as we saw in Chapter 1, the countries of the Arabian peninsula had been airing Disney animated cartoons and Japanese anime on their state channels in time slots dedicated to children. Therefore, the appearance of Islamic animated cartoons did not meet with as much hostility as one might have expected. The absence of religious criticism can also be explained by the fact that in the 1990s, the distribution of Saudi-style productions was relatively modest, usually restricted to VHS cassettes and video CDs, and may therefore have been missed or even ignored by most orthodox Islamic scholars. Moreover, the authors of these productions were consistent in stressing their Islamic identity and their goal of presenting Islamic values for Muslim children in the face of the one-way flow of foreign animations advocating alien values. As shown by its very definition, the authors of 'Islamic animations' claim an Islamic identity for their productions that is not tied to a particular nation-state or national identity. This claim is also supported by the production process in certain cases. When lacking local (i.e. national) animation industries, authors usually prefer to sign with Muslim animators from other countries. Such considerations are not priorities in the case of authors advocating national identities, as we have seen in the case of Dubai's *Freej*, which was animated in India, or the Jordanian *Ben wa 'Esam*, produced with American cooperation. Despite the 'Islamic' identities of the texts, if the conditions for claiming authorship are fulfilled by Arab individuals, I identify 'Islamic animations' as Arab productions. This is even more the case because the interpretation of Islam mediated by these productions usually stems from Saudi Arabian and Arab Gulf culture. One example of this is the exclusion of instrumental music. During the 1950s, the Committee for the Advancement of Virtue and Elimination of Vice in Saudi Arabia banned instrumental music and singing for its assumed connection to immoral behaviour and Sufi practices (van Nieuwkerk 2008). While instrumental music is still considered *haram* (forbidden) by Wahhabism and Salafi scholars, it is considered *makruh* (disliked) – and hence tolerated – by Sunni Muslim schools (*madhab*) such as the Shafi'i, which is dominant in Egypt and Turkey, and is accepted by Shia Islam, dominant in Iran.

Authors of Saudi-style Islamic animation went beyond the localisation of foreign cultural elements. The fusion of local cultural elements to animation as a global format resulted in a hybrid that was strikingly different from the original.

Starting in the mid-1990s, a number of companies and religious institutions became involved in the production of 'Saudi-style Islamic animations'. The most influential author of this genre is Saudi animation producer Osama Khalifa (b. 1956) and his company Ella (later OK Toons). Khalifa was born in the Saudi city of Medina. He studied management in the US and later worked with the Canadian Islamic Congress. According to him, he became fascinated with the Canadian animation industry at the time and decided to develop a similar industry in his homeland with the mission of presenting Islamic values to Muslim children. Mu'assasat 'Alla' lil-Intaj al-Fanniyy (Ella Endowment for Art Production) was established as a non-profit project in 1992. Financial support for the productions was raised from private individuals and charities, and Khalifa himself invested a significant amount of money. To underscore the Muslim identity of his productions, Khalifa decided to keep the production process in the Muslim world rather than outsourcing it to Western studios.[2] One of his priorities was to involve Muslim workers, as they had a cultural understanding that makes cooperation smoother.[3] He moved the production to Turkey and only later signed a contract with Star Animation in Syria. Very soon afterwards, Ella became the most prolific Arab company to produce feature-length Islamic animations. Ella's significance lies not only in being the sole company producing a number of films, but also in the constantly improving technical level of the animations. Before reorganising as OK Toons in 2011, Ella produced over a dozen works of improving visual quality. However, as the animation was done by Turkish animators who had an established style, both Ella and OK Toons failed to develop their own unique visual style.

In my analysis of Saudi-style Islamic animation productions I will focus on Ella's animations and will use them as case studies. The narratives of Saudi-style Islamic animations in general, and of Ella/OK Toons productions in particular, have three dominant features: retelling stories from Islamic history (both from the Qur'an and from later history), Islamising non-Muslim narratives (stories from Arab and non-Arab literature) and original fictional narratives.[4]

Remediating Historic Themes

Narratives from Islamic history are popular with the authors of Saudi-style Islamic animations. By presenting Muslim empires, rulers and peoples of the past, and highlighting Islam as their primary identity, these productions aim to create a community and common identity among Muslims regardless of their ethnic and national background.[5]

Rosenstone observed that the representational strategies mobilised by 'postmodern history' are 'full of small fictions used, at best, to create larger historical "truths," truths that can be judged only by examining the extent to which they engage the arguments and "truths" of our existing historical knowledge on any given topic' (Rosenstone 1995: 209). Likewise, Saudi-style Islamic animations dealing with historical events and personalities are not always historically accurate. At the same time, their ambition is to tell 'a larger historical truth' of the moral superiority of Islam. As the canonical facts of history are often at variance with the plots of plays, animated films and serials on Arab and Islamic history, their narratives fit into the category of 'historical fiction'. They choose to locate themselves in the 'past', known or otherwise, providing contextual details of that particular 'past' as an authenticating strategy. Thus, receivers 'believe in' or yield to the events partly because the background details are so accurately drawn (Sanders 2006: 138).

History is used for similar purposes regarding Islamic identities with the goal of forging a sense of belonging among Arabs and Muslims of various backgrounds. Here, the distinction is not merely one of content (Arabic versus Islamic identities), but is also one of narrative style (implicit messages about Arabness versus very explicit references to Islamic identity being more important than ethnic ones).

Saudi-style Islamic animations intend to spread the Islamic message and argue for an alternative historical understanding, by focusing on history per se. In so doing, Islamic animations also pose a challenge to pan-Arab cinematic and television productions. This can be observed in Syrian television dramas with historical themes, such as *Salahuddin al-Ayyubi* (Saladin of the Ayyubids, 2001) and *Al-Tariq* (Tariq, 2004). These productions present non-Arab historical characters, such as the Kurdish Saladin and the Berber Tariq Ibn Ziyad, as Arabs struggling for the good of the 'Arab nation'. In contrast, 'Islamic animations' do indicate the ethnic affiliations of Seljuk, Kurdish, Berber or Arab characters, but these are presented as being of secondary importance to their Islamic identity. Also, in their dialogues, the characters refer to their people not as a 'nation' defined by ethnicity or language, but as *'ummah*, the Muslim community.

Ella's first production, released in 1995, was *Mohammad al-Fatih* (Mohammad the Conqueror). The nearly two-hour-long animated epic on the life of the Ottoman Sultan Mehmet II paved the way and became a model for subsequent 'Islamic animations' with a historical topic in terms of the genre's characteristics. The title itself suggests an Islamic identity, as *al-Fatih* (literally meaning 'the opener') comes from the term *fath* (pl. *futuhat*) that is associated with Islamic conquests. While making no secret of his original ethnicity, the producers claim an Islamic identity for Murad II, Mohammad's father, whom the narrator refers to as an 'Ottoman Muslim sultan'. Likewise, his son calls him a *mujahed* (a warrior engaged in *jihad*). Throughout the film, the Ottomans are identified with *al-'ummah* (the Muslim nation), and the Islamic conquest of Constantinople is presented as the fulfilment of Mohammad's prophecy. At the same time, Islam is largely associated with universal human values. According to the film, the goal of the conquest of Murad II and, later, of his son Mohamed II, was to save the people of Constantinople from the tyranny of Constantine, the Byzantine emperor. At the beginning of the film, the cruelty of the soldiers and the social inequality of Byzantine Constantinople are contrasted with the justice in the Muslim lands on the other side of the Sea of Marmara. The film shows Byzantine officers revelling in the suffering of the people. Cast in the role of the 'other', the Byzantines often refer to themselves as *salibiyyun* (Crusaders), and are presented as a brutal people, accentuated by their sharp features and harsh voices. In contrast, the Muslim lands resound with religious conversations about how Islam and justice are connected. The plot also involves the Mongols, led by Timur Lenk, whom the Byzantines send to wage war against the Muslim Ottomans. The religious/humanist legitimacy of the Muslim conquests is represented through the Sultan Mohammad, who instructs the Ottomans to 'spread the words of God' before the battle against their enemies.

As generic characteristics, *anasheed* play an important role as narrations in the plot. The battle against the Byzantines is narrated in verse:

Oh lines of knights, Oh bravest of the brave, your enemy is deceptive and sly and cowardly.

His castles are weak and his army is defeated, and the people's hatred grew toward him, and his oppression does not last. (2x)

Go, rise and achieve what the people want, go forth, oh my brothers, and free the slaves!

Conquer, oh you, on whom we pin our hopes, conquer, oh sons, give us security and peace, go and carry your truth to victory.

At the end of the film, Mohammad and his army enter the city, and are surrounded by its cheering citizens, welcoming them with flowers and songs of joy. In the last scene, a Muslim call for prayer is heard from the Hagia Sofia, a former Christian church.

The characteristics of Mohammad al-Fatih became an important example for other productions of this type. Visually, the film mimics Disney characteristics: a hyper-realistic visual style, facial features as a mirror of the characters' personalities, and, in some cases, the presence of animal companions beside the protagonists. These imported characteristics are hybridised with

Figure 5.1 *Mohammad al-Fatih* (Mohammad the Conqueror): an idealised Muslim past. 1995 © Osama Khalifa.

a number of added features: they include Islamic idioms and expressions in the dialogues; Islamic references (such as prayers) in the narrative; the blend of 'Islamic' values with moral lessons; and the replacement of instrumental music with children's choirs or men singing *anasheed* or other songs, typically in the form of short interludes repeating the same verses several times that also assume the role of the narrator in some cases. The language of 'Saudi-style Islamic animations' is exclusively *fusha* Arabic, the official language of the Qur'an and Arabic religious discourses.

The characteristics of this type of Saudi-style Islamic animations echo those of Mohammad al-Fatih, sharing many, though not all, of the following traits: they have a historical plot featuring actual personalities, or a fictional plot set in a historical frame with fictional characters. Although not always historically accurate, they tell a 'larger historical truth' that proves the moral superiority of the Muslims. The moral contrast between the Muslims and their foes are highlighted by associating Muslims with belief (*iman*), goodness (*khayr*) and justice (*'adl*), while non-Muslim adversaries are connected to injustice (*zulm*), treason (*khiyana*) and destruction (*damar*).

The productions have a penchant for presenting spectacular battles, although they avoid showing blood. Also, they are cautious in directly associating Christian characters with Christianity as a religion or belief. They often include neutral non-Muslims who support the Muslim cause by acknowledging its humanist values.

These features can be noted in Ella's other production, *Rihlat al-Kholoud* (The Boy and the King), an Arab-Turkish co-production directed by Dervis Pasin in 1996.[6] The story is also a Qur'anic adaptation, as the basic idea is taken from a *hadith* that explores the reference to 'The People of the Ditch' in a verse of the *Surat al-Burooj* (Sura of the Bridges) in the Qur'an.[7] It tells the story of 'Ubaid, a talented young magician who sets off for the city after being chosen as an assistant by Shaytun, the sorcerer of the King Jahdoun. On his way, he finds a cave where he meets a wise old man, Talha, who was a judge under the former king, but was expelled by his successor. Talha tells 'Ubaid about Allah, the only God, and decides to look after the boy. Arriving in the city, 'Ubaid witnesses lawlessness, poverty and tyranny as King Jahdoun rules his people by encouraging them to worship idols and terrifying them with the magic of Shaytun. While both the king and the sorcerer are portrayed with unpleasant, sharp features, the king's physical appearance is somewhat more caricature-like, indicating his simple-mindedness. At first, 'Ubaid is tempted by dreams of power, influence and the possibility of becoming the king's next sorcerer. However, he continues visiting the old man in the cave, who tells him about God and his prophets. Very soon, 'Ubaid starts questioning his priorities and builds a faith in God. His transformation is encapsulated in a *nasheed*: 'The heart that builds belief [*eman*] searches for his merciful creator, the one of splendour, with masterful knowledge of human existence.'

After performing miraculous deeds, 'Ubaid challenges the authority of the king and his sorcerer. When showing 'Ubaid's followers and the king's people, the film's authors play with contrasts, by the rapid alternation of scenes showing the two companies. The scenes of a chaotic party with dissonant music playing in the background at the king's court (the only instance of instrumental music in the production) is contrasted with scenes of pleasant-faced, calm people listening to 'Ubaid's words on religion. The king's soldiers capture 'Ubaid, but repeatedly fail to execute him as God extends his protection over him. Finally, 'Ubaid pretends to offer Jahdoun the means of killing him: he should shoot an arrow at him in front of the city's inhabitants, after saying loudly, 'In the name of God, the God of this boy'. Jahdoun accepts the offer. After doing as he was told, Jahdoun manages to kill 'Ubaid, so the people witness the power of God and rise up against the king. The story ends with a quote from the Qur'an.

Sayf al-Qutuz 'Ayn Jalout, a feature-length animation made by Ella in 1998, shares similar characteristics. It tells the story of the life of Sayf al-Qutuz, the Mamluk sultan of Egypt (1254–60) from his childhood until the battle of Ain Jalut. While historians have proposed several theories about the origin of Qutuz, the script accepts his own rather dubious claims as recorded by official chronicles of his time (Amitai-Preiss 1995). According to the film, Qutuz's original name was Mahmud Ibn Mamdud, and he was a descendant of 'Ala ad-Din Muhammad II, ruler of the Khwarezmian empire in Central Asia. The plot starts in Central Asia, showing how the Mongols attacked Qutuz's homeland, and how he and his cousin Juljanar were separated and sold as slaves in the Syrian city of Aleppo and later in Cairo. The narrative follows the story of how Qutuz rose to become the vice-sultan of Cairo, and was then reunited with and subsequently married Juljanar. The story ends with the glorious victory at Ain Jalut on 3 September 1260.[8]

With a plot taking place in distant Muslim territories, the film shows a community and common identity amongst Muslims. To stress this point, the peoples of the Khwarezmian empire, Aleppo and Cairo are depicted in a similar manner (both in physical appearance and costume), and they use common Islamic figures of speech, without regional dialects or accents. The Muslim leaders, from Seljuk Jalal al-Deen, sultan of Ghazna, to Sultan Ayyub of Cairo, call their people 'Muslims', while referring to the Mongols by their ethnic origin as *al-Moghul*. Their ultimate goal as Muslim leaders is the defence of Muslims wherever they are. Sultan Ayyub, who is shown to be suffering from illness, repeatedly says, 'How could I rest when Muslims are in danger?', and in other instances describes himself as the 'Servant of the 'ummah'.

In contrast, the Mongols – in line with the dominant historical and literary narratives of the Arab Middle East that blame the Mongol conquest of Baghdad for the decline of the Muslim empire – are portrayed as violent and interested mainly in destruction, as a *nasheed* serving as narrator asserts:

> Phalanges of the Tatar, they come with destruction, have no mercy on women, and kill the children.

Fath al-Andalus – Tareq ibn Ziyad (The Conquest of Andalusia – Tareq ibn Ziyad), produced by Ella in 1999, tells the story of Tareq ibn Ziyad, the conqueror of Andalusia. Tareq ibn Ziyad is shown to have a strong Muslim identity, as in the frame story a grandfather who recounts the heroic deeds to his grandson describes him as a '*batalon 'arabiyyon mulsimon*' (Arab Muslim hero). The story portrays Tareq ibn Ziyad as a man of integrity who had no aspirations to power, but nonetheless accepted it for the good of the people, who are simply referred to as 'Muslims' by both the narrator and the protagonist. The Islamic identity of the film is also emphasised through the inclusion of a black African Muslim character called Omar, who strikes up a friendship with a fellow Muslim solider who has blond hair and blue eyes, as his mother was a Goth. The obvious message is that ethnic backgrounds matter less when people bond over their faith.

Here, the values of Islam are largely associated with general humanist values. In one scene, Tareq ibn Ziyad is shown imploring God to bestow good and justice on all humankind (*insaniyya*). In another scene, he makes a speech in front of his generals: 'The goal is to end the tyranny of the Christian Church's people and spread justice and equality in the lands'. Before the invasion of Andalusia, he also gives instructions to his people not to harm the innocent or to destroy anything. The personal qualities of Tareq ibn Ziyad as a servant and defender of Islam are indicated by showing him building a mosque with his own hands. Another scene has him travelling to Damascus together with two companions and slaying the bandits who terrorise the travellers. The rebellious act of his opponents, hiding in the mountains, is also framed in an Islamic way, by defining it as '*fitna didda Amir al-Mu'mineen*' (sedition against the Emir of the Believers).[9]

In order to justify Tareq ibn Ziyad's campaign, Andalusia under Qutiyya (Visigothic) rule is presented as a land of injustice and tyranny. To highlight this point, one scene even shows Hispanians seeking refuge in the Muslim lands, a feature unverified by credible historical sources.

King Roderick of Hispania is shown as a proud, intimidating man. In general, Hispanians are presented as forceful, indicated by a male choir singing about the 'glory of Hispania' at the beginning of the Hispanic scenes. On the other hand, the rulers of Hispania are shown as oppressing people on religious grounds. The animation shows how the number of Muslims increased in Andalusia through conversions, and how even non-Muslims suffering under the tyrannical rule longed for the Muslim armies to liberate them. It also casts Julian, governor of Ceuta, in a favourable light, calling him *al-muta'awin* (the co-operator) because of his collaboration with the conquering armies. The film also features a Hispanian noblewoman who converts to Islam by choice, and Cyrcon, a wise historian, who greatly admires Islam.

Islamicising Non-Islamic Narratives

In a number of cases, authors of Saudi-style Islamic animations adapt and alter existing narratives, in order to give the text an Islamic identity. 'Islamisation' of this type can take many forms, ranging from the inclusion of phrases, adding or deleting scenes, to even changing the entire plot. These productions can be considered 'adaptations', if adaptation is defined as 'repetition without replication', or 'repetition with difference' (Hutcheon 2006: xvi, 4, 7, 142,

149, 173, 176). The source texts are largely produced by Muslim authors who originally had no intention of giving their text an 'Islamic identity', and only use Islamic references in the context of local culture. In all cases, the authors of Islamic animations strip the original texts of their identities and add visual and linguistic markers with direct, unambiguous references to the preferred Islamic identities. This process of adaptation was described by Osama Khalifa as the 'presentation of Islamic literature to the children', an expression that strongly indicates that the authors do not regard the production process as an 'Islamisation' of non-Islamic narratives, but treat the source texts as Islamic because they were conceived in a Muslim environment. I will examine the productions of Ella, but I will treat these animated cartoons as adaptations because of the fundamental differences between the source texts and their animated counterparts.[10]

Texts from Arab literature are natural choices for the authors of Saudi-style Islamic animations. One case in point is *'Ali Baba wal-Arba'ina Lissan* (Ali Baba and the Forty Thieves), an Ella production released in 1996 that is an adaptation of the story of Ali Baba of *The Arabian Nights*, with the inclusion of a few scenes that are not particularly relevant to the narrative, but showcase Islamic identity, such as Ali Baba praying upon hearing the call for prayer (*adhan*). The dialogues, too, include Islamic messages: for example, Ali Baba is shown saying, 'We are satisfied with what God gives us for sustenance (*rizq*), and praise him in the mornings and evenings'.

Another example of the remediation of non-Islamic narratives is *Hikayat al-Amm al Hakim* (Stories of the Wise Uncle), released by Ella in 1999. The story is an Islamicised adaptation of the *Fables of Khalila and Dimna*, the secular fables of two jackals translated from the Sanskrit in the eighth century (Brockelmann 1978: 503–6). Each episode of the three-part series recounts several short, moralistic stories of animals framed by Islamic terminology. Islamic morals are also presented as having an overall human validity. Each story ends with a moral being highlighted, such as the importance of listening to advice offered by others, respect for each other, the harm of spreading sedition (*fitna*), the importance of telling the truth, all of which are explained through Islamic phrases and are often summed up at the end of the stories in the form of short *anasheed*.

One production that involved numerous changes to the narrative was

Jazeerat al-Nur (Island of the Light), an Ella co-production written and directed by Hasim Vatandas, from Turkey.[11] The feature-length film is an adaptation of Ibn Tufayl's *Hajj Ibn Yaqzan*, an eleventh-century philosophical 'Robinson Crusoe' story, inspired by Avicennism and Sufism, that later influenced the works of Daniel Defoe and John Locke.[12] Scholars generally agree that Ibn Tufayl had no Islamic intentions with his work (Hourani 1956). In contrast, *Jazeerat al-Nur* claims a strong Islamic identity. Similarly to Ibn Tufayl's original work, it tells the story of a boy who was brought up by a gazelle on a deserted island. Hajj, the original protagonist, is renamed 'Abdullah (literally meaning 'servant of God'). While Tufayl's work has little to say about Hajj's original homeland, the animation describes it as a place where people believed in Allah and followed 'the true religion' (*al-Din al-Haqq*). There are also references to Abraham and Moses, both prophets in Islam. The animation narrates how 'Abdullah's island home was destroyed by an earthquake, sent by God as a punishment for the corrupt governor. The greater part of the plot shows 'Abdullah growing up on the deserted island and eventually coming to the conclusion that the world around him is a created one. In the concluding part, a Muslim preacher called Saleh, described by the narrator as a preacher of the 'true faith', arrives on the island and meets 'Abdullah. After learning to speak and hearing about Islam, 'Abdullah realises that everything he had discovered while growing up is the same as the teachings of Saleh. When told about the Prophet, 'Abdullah accepts him without reservation. At the very end, the two depart from the island with a plan to help humankind and tell people about God's path.

In all cases, the extremely versatile animation format is used to Islamicise narratives of different identities. On the visual level, the style does not differ from that of other Ella productions, animated in Turkey by Turkish artists.

Creating Original Narratives

Writing original narratives is the third path to creating Saudi-style Islamic animations. While the similarities in tropes and plots may exist, they are so slight that the overall narratives can be regarded as originals.

One such example is *Al-Qarasina wa Kanz al-Dhahab* (The Pirates and the Gold Treasure), an Ella adventure animation released in 1998. While both the environment presented in the cartoon and the script obviously resemble the adventures of Sinbad as recounted in *The Arabian Nights*, the producer, Osama Khalifa, insisted that the plot itself is original.[13] The hero of the story is Omar, a ship's captain, who is asked by the merchant Sulayman to take cases of gold from one port to another.[14] While at sea, Omar's ship is attacked and sunk by pirates. Omar is shipwrecked, together with one of his sailors and a small boy called Bunduq ('hazelnut'). In search of a city, the three cross the desert. Upon reaching an oasis, they are attacked by bandits, but 'Imade, one of the bandits, recognises Captain Omar who had earlier saved his life, and he helps them to escape. Soon they reach a coastal town, where they mobilise the inhabitants and, with their help, defeat the pirates. Although the plot itself is not Islamic, the text is loaded with Islamic references such as the sound of the call to prayer and the inclusion of Islamic phrases and *anasheed*. In addition, the Islamic identity of the good characters (such as Omar, Bunduq and 'Imade) is clearly expressed, while leaving the religious and general identities of negative characters such as the pirates vague. The 'ownness' and 'otherness' of the characters is also indicated on the visual level: the protagonists and their helpers, such as the sailors and inhabitants of the town, have a 'localised' appearance, indicated by turbans, beards and dark hair. In contrast, pirate captain Shaddad and several of his pirates have red hair and light-coloured eyes, while other evil characters such as the desert bandits are presented as being of a mixed ethnic background.

The second original narrative of Ella was *Masrour fi Jazirat al-Lu'lu'* (Masrour on the Pearl Island), released in 1998. The story revolves around a young boy called Masrur who is sent by his father to a village to learn fishing from his old friend Misbah. Misbah is an honest man, who worries about his ne'er-do-well son Ziyad. Misbah is shown imploring God to steer his son onto the right path, a sign of the Islamic identity of the film. There are other Islamic references in the text, such as Masrur's father instructing him to pray. At one point in the story, Misbah tells Mansur about the source of his wealth: once, when he was fishing and his boat was caught in a storm, he saved a man from a giant octopus. He was shipwrecked on an island full of pearls. Ziyad listens to his story and sets off for the island to find the treasure. When they discover he has gone, Masrur and Misbah decide to go after Ziyad. On the island of pearls, they find Ziyad and save him just before a volcano erupts, leaving the treasure behind. In the end, Ziyad apologises to his father for being greedy and promises to work as a fisherman.

Portraying Islam as a Moderate Religion: Productions Supervised by al-Azhar

Religious Programming in Egyptian Television Since the 1990s and the Emergence of Egyptian Islamic Animations

The appearance of Egyptian animated cartoons featuring Islamic topics started in the mid-1990s. Similarly to Saudi-style Islamic animations, Egyptian productions can be linked to a local cultural and religious environment, forming a genre that articulates an Egyptian Islamic identity.

Al-Azhar is the highest religious authority in Egypt and also commands a considerable reputation across the entire Sunni Muslim world (Barraclough 1998). Under the presidency of Gemal ʿAbdel Nasser, al-Azhar came under government control in accordance with the reform law of 1961. In the same year, Al-Azhar University, which originally had a curriculum of exclusively Islamic studies, also became host to a number of secular faculties. In addition to higher education, it also established a national network of primary and secondary schools. According to an informal agreement, al-Azhar supported the socialist politics of Nasser. Under the presidency of Anwar al-Sadat, al-Azhar continued to function as an organ of the state, in support of the president's *infitah* policies (Ismail 1999). The 1981 assassination of al-Sadat by Islamists and the increasing activity of militant groups such as Takfir wal-Hijra and al-Jamaʿa al-Islamiyya as well as that of more moderate organisations such as the Muslim Brotherhood increased al-Azhar's role. Under Mubarak, al-Azhar became the government's partner in justifying campaigns against the Islamist opposition and its legislation directed against opposition activism.

As part of the deal between al-Azhar and the Egyptian state, in 1994 the government granted al-Azhar new powers in providing an Islamic dimension to printed and electronic media. Ruling No. 58/1/63 of the Council of State also gave al-Azhar the power to censor artistic and intellectual productions of the electronic media. In terms of television programmes, this meant that scripts had to be sent to al-Azhar for approval before production began. This also applied in the case of Islamic animated cartoons. The scripts are largely based on sacred texts, while the narratives about sacred figures are mostly written by professionals who are involved in the production business. Therefore, as the highest religious authority and the ultimate censor, al-Azhar acts as a gatekeeper for religious animations before they arrive on screen.

Beginning in the late 1990s, Islamic TV serials – censored by al-Azhar – went mainstream and moved to prime time as the state 'tried to appropriate for itself the role of supporter of a legitimate Islam'. Simultaneously, the production of religious programmes started to flourish. Al-Azhar's image as a representation of the orthodox authority of religion fuelled the desire of intellectuals and officials to align themselves with it, even though it has simultaneously been criticised by Islamists for 'being under the state's thumb' and regarded with some anxiety by state officials for 'harboring scholars with strong Islamist sympathies' (Abu Lughod 2006: 170).

Writing about visual culture, Armbrust also noted, 'the [Egyptian] state regularly televises calls to prayer, special religious programming, and sermons, some of which are extremely popular' (2002: 923). In the new millennium, the preservation of Arab-Islamic identity became a goal of Egyptian television (Sakr 2001: 33).

Because of the improved status of religious programming, a growing number of directors and popular actors began participating in these productions, which now enjoyed larger budgets and increasing popularity (Abu-Lughod 2008: 157). The trend was also joined by private television production companies and investors, who – according to Abu-Lughod – had not been separated from governmental production systems as it involved the very same actors and professionals working in state television. The authority of al-Azhar could not be bypassed in the case of productions with a religious topic.

In the mid-1990s, satellite channels began to proliferate. The Egyptian state responded to the challenge set by local and other Arab players in a political way, through agreements about standards and morals, as well as through the creation of works that could compete with what was offered on satellite.[15]

The start of the production of Islamic animations in Egypt largely coincides with the growing prestige of religious programming on Egyptian television (Sayfo 2018). The first Islamic animated cartoon produced in Egypt was *Qissat 'Ayah* (Story of the Ayah) created by al-Shahar in 1995 and broadcast on the newly established ART channel. Even though al-Shahar was based in Cairo, it was not entirely tied to local hierarchies, as its owner, 'Abbas ibn 'Abbas, was a Saudi national whose business plan was to focus on countries other than Egypt too.[16] In addition, ART, the very first Arab children's television channel, was based in Cairo and was owned by Saleh Kamel, a Saudi businessman. As its title indicates, *Qissat 'Ayah* draws from Qur'anic stories. The series included six episodes on Moses, four episodes on the story of Yousef (Joseph) and one about Nuh (Noah). Even though several Egyptians were involved in the production, the series blends the characteristic traits of religious television programmes of both Saudi Arabia and Egypt. Similarly to Saudi-style Islamic animations, *Qissat 'Ayah* involves instrument-free *anasheed* as both theme songs and narration. However, similarly to Egyptian television dramas, there are also instrumental soundtracks. Like the vast majority of Islamic animated cartoons, *Qissat 'Ayah* was dubbed in *fusha* Arabic. The circulation of *Qissat 'Ayah* remained limited, although it was later also sold to Iqra TV, a Saudi-owned Islamic channel.

The first genuine Egyptian Islamic animated productions were two clay animations: *Yunus*, recounting the story of Jonah, and *'Ashab al-Ukhdud* (People of the Trenches), released in 1995 by Egyptian Television and directed by Zainab Zamzam. After the first clay productions, Zainab Zamzam established her own production company, Zamzam Media, which became the executive producer of later Islamic clay animations produced under the auspices of Egyptian Television.

In the following years, Zamzam Media continued to produce clay animations with Islamic topics. In 1999, it released thirty episodes of *Min Qisas al-'Anbiya'* (From the Stories of the Prophets), followed by a ten-episode series about the life of the Prophet Muhammad in 2002, entitled *al-Sira al-Nabawiyya* (The Prophetic Biography). It then released fifteen episodes of *Qisas al-Qur'an* (Stories from the Qur'an) every year for the next three years. In 2005 and then again in 2006, it produced fifteen episodes of *Asbab al-Nuzul* (The Occasions of Revelation), which explain the context of a particular Qur'anic *sura* (chapter) or *'ayah* (verse). The years 2007 and 2008 saw Zamzam Media release thirty episodes – fifteen per year – of a religious educational series, *Min 'Asma' Allah al-Husna* (Of God's Most Beautiful Names).

The characteristics and narratives of Zamzam Media's productions paved the way for later Egyptian Islamic animations. They feature most of the characteristics shared by the vast majority of similar Egyptian productions ever since, characteristics that at the same time distinguish them from other productions of the region: they are dubbed in *fusha* Arabic and they include instrumental theme songs and soundtracks. Regarding the characteristics of the narrative, they often feature fictional dialogues and other elements that go beyond the sacred text of the Qur'an and the *hadith*, but without contradicting them. They often involve short spots showing original Qur'anic lines in order to highlight the authority of the animated text, and, like Islamic cinematic and television productions, they avoid the portrayal of the prophets. Unlike productions advocating national identities, the language of Egyptian Islamic animations is *fusha* Arabic. This can be ascribed to educated Egyptians' low opinion of local dialect: Haeri notes that in state schools and the Al-Azhar University system alike, Egyptian ʿ*ammiyya* and other vernaculars are disdained and viewed as markers of ignorance and illiteracy (Haeri 2003). Meanwhile, *fusha* Arabic is the official language of religious discourse as well as of education.

In the early 2000s a growing number of Egyptian producers entered the animation business. Inspired by the critical acclaim of Zamzam Media's output, many producers became involved in the production of religious animated series. These decisions were often based on financial considerations, as Islamic animated cartoons could be potentially distributed not only in the national market, but also in other Arab and Muslim markets (Sayfo 2018).

The distribution of the growing numbers of Egyptian Islamic-themed animations generally reaches beyond the national level. As with the Arab world – a geolinguistic market where the common language and culture support a cross-border flow of cinematic and television productions – the Muslim world is also a cultural market where shared religion facilitates the flow of cultural and media productions, including Islamic animated cartoons.

Drawing narratives from the Qur'an and the deeds of the prophets is an obvious choice, as it does not contain any topics that would divide Shia and Sunni viewers.[17] Also, the authority of Egypt's al-Azhar on Islamic topics makes Egyptian Qur'anic adaptations marketable in other Muslim countries too. According to the Egyptian producers I interviewed, once an animation is approved by al-Azhar, it is rarely questioned by other Arab and Muslim authorities, including those of Iran and Saudi Arabia.[18]

Thus, it has been a natural choice for Egyptian production companies and animation studios to become involved in the making of such animated series, especially after the fall of President Mubarak in 2011, when government television channels ceased purchasing animated series from local companies, pushing them to find alternative sources of funding and customers for their productions. One case in point is the producer of *Bakkar*, Cairo Cartoon, which in 2013 signed a deal with JCC to produce *'Ulama' al-Muslemeen* (Scientists of the Muslims), an edutainment series recounting stories of the famous Muslim (mainly Arab) scientists of the past.

Qisas al-Qur'an

Adapting Qur'anic stories and stories about the prophets has been a long tradition in Arab literature. In the late twentieth century, children's book publishers also paid a great deal of attention to religious topics. Bringing the stories of the prophets to the screen can be challenging, considering the general prohibition on portraying the Islamic prophets. In 1930, al-Azhar

Figure 5.2 *Qisas al-Hayawan fil-Qur'an* (Stories of the Animals in the Qur'an): an Islamic identity for domestic consumption and export. 2011 © Cartoonile.

passed a general ruling, still in force, prohibiting the portrayal of Mohammad (Shafik 2007b: 48–9). The ruling prohibits depictions of Mohammad – image and voice alike – as well as those of other prophets mentioned in the Qur'an in any way, a problem encountered and somehow dealt with in a number of Arab cinematic productions and television dramas covering Islamic history.

Qisas al-Hayawan fil-Qur'an (Stories of the Animals in the Qur'an) debuted in the month of Ramadan 2011 on Egyptian al-Hayat TV. The series, consisting of thirty half-hour episodes, was produced in 2D interaction technology with 3D backgrounds, and dubbed in *fusha* Arabic. The production had a budget of $2 million.[19] It was the first animated production by Ashraf al-Mallah of Associates Media Production, a Cairo-based private production company largely involved in making television dramas. Lacking an animation department of its own, it signed up with Cartoonile, a local animation company owned by Mustafa al-Faramawy, a director and animator who started his career as an animator at Mona Abu al-Nasr's Cairo Cartoon, participating in the production of *Kani wa Mani* (Kani and Mani).[20] Al-Mallah enlisted renowned Egyptian actors and actresses who gave their voices to the characters, while the narrator was TV and film actor Yahya al-Fakharani (Sayfo 2018). The script is an animated adaptation of the book *Qisas al-Hayawan fil-Qur'an al-Kareem* (Stories of the Animals in the Glorious Qur'an), written by Ahmed Bahgat in 1983.[21] Like all Egyptian Islamic animations, the scripts were reviewed by Al-Azhar University before the animation phase started. This production background undoubtedly played a prominent role in making *Qisas al-Hayawan fil-Qur'an* widely popular among other audiences beside the local. In the year of its release, it was sold to a number of other Arab countries. The series was later translated into English, Malay and Turkish, and was distributed in various Arab and non-Arab countries. Encouraged by the immense success of the first season, the producers released new series in the coming years. *Qisas al-Insan fil-Qur'an* (Stories of People in the Qur'an) was screened in 2012, followed by *Qisas al-Nisa' fil-Qur'an* (Stories of the Women in the Qur'an) in 2013 and *Qisas al-'Aja'ib fil-Qur'an* (Miracle Stories in the Qur'an) in 2014.

On the visual level, Mustafa al-Faramawy strove to create a Disneyesque, hyper-realistic world using 2D characters and 3D backgrounds. However, both the characters and the backgrounds represent a Middle Eastern environment, as al-Faramawy is among the few Arab authors who have developed a unique style.

All episodes of the three series revolve around characters appearing in the Qur'an, without telling their actual stories in detail. The series therefore had a self-imposed educational mission to spread religious knowledge to its viewers.[22] Similarly to other Arab cinematic and television productions about the prophets of Islam, the *Stories in the Qur'an* series avoid presenting images of the prophets or the sound of their voices. The audience learns about the deeds of the prophets from other characters speaking about them. In episodes where the prophets should be present, the scene focuses on the other characters, showing them talking to the prophet, then the voice of the narrator comes in, quoting the prophet's answer.

Although the basic narratives of the animated stories are based on references made in Qur'anic verses, the narratives also draw heavily from other religious texts such as Qur'anic exegesis. The episodes also include additional, fictional characters, dialogues and narratives, but these never contradict the Qur'anic phrases. One episode that best illustrates this point is about the Whale of Yunus (Jonah).[23] The story begins with the dinosaurs (referred to as *wuhus* 'beasts' *or tananin* 'dragons') that lived a million years before Adam and Eve. The choice of narrative is an attempt to reconcile modern views about 'prehistory' with religious ones about Adam and Eve as the first humans. The plot shows how the dinosaurs killed each other while fighting for food, and how some of them moved to the seas and became whales. The story continues with a young whale called Anbar. He is miserable because his father, the strongest whale in the ocean, is dissatisfied with him and wants the friendly, peaceful Anbar to be a fearsome whale. The story also includes educational messages, showing how humans are 'the most dangerous enemies of whales'. One day, a black whale fights Anbar's father and becomes the mightiest whale in the sea. Anbar vows to defeat the black whale. After training for a long time, he takes his revenge and becomes the lord of the sea. One day, he swims by a ship at the very moment that Yunus is cast into the sea by his companions in order to calm the storm. After swallowing the prophet, Anbar's spiritual journey begins. He listens to the prayers of Yunus from his belly, becomes the prophet's first follower and brings Yunus to the shore.

Considering the many non-Qur'an-based narratives, the series can be best defined as Qur'an-based stories rather than Qur'anic adaptations. The episodes also include Western cultural elements, creating a hybrid text. One example is the use of characters giving a thumbs-up as a sign of approval, an unmistakably Western gesture.

The episodes in the *Stories in the Qur'an* series have a similar structure. They start with an animated frame story in which a storyteller addresses other characters, relating moralistic stories from the Qur'an. In *Stories of the Animals in the Qur'an*, a shepherd addresses his sheep, in *Stories of the People in the Qur'an*, a ship captain addresses his crew, while in *Stories of the Women in the Qur'an*, a judge (*qadi*) tells stories to his daughter, Salma. The voice of the storyteller in the frame stories is also used to narrate the main stories, following on after the frame and centred on the title character of the episode. At the end of each episode, relevant quotations from the Qur'an, recited by a deep male voice, appear on the screen, illustrated with screenshots taken from the main story shown earlier. At the very end, the closing scene reverts to the narrator and his audience with various closing remarks.

The identity advocated by the *Stories in the Qur'an* series is an Islamic one, associating Islam with tolerance and with the acceptance of diversity, and hence shows a difference with Saudi-style animations, which sometimes have little trouble portraying the 'other' as barbaric. Considering the involvement of al-Azhar, it can also be defined as a regionalized Islamic identity with slight pan-Arab as well as educational tones. In the second series, the sailors travel to India, where Ziyad learns that Hindus worship their cows as saints. After expressing his astonishment, the captain reflects: 'We should respect the beliefs and culture of others. This is what our religion teaches us.'[24] Evil characters are not demonised on a religious basis, but according to their role in the stories. Their visual presentation, drawing on the traditions of Walt Disney, also follows suit. The 'good' Banu 'Isra'eel (People of Israel) are portrayed as pleasant-looking, while the 'evil' ones are drawn with sharp features and cruel eyes, and are either markedly fat or markedly thin. The same applies to the Arab characters, as the followers of Muhammad are presented as friendly people, while his opponents are drawn as ugly people.[25] The portrayal of women also points to a moderate Islamic identity, as some of them (for example, the *qadi*'s daughter in Season 3) do not wear a hijab, and their depiction as courageous reflects an emancipated perception of women, in contrast to Saudi-style Islamic animations where Muslim women are always veiled. In one of the episodes of *Stories of the Women in the Qur'an*, the *qadi* confronts his daughter when she tells him that she had heard that the expulsion of Adam from the Garden of Eden was because of the temptation of Eve (Hawwa'). He dismisses these ideas as ignorance (*jahl*) and refers to the Qur'an as a source of truth.[26] It should be noted that the idea of Eve being the first to sin in Paradise can be found in Genesis 2, and that while this also appears in early Islamic tradition and in Qur'anic exegesis, it cannot be found in the Qur'an itself. However, the scholars of al-Azhar reject the idea of Eve being the first sinner by exclusively basing themselves on the Qur'an and rejecting the post- Qur'an traditions on the matter. In the case of *Stories of the Women in the Qur'an*, this approach, which is in line with al-Azhar's statement, is an indicator of a moderate Islamic attitude towards women.

Islamic belief is presented as a state of mind attained by logic and sense. In one episode, Umm Kulthum, daughter of Utba, one of the Prophet Muhammad's foes, is described by the narrator as follows: 'Her intellect (*'aql*) and knowledge (*'ilm*) led her to the belief in God. She became a Muslim out of "intellectual conviction and logical thinking" (*iqtina' 'aqli wa tafkir mantiqi*)'.[27] Following this logic, non-believers are often presented as dim-witted.

In some rare instances, the plots engage in religious discourses, as, for example, in the case of 'Eve's sin'. One episode tells a story of two brothers, one a poor, God-fearing man, the other a rich, conceited man. At the end of the story, the narrator acknowledges that there is no actual proof of them being brothers in the Qur'an, and although references are made by the Prophet's companions (*al-Salaf al-Saleh*), the story makes no mention of the time and place – however, there is a common consensus that they were brothers, but ultimately only God knows (*Allahu a'lam*).[28] When there is engagement in religious debates, the speakers never mention the names of those holding contrary opinions in order to avoid direct confrontation.

The texts advocating social engagement are not entirely devoid of political references. The frames of the episodes from one season to the next show a subtle shift from avoiding any political content to statements that could be interpreted as political. Regarding the shepherd of the first season, there were no references to the actual time or place of the frame story. In contrast, the time and places of the frame story of the second season are more definite. The captain and his companions visit Paris, and remark that the Eiffel Tower had been constructed 'a few years ago', possibly indicating that the story takes place in the late nineteenth or early twentieth century.[29] In addition to its moralistic messages, the frame story of the second season also has slight political undertones: When visiting European locations like Marseille, Malaga and Sicily, and Far Eastern ports like Calcutta and Hong Kong, the captain never fails to mention the cultural influence of the 'Arab' presence in the past and the positive impacts of Muslim conquests (*futuhat*). Most of the frame stories revolve around the characters visiting Arab cities such as Aden, Alexandria, Beirut, Duba, Kuwait City, Muscat and Tartus, and they also make a *'umra* (small pilgrimage) to Mecca and Medina. These episodes include educational content about the Arab cities, highlighting the similarities between Arabs: they all speak *fusha* Arabic and have more or less similar features, suggesting unity amongst Arabs regardless of their country of origin. While the first two seasons are relatively free of political references, the frame story of the third season is more loaded. The story takes place in an unnamed Arab city of the past, governed in an idealised Islamic way. The only hints at the possible timeframe are in the form of references to the caliph, suggesting that the episodes take place in the Abbasid era (CE 750–1228). The main characters are the old judge (*qadi*) of the city, his daughter Salma and the police chief. The *qadi* is depicted as a man of justice, explaining his decisions with moralistic and Islamic references. In the *qadi*'s city there is equality before the law, regardless of financial status. In one episode, the judge gives priority to a case of stolen shoes over larger issues, as it affects many people.[30] Corruption is non-existent, as is illustrated in an episode in which the *qadi* refuses a business offer to sell the perfumes which he concocts at home as a hobby, seeing it as a source of corruption.[31] The *qadi* does not even need a bodyguard, confidently explaining, 'Who applies justice and fears (*yattaqi*) God in everything does not need guards'.[32]

The series includes even more concrete political references. On one occasion, the police chief catches a carrier pigeon and reads its message. When asked by his wife why he is doing this, he explains that it is part of his job. Reading the letter, he learns of the activities of a foreign (*ajnabi*) spy, who is gathering information for the enemy (*firanja*).[33] The police chief searches some homes after obtaining the *qadi*'s permission to do so; the *qadi* warns him not to hurt innocent people. After the investigations, the police chief arrests an Indian man who is acting suspiciously, looking at buildings and people. Finding the case against the man to be weak, the *qadi* frees him. It soon turns out that the real spy is a beggar pretending to be lame, who is caught in front of the town's mosque. After being arrested and asked why he was standing in front of the mosque, he answers, 'The mosque is the heart of Arab society. It is an indication of a society's strength or weakness.' The spy explains that the number of old preachers in the mosques means that a society is not ready for war.[34] This particular story has a number of conclusions: first of all, the activities of the secret services are justified if they do not harm innocent people. Second, innocent people cannot be held in custody without proof. Third, old religious hierarchies represent a setback for the Muslim community.

In the *qadi*'s town, all citizens are equal before the law. The very first episode starts with a policeman who is arrested and convicted for stealing a hen. The last episodes revolve around the unlawful expropriation of a piece of land by the ruler.[35] After hearing the complaints of the previous owner, the *qadi* orders the caliph to appear in person in court to testify. The caliph obeys the *qadi* without complaint and pays compensation to the owner, who withdraws the case. The *qadi* rules that the caliph is also obliged to compensate society. After accepting the judgement, the caliph asks why he is receiving such a harsh punishment, even though it is not he, but one of his viziers, who is the guilty party. The *qadi* answers: 'He works for you and you share responsibility with him. Governance (*huqm*) and judgment (*qada'*) are the greatest responsibility and the heaviest burden (*'aba'*)'.

References to an idealised Muslim society can be set in the context of the political circumstances in Egypt at the time when the series was made. Production started in 2012, more than a year after the Arab Spring protests had toppled President Mubarak and a new government led by the Muslim Brotherhood had been installed. After long decades of illegality and repression, the Islamist Party aimed to apply their interpretation of Islamic principles to governance. It was also a time when Egyptian television had cut funding for a number of homegrown cultural productions, including animation. Therefore, creating politically aware content might have been a strategy for producers of Islamic animation to maintain government funding and to find a way to the well-off Qatari market, including JCC, which was hungry for Egyptian Islamic content at that time. As the political tides changed following 'Abdel Fattah el-Sisi's coup in 2013, Egyptian Islamic animations lost this political edge.

While both Saudi and Egyptian Islamic animations are officially produced for a transnational Muslim audience, in fact they mainly addressed those within a specific geopolitical realm. When it comes to mediating identities, Muslims living in established diasporas have a different set of needs from those living within the geopolitical borders of the Arab world.

Merging Muslim and Western Identities: an American-Kuwaiti Production

The Adaptation of the Superhero Genre to the Arab World

The number of Arabs and Muslims living in Western diasporas runs into tens of millions. Hybrid identities of Muslims living in the West have resulted in cultural productions articulating a specific form of Islamic identity (Kraidy 1999). *The 99*, a Muslim superhero saga that started out as a comic book in 2006 and was later adapted into an animated cartoon format is a telling account of a Muslim diaspora identity formation.

The creator of *The 99* is Naif al-Mutawa, a Kuwaiti-American. Al-Mutawa founded Teshkeel Media in 2005, and established his publishing business by gaining the rights to distribute Arabic versions of Archie, DC and Marvel comics in the Middle East (Mujtaba 2008). The first printed issue of *The 99* was published in 2007, and was followed by several more issues. For the production of *The 99*, al-Mutawa cooperated with artists such as comic book writer Fabian Nicieza, author of *X-Men* and *Captain America* stories. Similarly, the artists involved in the design of the comics that became the basis of the animated series gained experience when working for companies like DC Comics and Marvel.[36] Al-Mutawa explained that his goal was to make the stories look like original American productions, but featuring Islamic archetypes and including strong references to Islamic culture.

The comic debuted in Arabic and English, and was later published in other languages, including French, Spanish, Indonesian and Mandarin

Figure 5.3   *The 99*: homegrown Muslim superheroes. 2011 © Teshkeel Media Group.

Chinese. Inspired by the success, in 2008 Teshkeel signed a partnership deal with British Endemol Productions to produce an animated TV series based on the comic books. Endemol outsourced animation phases to an Indian company, Sanraa Media, based in Chennai. By 2010, a twenty-six-episode 3D series had been completed. Through the partnerships of Endemol Worldwide Distribution, 'The Hub', a joint venture between Discovery Communications and Hasbro, acquired the rights to air all twenty-six episodes in the United States. On 22 October 2011, *The 99* premiered on a PBS Independent Lens Livestream broadcast. While agreements were signed with a number of television channels, *The 99* was also distributed digitally. In 2012, Teshkeel signed a deal with Yahoo! Maktoob to offer episodes on demand to Middle Eastern and North African subscribers (The 99 Newsletter 2012). Later in 2012, Teshkeel partnered up with Netflix to stream the first season (The 99 Newsletter 2013).

Teshkeel declared its mission 'to fill a significant void in positive, high quality children's content in the region, including in print and electronic media, film and television' (Teshkeel Media Group 2006). The concept of *The 99*, as a Muslim superhero brand, can be analysed in the context of the post-9/11 anti-Islamic discourse in the West, which was a traumatic experience for Arabs and Muslims living in diasporas in general and the United States in particular (Peek 2011). Al-Mutawa made it his goal to promote positive narratives of Islam to both young Muslims and non-Muslims during the growing Islamophobia in the course of the Bush administration (Al-Mutawa 2010).

While the number 99 is a reference to the ninety-nine names of God and their associated attributes in the Qur'an, al-Mutawa also links the name to the 9/11 attacks:

> I had already made a decision that I needed to find a way to take back Islam from its hostage takers, but I did not know how . . . So at the age of thirty-two, I uncapped my pen to create a concept that could be popular in the East and the West. I would go back to the very sources from which others took violent and hateful messages and offer messages of tolerance and peace in their place. (BBC 2009a)

The concept of *The 99* mediating a moderate Islamic identity compatible with Western values became especially timely when Barack Obama became US president. Obama's speech in Cairo in 2009 was seen as a symbolic act for the rebuilding of trust between the United States and the Muslim world (Obama 2009). Later, in April 2010, Obama himself recognised the importance of al-Mutawa's initiative during his speech at the Presidential Summit on Entrepreneurship in Washington, DC. In his remarks, Obama praised al-Mutawa for 'his comic books [that] have captured the imagination of so many young people with superheroes who embody the teachings and tolerance of Islam'.[37] Such recognition opened new, iconic perspectives for Tashkeel's project, and led to *The 99* partnering up in comic books with DC Comics' Justice League of America, featuring superheroes such as Superman, Batman and Wonder Woman.

The 99 is involved not only in the rebranding, but also in what Avi Santo labelled as the marketisation of Islam. As he pointed out, '*The 99* works to re-brand Islam, not by commercialising Muslim spaces as much as by reconfiguring the consumer spaces in which Islam circulates, with "American"-style Muslims serving as examples of the brand's trajectory and final destination' (Santo 2013).

The Formation of Hybrid Identities in the Muslim Diasporas of the West

The 'superhero' is a 'modern mythology' that blends elements from ancient mythology with pulp and science fiction stories, resulting in a unique

American cultural production (Reynolds 1992; Wright 2001). For Matthew Costello, superhero stories are appropriate forums for studying cultural change, and, more precisely, an exploration of national identity (2009: 14). Ryan Edwardson agrees that superheroes 'engage this act of [imagining nations], and in turn facilitating the mental construction of the nation and national identity' (2003: 185).

As an American genre, superhero literature largely stems from the multicultural society of the United States. A case in point is the first popular American superhero, Superman. Like many authors, Aldo Regalado agrees that Superman's origin as the last survivor from the Planet Krypton makes him a 'foreign-born immigrant', the son of a great civilisation who wants to assimilate to American culture (Regalado 2005: 92). Some scholars of superhero literature even assert that the Jewish creators of *Superman, Man of Steel*, and other superheroes transferred their Jewish identities to the characters (Murray 2011). Danny Fingeroth goes even further, seeing Superman as a sort of wish fulfilment of the Jewish (American) Dream to become 'the quintessential American, unafraid to speak truth to power, especially to the types of petty tyrants that people face on a day-to-day basis' (Fingeroth 2007: 49).

Double identity is not a characteristic unique to Superman, but a general phenomenon seen in the vast majority of superheroes like Bruce Wayne–Batman, Peter Parker–Spiderman, Dr Bruce Banner–Hulk and members of the X-Men, a team of mutants who are despised and feared by society and learn from their leader Professor X how to be proud of their otherness, and become defenders of humankind.

Similarly to large parts of his target audience, Naif al-Mutawa is an Arab and a Muslim living in the Western world, specifically in the United States. Abu-Lughod described 'people whose national or cultural identity is mixed by virtue of migration, overseas education, or parentage' as 'halfies' (1991: 137). According to Abu-Lughod, their anthropological practices blur the boundary between 'self' and 'other'. Kraidy argued that by belonging simultaneously to both local and global realms, the people whom Abu-Lughod described as halfies are capable of understanding the hybridity inherent at their intersection (1999: 456–76). In this regard, Naif al-Mutawa created heroes with whom the audience can connect, because they recognise their struggles and identities.

Indeed, hybridity is a critical concept for understanding both the identities and the cultural production of diasporas living in multicultural societies.[38] Regarding the hybrid identities and media texts produced by Arab Muslims living in Western societies, there is a likely possibility of the articulation of identities that are part of both Western and Arab/Muslim discourses, but simultaneously different from both.[39] I read *The 99* as a mediation of hybrid identities of children growing up in Arab/Muslim families of the West in general, and the United States in particular. In this regard, it was the first Islamic diaspora animation and is the most renowned so far.

The Hybrid Islamic Identity of The 99

The background story of the animation series is based on that of the comic book. The story takes us back to 1258, when the Mongolian armies invaded Baghdad. The event itself is of symbolic value, as it led to the destruction of the Abbasid empire and the 'Islamic Golden Age', whose loss has long been a trauma both in Arab and Islamic history. While the Mongolian invaders besiege the city, the librarians are racing against time to preserve the knowledge accumulated in the library called Dar al-Hikma (House of Knowledge). By using alchemy (originating from the Arabic word *al-kimya'*), they prepare a liquid called the 'King's Water', with which they distil ninety-nine gemstones. At the last minute, the ninety-nine 'Noor Stones' (*noor* means 'light' in Arabic) are smuggled out of the besieged city. When the books are thrown into the Tigris River by the Mongols, the librarians immerse the stones in the water in order that they absorb the knowledge from the books, before fleeing Baghdad with the stones. The three bearers of the gemstones reunite in Andalusia, then under Muslim rule, and place the gemstones in a monument built by the librarians, called Husn al-Ma'rifa (The Fortress of Knowledge). The monument, watched over by a council of guardians, becomes a place of pilgrimage for scholars who seek knowledge. In 1420, a boy called Rughal becomes one of the guardians. A talented scientist, he discovers that the gemstones can vest certain people with extraordinary powers and capabilities, enabling them to regain the knowledge that was lost in the destruction of Baghdad. The guardians recognise his obsession with the stones and restrict his access to them. Husn al-Ma'rifa is destroyed during the Reconquista in the late fifteenth century. In order to prevent the capture of the gems, the guardians divide them into three batches: one is shipped to the New World, one is scattered throughout Europe, while the last is sent to Asia along the Silk Road. As al-Mutawa remarked, the scattering of the gems is meant to be a symbol of Muslim communities and diasporas around the world (Mujtaba 2008). It may perhaps also be understood as an allusion to a globalised vision that power and knowledge can be found anywhere in the world, not only in the heartland of Islam. Mary-Jane Deeb also observes that the background story of *The 99* suggests that the superheroes are not a modern invention, based on models from the West. They are the product of forces that go back to the depths of Islamic history – not just to any point in history, but to the time of the downfall of the Abbasids, under whom a great civilisation had flourished (Deeb 2012). The concept also highlights the Arab contribution to what is called 'civilisation', and hence forges a connection between the Arab/Islamic cultures of the past and the Western culture of the present.

The comic book provides a chronological order, telling how Dr Ramzi Razem, a psychologist and historian, struggles to gather the young holders of the gemstones around the world, as Professor X did with the young mutants of *X-Men*. The first issue tells the story of how a Saudi boy, Nawaf al-Bilali, turns into Jabbar ('powerful'), a Hulk-like character made of muscles, after a Noor Stone becomes lodged under his skin in an accidental mine blast. The episodes of the animated series do not follow the narrative of the comic books. The first episode of *The 99* begins in medias res. The story starts with Dr Ramzi and two gemstone holders, Jabbar and Noura (Dana Ibrahim, an Emirati woman who has the power to control light), visiting John Weller, a disabled young man and holder of a gemstone, at his home in Missouri in the United States. They save him from the immortal villain Rughal and his men, who try to kidnap him for their evil schemes.[40] Joining the 99, John becomes Darr and channels his superpower to cause other people pain into relieving them of their pain instead. Later episodes revolve around Dr Ramzi and his group of young gemstone holders going on missions around the globe in order to find other holders of the gemstones before Rughal and his henchmen do, and to convince them to join their fight for the good of humanity. A number of episodes also show how the group fight against evil people and criminals around the world.

While several episodes are set in non-Muslim countries, the stories and characters refer to actual problems and traumas of the Arab and Muslim people. One of the episodes shows Jabbar returning for a short visit to Saudi Arabia, where he first experiences general hostility from the people who fear his abilities, before they realise how they misjudged him and celebrate him instead.[41] The story could be interpreted as a reflection on a common experience of young people of Arab/Muslim immigrant background being misjudged in their new and old homelands, and as an expression of their wish to be admired. Another story shows how two members of the group, Rafeʿ and Sameda, save an entire Bangladeshi village from being destroyed by a storm.[42] Deeb also sees Rughal as a possible reference to the charismatic leaders of the Arab and Muslim world such as Ayatollah Khomeini, Osama bin Laden and Muammar al-Qaddafi, all of whom advocated ideologies that were meant to serve the greater good, but in reality only served their personal desire for power. His group is called al-Mamalik ('owned' or 'slave'), a reflection on the undemocratic nature of his worldview. With such allusive criticism of radical Islam, *The 99* advocates moderate notions of religion.

American superheroes are rooted in American individualist culture, representing individualistic values and responsibilities. Gary Engle pointed out that superheroes like Superman (Clark Kent), Spiderman (Peter Parker) and Batman (Bruce Wayne) are orphans, and are therefore not only free but also obliged to invent their own history (Engle 1987: 80–3). Collectivist Arab/Muslim values are reflected in the very concept of showing the 99 as a team of superheroes. Even though American superheroes occasionally team up in later stories, they remain individualistic characters, often sharing ambivalent feelings towards each other and occasionally even getting into fights with each other. In contrast, the 99 are defined by collectivism, working together in teams towards a common goal.

Representing the collectivist values of Arab/Muslim societies, the heroes of *The 99* are vested with the virtue of responsibility towards their elders and kin. One of the episodes revolves around Sharifa, a Muslim Malaysian girl, who uses her powers provided by the Noor Stone to win a television quiz show in order to help her grandfather, who is being blackmailed by criminals.[43] While obviously a general human value, respect for the elderly is also one of the pillars of traditional Arab culture and an essential principle of Islam. Another episode tells the story of a Jordanian gemholder, a child named Fadi, who helps an arms smuggling network operating from the caves of Petra with his teleportation powers.[44] The plot shows how the smugglers exercise control over Fadi's village, hence freeing the boy from moral responsibility. Of course, at the end of both episodes, the criminals are beaten by the 99, and the team gains a new member. The plot of the episode about Jabbar shows how he is under pressure and facing the dilemma of whether to leave his new friends and work for his father's business. His mother explains how he owes his father (*mudin lahu*) help and loyalty. His friends in the 99 understand Jabbar's dilemma and reassure him that they will always remain his friends and will be ready to help him if he is in need. Later, the 99 help Jabbar to defeat his father's enemy Shirrir (literally 'evil'), a greedy entrepreneur who exploits his workers. At the end of the episode, the father gives Jabbar his blessing to return to his friends.

In the series, the 99 are presented as a multinational community, with members hailing from different countries. Al-Mutawa explained in an interview that while the characters are modelled on Islamic archetypes, religion is not discussed directly, and Islamic values are largely associated with universal values. In another interview, responding to the criticism of Islamist opponents and a ban from Saudi Arabia, al-Mutawa asserted that the superheroes represent the values of Islam and not the intrinsic qualities of God.[45]

Regarding its visual style, *The 99* can hardly be regarded as a hybrid, as it largely follows the characteristics of Western 3D action series. In my opinion, the influence of *Action Man*, a Canadian 3D series distributed on Fox Kids Network in 2000–2 is visible. This visual style can perhaps be explained by al-Mutawa's goal to target Muslim children living in diasporas, who are used to watching high-quality animated cartoons.

With the presentation of a set of heroes of diverse backgrounds, *The 99* embraces the diversity of Islam, rather than choosing a particular appropriation. However, as Jason Dittmer observes, al-Mutawa 'succeeds in externalizing certain aspects of Islamist discourse in that he is pluralist without resorting to complete relativism' (Dittmer 2014). Therefore, *The 99* presents a rebranded, hybrid approach to Islamic identity; it is an indicator of the identity dilemmas of young Muslims and Arabs living in diasporas. At the same time, it encourages young Muslims in the diaspora to carve out a space for themselves, challenging the validity of any essentialist cultural identity.

Conclusion

This chapter has shown how the animation format has been adapted to advocate Islamic identities and also to create different worlds on the visual level in order to promote different approaches of Islam.

In all cases, *fusha* Arabic, the language of the Qur'an and religious discourse, is used as a symbol to emphasise the Islamic identity of the productions, regardless of their background. Therefore, unlike in the case of pan-Arab animated cartoons discussed in Chapter 4, *fusha* Arabic here is used not as a symbol of Arab unity, but one of Islamic identity. On the visual level, animation is used to create different worlds, constructed according to the preferences of the authors and representing different approaches to Muslim identities. In this regard, Saudi-style productions as well as Egyptian Islamic animated cartoons have hybridised the hyper-realist style (often associated with Disney) to create different representations of Muslim characters and environments. Regarding the characters, the 'own' and the 'other' are represented in various ways in order to arouse a sense of sympathy or antipathy.

Animated Islamic identities are specific as they follow broader notions and understandings of religion. The individual charactistics of 'Saudi-style' Islamic identity are expressed by the exclusion of instrumental music and the inclusion of *anasheed*. On the visual level, racial differences are downplayed when representing the Muslim 'own', while markers of otherness regarding physical appearance are highlighted when representing the 'other'. On the narrative level, the approach to Islam often claims an exclusive ownership of an ultimate truth that struggles with an often demonised 'other'.

Islamic animation production in Egypt cannot be separated from the wider Egyptian political and religious environment, as it was principally facilitated by the Egyptian government's efforts to create a controlled Islamic public sphere in the media in order to strengthen its own legitimacy. The inclusion of instrumental music can be regarded as a particularity of this approach as is how the series discussed here are based on adapted stories from Islam's most fundamental sacred texts, the Qur'an and stories of the prophets. Egyptian productions largely associate Muslim identity with moderation and harmony. To facilitate the transnational flow of the productions and make them marketable beyond the borders of Egypt and the Arab world, the producers mostly avoid touching on sensitive religious issues, and also create a narrative fusing Muslim and popular Western elements.

Meanwhile, in the case of the series *The 99*, the hybrid concept of 'Muslim superheroes' largely stems from the hybrid identities of Muslim diasporas and individuals. The fusion of values and cultures has resulted in the promotion of a Muslim identity that goes hand in hand with modern, Western identities, creating a hybrid approach between Muslim and Western values, which in turn leads to the presentation of 'universal' values through Islamic archetypes.

These three approaches and productions all represent rival approaches of Islamic identities, tied to particular countries and elites. Because of the wide international distribution, Islamic animated cartoons have the potential to participate in the creation of globalised Muslim identities and present Islam as the main bond between Muslims, regardless of their country of residence.

Notes

1. Another possible explanation for the prohibition of *The Prince of Egypt* was an objection to the way it depicted relations between Jews and Egyptians.
2. Telephone interview with Osama Khalifa (15 May 2014).
3. Interview with Osama Khalifa: Haitham al-Ashraf, 'Al-Ustaz Osama Khalifa fi Hiwar Muthir 'an Tajribatihi fi Intaj Aflam al-Kartoun', 14 December 2004, http://www.odabasham.net/show.php?sid=592
4. Telephone interview with Osama Khalifa (15 May 2014).
5. Ibid.
6. Unlike the Arabic film, the English version of the production does have instrumental music.
7. Qur'an 85: 4.
8. The plot does not recount how Qutuz was assassinated by Baybars on the triumphant journey back to Cairo. See Holt et al. 1977, p. 215.
9. *Fitna* (pl: *al-fitan*) is a word largely used in Islamic terminology to refer to an 'artificial' division between Muslims.
10. Telephone interview with Osama Khalifa (15 May 2014).
11. Given the fact that the director and the majority of the crew were Turkish, the production could be regarded as Turkish. However, as Osama Khalifa was the producer and hence maintained his control over the text, I have chosen to include it among Arab animations.

12. Avicennism is a medieval Islamic school of philosophy founded by the eleventh-century Persian philosopher Ibn Sina (known in the West as Avicenna), with the aim of reconciling Islamic theology with Aristotelianism and Neo-Platonism.
13. Telephone interview with Osama Khalifa (15 May 2014).
14. It must be noted that Omar is generally considered to be a Sunni Muslim name, after the second caliph who followed the Prophet Muhammad.
15. These coordination plans were proposed by the Egyptian Minister of Information Safwat al-Sharif in a speech to the 1998 Annual Radio and Television Festival in Cairo. See Sakr 2001, pp. 64 and 162 and Abu-Lughod 2008, p. 197.
16. Personal interview with Abbas ibn Abbas (Cairo, 1 September 2012).
17. Personal interviews with Mustafa al-Faramawy (Cairo, 6 September 2012) and Omar Moghazy (Cairo, 6 September 2012).
18. Ibid.
19. Personal interview with Mustafa al-Faramawy (Cairo, 6 September 2012).
20. Mustafa al-Faramawy also produced *Youmiyyat al-Ustaz Sahlawi* (Everyday Stories of Mr Sahlawi), an educational animated series. He was presented with the Award of the Children's International Jury Committee in 2004 and with the Bronze Award at the Children's Film Festival in 2004. He also received the Academy Award, the highest accolade given to an Egyptian work, by the Cultural Development Fund in 2009.
21. Ahmad Bahgat was in charge of the film *Ayyam al-Sadat* (Days of al-Sadat), for which he received the Order of Arts and Sciences and a special honour from former president Hosni Mubarak. Bahgat has written social satires that portray his understanding of daily life as a columnist for *Al-Ahram*, in the daily column 'The Box of the World', and is the author of the socially critical piece, *Kilmitayn Wa Bass* (Only Two Words), written for radio.
22. Personal interview with Mustafa al-Faramawy (Cairo, 6 September 2012).
23. Season 1, episode 9.
24. Season 2, episode 23.
25. Season 3, episode 2.
26. Season 3, episode 1.
27. Season 3, episode 29.
28. Season 2, episode 28.
29. Season 2, episode 2.
30. Season 3, episode 6.
31. Season 3, episode 3.
32. Season 3, episode 6.

33. *Firanja* is a politically non-loaded term generally associated with Europeans in general, and Franks in particular.
34. Season 3, episodes 25 and 26.
35. Season 3, episodes 27–30.
36. The graphics team includes character designer Dan Panosian, penciller John McCrea, inker James Hodgkins and colourist Monica Kubina.
37. See President Obama's remarks at the Presidential Summit on Entrepreneurship, Washington, DC (26 April 2010), https://obamawhitehouse.archives.gov/the-press-office/remarks-president-presidential-summit-entrepreneurship
38. See also Chapter 1.
39. A similar phenomenon was observed by Kraidy regarding the identities and media texts produced by Lebanese Maronites. See Kraidy (1999).
40. In a later episode we learn that Dr Ramzi was actually played by Rughal, who made Jabbar and Noura fight against the real Dr Ramzi, whom they thought to be the villain Rughal.
41. Season 1, episode 19.
42. Season 1, episode 23.
43. Season 1, episode 11.
44. Season 1, episode 18.
45. See the criticism of some Islamists at PBS, 'Kuwait: *The 99*: Super Heroes of the Muslim World', 26 June 2007, www.pbs.org/frontlineworld/stories/kuwait605/video_index.html

6

The Arab Spring of Animation

Introduction

The so-called 'Arab Spring' was not merely a political, social and economic uprising; it was also a cultural and artistic one. It brought an outpouring of creative talent from people who were neither professional artists nor part of the intellectual elite. Countless mediums and forms of revolutionary self-expression emerged. It was a 'revolution of the imagination' that enabled people with limited access to resources to consume new kinds of media and also to produce and distribute their own mediated narratives (Elseewi 2011).

Very soon after Zine el-Abidine Ben Ali of Tunisia announced his resignation, a short, edgy animation appeared online. The spot featuring cut-out animated characters was created by a small Jordanian company called Kharabeesh ('Scribbles'). It showed the president fleeing his country by plane and phoning his former Middle Eastern and European allies, begging for refuge. The popularity of the animation prompted Kharabeesh to release more productions of this kind, and it inspired others across the region to follow suit. Soon, short sarcastic animations, produced mainly by Flash, Post Productions, 3D Studio and other easy-access software mushroomed on social media, making animation production an integral part of this 'creative insurgency' (Kraidy 2016a) and a platform for the mediation of revolutionary identities.

In the enthusiastic revolutionary public discourse, individuals and creative groups behind popular animation projects such as the Syrian WikiSham, the Tunisian Captain Khobza, the Egyptian Egyptoon and others were hailed as champions of the democratisation of media production. However, this approach, at least in the case of animation, was overly optimistic from the very beginning. Producing even low-scale animated content and then distributing it online requires capital as well as a certain level of artistic talent and know-how, which is not available to the vast majority of social media users. Even though the internet was widely available in the Middle East and North Africa from the mid-1990s onwards, access had been largely limited to internet cafés for lower- to average-income citizens, which predestined the vast majority to the role of cultural consumers rather than of producers. Computer ownership and private access to the internet were the privilege of the middle- and upper-middle-class youth. Thus, at the time of the uprisings, developing homegrown Arabic multimedia content and using the internet for business purposes was mainly the prerogative of the middle and upper-middle classes, as was the revolutionary animation production, which was mainly pioneered by those who had established themselves as online animators well before the uprisings.

Technically, the local and transnational flow of creative content was facilitated by the proliferation of the internet and the increasingly easy access to computers and smartphones that enabled citizens to bypass traditional media hierarchies. Starting from the early and mid-2000s, countries like Jordan, Egypt, Syria and Tunisia became a home to bloggers and internet users distributing their creative work online (Cambie 2012). Websites and blogs became platforms for defying autocratic regimes and challenging official narratives (Khamis and Sisler 2010). However, these were not taken too seriously, as several governments and autocratic regimes encouraged internet proliferation as a means of boosting economic development. In fact, for a very long time, regimes had little to be afraid of: although the internet enabled content to be hosted on servers beyond the reach of state censors and afforded anonymity, the vast majority of locally based online artists and bloggers opted for self-censorship in order to avoid provoking the ire of the authorities responsible for monitoring their activities. The revolutionary climate of the Arab uprising tore down the walls of fear, if only temporarily. As the censorship boards in countries like Tunisia, Syria, Libya, Yemen and elsewhere began to loosen their grip, YouTube and social media quickly rose as the main platform for revolutionary artists and political activists to distribute their works and narratives.

In 2011 and 2012, independent online artistic projects and initiatives mushroomed, bringing people together, amplifying their voices, and spreading their messages and revolutionary identities beyond national borders. Although demonstrators in Tunisia, Egypt, Libya, Syria and other countries involved in the Arab Spring embraced different ideologies, they put their differences aside, particularly in the early days of the Arab uprisings, which gave protesters a sense of collective action and a feeling that all factions of society were in agreement (Barber and Youniss 2013: 68). This sense of belonging, coupled with a collective opposition to the governments, conforms to Günther Schlee's concept of 'conflict identities', which he uses in the context of an open war between two (mostly) different people (Schlee 2004). In this chapter, I adapt this concept to a context where segments of the population identify themselves as being opposed to the regime and develop a kind of collective self-understanding, solidarity or 'groupness'.[1] Like wars, revolutions are conflict situations with a strong potential to make or break existing alliances and patterns of identification they follow, facilitating a distinction between those who are willing to embrace the emerging identity and those who are not. Such situations are often accompanied by prompt and schematic identity discourses, emerging in the form of slogans and revolutionary art, among other things. The Arab Spring's transnational slogan '*al-Sha'b yureed isqat al-nizam*' (The people want the fall of the regime) itself stresses a collective will and identity of all those who oppose the regimes, regardless of their social status or political affiliations. Such revolutionary identities are essentially temporary given the prompt shifts in participants' considerations regarding costs and benefits followed by renewed politics of inclusion and exclusion – and they are a product of a historical momentum when people, united by a common goal, put their differences to one side in order to face a regime that they all regard as their enemy. Certainly, revolutionaries are often self-styled, and the term 'revolutionary' itself is loaded and controversial. Therefore, in the following chapter I will use the word in its widest sense, considering the fact that the Arab uprisings found different expressions depending on time and location.

From an art production perspective, this revolutionary identity had a generational dimension. The art and animation of the Arab uprisings often referenced intellectual and cultural tropes, symbolism and experiences shared by young people across the region, which enabled them to imagine their relationship to the world differently. The wide use of humour in videos, graffiti and other formats highlights a generational struggle in which young artists deconstructed myths and redefined identities outside their parents' 'regimes of truth' (Elsayed 2016: 5120). Revolutionary Arab and national identities did not seek pride and unity in an imagined glorious past, but rather in a generally critical attitude towards social and political hierarchies. Particularly in the case of online humorous Arab content, this identity was often also redefined along class lines, where secular artists and comedians utilised Western cultural references as a way of reaching out to like-minded working- and middle-class people.

Many of the animators of the uprisings displayed a confrontational, no-holds-barred, high-stakes, high-risk and potentially high-rewards gambit. Their creative labour entailed the convergence of expression, production and revolution, and much of it remained unrecognised, but occasionally also reflected a commercial and political co-optation of revolutionary creative labour (Kraidy 2016b).

Similarly to other oppositional social media content, a number of online animations of the Arab uprisings bypassed the boundaries between old and new media, and were received with acclaim by transnational channels such as BBC, Al Jazeera, Al Arabiyya and others. In this respect, they participated in the consolidation of a 'synchronization of new social media and satellite media' (Aouragh and Alexander 2011: 1351). Kraidy notes that similarly to satellite television a few decades earlier, the entry of the internet into the tightly policed Arab world enabled a 'transfer' of political and social relations into a 'potentially subversive space created by various interacting [online and offline] media and information technologies' (2006: 2). However, this shift in media did not occur in a power vacuum. Writing about the Egyptian scene, Sakr notes that

> business elites set parameters for television, while international firms intervened over content on YouTube, Facebook, and mobile phones. In other words, offline–online media interaction was constrained by the way hierar-

chies in offline power relations shaped the points of access to hypermedia space. (Sakr 2013a: 334)

Dynamics of this type were also apparent in the development of the online animation scene of the Arab uprisings and beyond. This chapter analyses how the political turmoil of the Arab uprisings provided a unique major event for young animation producers who were not part of traditional media elites to articulate oppositional identities and gain recognition, and how they kept operating after the uprisings.

Kharabeesh: Revolutionaries from a Country of No Revolution

Jordan's internet scene had proliferated since the mid-2000s. Engaging in media and cultural production, however, remained the privilege of the middle classes and above, who had the necessary resources to invest in hardware and private internet access, and the time to spend on creative production.

Kharabeesh, a small company dedicated to the online distribution of creative content, was founded in Amman in 2008 by five young upper-middle-class Jordanians: Mohammad Asfour, Wael Attili, Wafa Nabulsi, Firas Otaibi and Shaher Otaibi, as part of ThinkArabia, a conglomerate of six small-scale digital media companies (Tarawnah 2011). Kharabeesh CEO Wael Attili already had experience in online branding and also ran a blog dedicated mainly to non-political social commentary. This blog provided the first platform for Attili's sketchy Flash-animated spots.

As online platforms for professional video distribution were rarely available at the time, Kharabeesh partnered up with Zain, one of Jordan's largest mobile companies, to distribute animated content via MMS and Mobile Aggregator.[2] Soon, the first series of Kharabeesh's Flash animation, *Khatt Ahmar* (Red Line), was released, featuring two rough, poorly drawn characters arguing over social and even political issues. With a primarily Jordanian audience in mind, *Khatt Ahmar* articulated a national identity, indicated by locally relevant topics and the use of Jordanian dialect. Despite its bold title, the spots took care not to cross the 'red lines' of Jordanian public discourse; they revolved around relatively safe topics, already widely discussed in Jordanian media, such as the issue of corruption in general and the politics of the United States in the Arab world.

In 2009 and 2010, in cooperation with Zain, Kharabeesh released a number of locally relevant animated projects. These included *Ehsebha Sahh* (Count it Well), a religious educational series with the aim of spreading moderate notions of Islam in line with the government's religious policies, *Hawwa'* (Eve), exploring the role of women in Jordanian society, and *Hazzaz* (Shaker), a series of animated adaptations of folkloric Jordanian jokes. Although the approach of these productions to politics, society, religion and identity conformed to Jordan's official discourse, Kharabeesh did not abandon politics and did not limit itself to mediating national identities.

One of the most political among the series of that time was *Kharabeet Alf Layla wa Layla* (Scribbles of the Thousand and One Nights) that placed the characters of *The Arabian Nights* into the modern Arab world. The episodes involved mild political and social criticism by indirect references to the overall issue of the state's attitude towards the people. By drawing from pan-Arab literature and building on the experiences of Arabs irrespective of their homeland as well as using *fusha* Arabic, the show claimed a transnational Arab identity. In one episode, the sultan is challenged by protesters gathering around his castle. After rejecting the plans of his advisers to dispel them by spreading rumours about bird flu or by using force, the problem resolves itself when the soccer match between Barcelona and Real Madrid starts, and the protesters rush off to the cafés to watch it. This infantilisation of the people largely reflects the opinion of the upper-middle-class creators regarding the lower classes' priorities and engagement in politics. However, they were soon to be proven wrong.

This regionally exceptional portfolio in animation production helped Kharabeesh to sign a contract with Google's Dubai office in 2010 to produce short educational animated cartoons called *Google Ahlan*, the aim of which was to teach Arab audiences how to use Google as part of a campaign to expand Google's business in the Arab world.[3] This project led Kharabeesh to the next level, as it signed a partnership deal with YouTube which, like its parent company, Google, aimed to expand its profile in the Middle East by distributing original content by local producers.

In less than a year, Kharabeesh established a profile in producing one- to four-minute online distributed animation spots of both local and regional relevance. Most of the projects during this period were driven by the creative input of Omar al-'Abdallat, a cartoonist who in 2010 merged his own creative company, 'Ala Ra'si (founded in 2007), with Kharabeesh. Al-'Abdallat's flagship production, *'Ala Ra'si* (Anything For You), was a satirical animation show of more than 100 one- to three-minute episodes revolving around the characters of a thin, poorly educated Jordanian man called 'Awad and his strong, but dull friend, both living in Al-Zarqa', a lower-class suburb of Amman. The characters portrayed young people of their age and class, whom middle-class Jordanians perceived as being ignorant of social affairs and as wasting their time by watching television, gossiping and listening to music. In this respect, the show followed in the footsteps of *Abu Mahjoub*, in the sense of stereotypically representing a Jordanian social class and age group and making it the focus of mockery. In contrast, *Al-Shaikh Khaffash* (The Bat Sheikh, 2010), another al-'Abdallat production, claimed a regional identity, with the declared aim of enabling Kharabeesh to gain a foothold in the media markets of the Gulf countries.[4] This goal is underscored by the characters speaking a Jordanian Bedouin dialect, while wearing clothes resembling the garments of the Bedouins of the Gulf. According to the narrative, Khaffash differs from the other Bedouin sheikhs by travelling to New York to study and then returning to take up his position as a clan elder in his tribe. The episodes show how he struggles with the clash between American cultural values and traditional Bedouin society. *Khaffash* fulfilled its mission to expand Kaharabeesh's viewership in Saudi Arabia; still, the real breakthrough to international fame required a historical momentum.

The Golden Opportunity of the Arab Spring

The expansion of Kharabeesh was also facilitated by technological trends. By 2010, affordable smartphones and increasingly cheap access to the internet was heralding a change in Middle Eastern media consumption. Between June 2010 and June 2012, the number of Arab Facebook users tripled, and from June 2010, YouTube views and uploads in countries such as Jordan, Saudi Arabia and Egypt rose by up to 240 per cent (Dubai School of Government 2013).

As a pioneering for-profit online company in Jordan, Kharabeesh became a hub for young Jordanian creative individuals. In early 2010, Bechir Omran, a Tunisian student in Amman, joined the team and Omar later became head of Kharabeesh's Tunisian office.

When protesters took to the streets of Tunisia, and then Egypt and Libya, demanding change, Kharabeesh was able to reflect on the events quickly, and was in a strong position to become a regular distributor of animated commentaries on the Arab uprisings. On 19 January 2011, immediately after Tunisian President Ben Ali had fled the country, Kharabeesh released a three-minute satirical animation on YouTube and other social media channels. The show, called *Youmiyyat Zayn al-Abedine Ben 'Ali* (Everyday Stories of Zayn al-Abedine Ben Ali) imitated the visual style of JibJab, an American online satirical show that used a simple cut-out animation style combining photographs, vector graphics and computer-generated animation to make the characters move. This technique enabled Kharabeesh to reduce both production costs and time, offering satirical commentaries on actual political events within less than a week. Provocative dialogues compensated for the low visual quality. In a 2012 interview, Wael Attili explained how this simple quality was intended to democratise creativity, making production available to the widest possible audience (Alrimawi 2013). While such sentiments fit perfectly into the enthusiastic revolutionary narrative of the democratisation of the public voice via new means of communication, this proved to be overly optimistic.

Figure 6.1 *Youmiyyat Zayn al-Abedine Ben 'Ali* (Everyday Stories of Zayn al-Abedine Ben 'Ali): JibJab meets the Arab Spring. 2011 © Kharabeesh.

The popular acclaim of *Youmiyyat Zayn al-Abedine Ben 'Ali* inspired Kharabeesh to produce similar pieces mocking two other struggling leaders: Hosni Mubarak of Egypt and Muammar al-Qaddafi of Libya. When I met them in their Amman office in February 2014, Wafa Nabulsi and animator Saleh Habbab told me that they hesitated to comment on powerful political figures while they were still in office, fearing official backlash. As Mubarak resigned on 11 February 2012, and an international coalition declared war on al-Qaddafi in the same month, mocking them became safe.

Kharabeesh released several spots framing the uprising as a pan-Arab rather than a national phenomenon, hence articulating a transnational Arab revolutionary identity. For example, the one-minute black-and-white animation *Rabee' al-'Arabiyy al- Shu'oob* (The Spring of Arabic Nations) begins with a flower growing and blossoming to the tune of a well-known patriotic Palestinian song. Suddenly, the foot of a policeman who is wearing an Egyptian-looking uniform and heavy boots stomps on the flower that symbolises the revolution. Soon, a new flower pops up through his boots and countless other flowers grow and blossom around him. These videos did not take pride in an imagined past, nor did they present optimistic visions of the future, as their goal was to reflect on the current events by releasing fast-produced animated commentaries. This approach became widespread for revolutionary animations of other countries too.

Though Kharabeesh's creativity was confrontational, it was relatively low-risk. The edgy spots caught the attention of international channels like CNN, France24, ABC News and Al Jazeera, and in November 2011 Kharabeesh received its first angel investment from Mena Venture Investments (MVI) and DASH Ventures, enabling the team to increase production. In 2013 the company signed a contract with MBC Ventures, the capital arm of the Saudi MBC media group, to participate in the synchronisation of new media and satellite media.

From Revolutionaries to Businessmen

By 2013, the enthusiasm of the Arab Spring had been replaced with disillusion. On 3 July, as a response to the popular protests, a military coup ousted Egyptian president Mohammed al-Mursi from office, and military strongman 'Abdel Fattah el-Sisi pushed forward an autocratic restoration.

Post-Qaddafi Libya fell apart, while the once-peaceful Syrian uprising turned into a full-scale civil war.

As a result, Jordan's revolutionary climate also faded. The series of demonstrations that started in Amman and other major cities in January 2011 over unemployment, inflation and corruption were defused when King Abdullah sacked three ministers and called for early elections in 2013. Simultaneously, the unrest in neighbouring Syria and the influx of Syrian refugees pushed public opinion to treasure peace and established Jordan's self-image as an island of stability. Although barely affected by the unrest, the regional political climate led to a chilling setback for freedom of expression in Jordan. As a reaction to the role it had played in the Arab uprisings, the media laws of 2011 brought online media, until then generally exempt from the 2007 Press Law, under the same regulations that applied to traditional outlets (Yom 2009; Human Rights Watch 2012). Very soon, online self-censorship became widespread.[5] As a general consequence, freedom of expression online took a plunge in 2014–15, when Jordan started cracking down on activists for their social media posts and closed some critical news websites for not obtaining a licence (Elsayed 2016: 5104).

During this time, Kharabeesh experienced significant growth, and evolved from a small venture into a professional, medium-sized online company.[6] The potential market also expanded, as the uprisings inspired popular online participation, and by 2013, there were 2.6 million Facebook users in Jordan, a country of 6.5 million (El-Rayyes 2014). This growth enabled Kharabeesh to gain revenue through online advertising (YouTube and Google ads), product placement, product experience, banner ads on its website, sponsorship of various events and, occasionally, selling content to traditional media outlets such as TV channels. Another major source of income was signing up with artists and individual animators, rebranding the creative content and then offering it to relevant advertisers.[7] Kharabeesh had expanded its portfolio to include live-action videos by mid-2012.[8] Very soon, it reached a peak in production, with approximately 300 short videos per month, and consolidated its regional position.[9] Shortly afterwards, Kharabeesh received investments from the Gulf and the United States, and signed sponsorship deals partnerships with a number of renowned Jordanian companies as well as with local branches of international giants like Samsung and Pepsi (Montauk 2014).

This success, however, came at the cost of direct political engagement. In a series of personal interviews, members of the Kharabeesh team recalled that the quick expansion increased the pressure to create a sustainable business model.[10] In late 2012, representatives of multinational companies operating in Arab countries discreetly warned them that remaining engaged in the political affairs of other countries could damage their potential business growth. Kharabeesh heeded the advice. From late 2012, the focus of their animated spots shifted from direct engagement towards social criticism and non-political humour.

One example of these less political shows was the new flagship live-action comedy show, *Female* (renamed *FemaleShow* in English-language contexts), featuring two young amateur actors, Rajae Qawas and Tima Shomali. The show revolved around the marital squabbles of an open-minded, middle-class couple. The show brought Rajae Qawas immense popularity, attracted several sponsors and inspired Kharabeesh to launch an animated series based on his character. The 3D comedy series *Rajae al-Ka'en al-Fada'eyy* (Rajae the Space Creature) recounts the daily life of a virtuous young man who rejects all socially accepted ways of gaining advantages such as paying bribes, which makes people think that he is some creature from outer space. By using the Jordanian dialect and drawing on the cityscape of Amman, the show expresses a national identity and simultaneously contains indirect social criticism.

Kharabeesh did not abandon politics completely. In early 2013, it released *Al-Za'eem* (The Leader), a series of one- to two-minute animated spots drawn and written by Omar al-'Abdallat centred on the stereotypical character of an Arab dictator, portrayed as a moustached man wearing a blue uniform. In a personal interview, al-'Abdallat claimed that with *Al-Za'eem*, he intended not only to mock dictators and the docility of the people but to criticise the overall concept of 'authority' by holding up a mirror to the pompous leaders who are admired despite their lack of significant achievements. One episode shows the leader making his way to the toilet, walking on a red carpet between two lines of uniformed soldiers. Once he finishes urinating, we hear the voice of a crowd celebrating, making the leader smile proudly. Thus, *al-Za'eem* remains fundamentally political, mocking familiar phenomena such as personality cults in the collective experience of Arab people who have lived under totalitarian regimes, hence mediating an all-Arab identity.

Figure 6.2 *Al-Za'eem* (The Leader): an archetype of every (Arab) dictator. 2013 © Omar al-'Abdallat.

A more overt political engagement can be noted in al-'Abdallat's 2014 project, a series of short animated videos of various visual styles, illustrating the poems of deceased and living Arab poets such as Hisham al-Akhras, Iraqi Ahmad Mattar and the Palestinian Mahmoud Darwish, known for their critical attitudes towards oppressive regimes. The poems were selected for their capacity to express the experiences of Arabs, regardless of their country, concerning oppression and social injustice, hence articulating an all-Arab identity. One example is *Kalb Waleena al- Mu'azzam* (Our Leader's Esteemed Dog) by Ahmed Matar: '*Our leader's esteemed dog / Bit me today and died / So the head of security / called me to my execution / When the autopsy proved / That the great leader's dog / had been poisoned.*' Another poem by Matar, *Al-Thowr wal-Hadheerah* (The Ox and the Barn) recounts how an ox that fled from the barn was ridiculed and despised by his fellow oxen who stayed behind, until the day came that the other creatures who had previously mocked him followed suit. While the first poem refers to the inequality before the law of the ruling elite and the people, the second criticises society for oppressing those who dare to think outside the box. As Omar al-'Abdallat told me in an interview, this shift from direct to indirect political engagement was intended to reduce the risk of hurting sensibilities.[11]

From 2013 on, Kharabeesh's explicit animated political statements were restricted to safe topics and safe targets. One of them was the Islamic State (mocked as *Daesh* in Arabic), a terrorist group despised by all political entities in the region. A two-minute short animation released in January 2014, *Kayfa tasnaʾ daʾeshiyy* (How to Make a *Daesh* Member) showed Islamic State terrorists as Lego figures, ridiculed as drug addicts of low intellect. Kharabeesh also produced several spots for the Jordanian BDS Movement that enjoyed consensus in Jordanian public discourse and was also backed by members of the political elite.[12]

As a general tendency, following its transformation from a politically provocative creative group into a media enterprise, Kharabeesh increasingly focused on cheap and quickly produced live-action shows; they abandoned their revolutionary identity and instead embraced national and regional identities, in line with the popular discourse in Jordan. In this process, a live-action show, *N2OComedy*, emerged as a flagship project, featuring young Saudi and Jordanian stand-up comedians addressing topics ranging from parent-child relationships, peer relations, relationships between the sexes, education, psychology and social habits.[13] Another show, *Mashrooʾ Haqeeqah* (Reality Project), supervised by Wael Attili, was launched in 2014, dealing with issues relating to regional politics from a young Jordanian middle-class perspective. The programme focused on safe topics such as American stereotypes about Arabs and criticism of the lack of Arab solidarity. One episode even featured an interview with Prince Hamzah bin Hussein, son of King Hussein, as a symbol of Kharabeesh's consolidation in the mainstream Jordanian media, and moving into the region's new online markets.

Captain Baguette of Tunis

On 18 January 2012, an AFP photographer shot a photo on Tunis's Habib Bourguiba Avenue. It shows a lone man defying anti-riot police with a baguette held like a machine gun. The image went viral, striking a deep chord in the country's popular culture. For many, the baguette evoked memories of the bread riots of 1984 (News24 2011).

The image inspired five young communications professionals who used the pseudonyms of Baker 1, Baker 2, Baker 3, Baker 4 and Baker 5 and adapted the idea into animation. In early February 2012, *Captain Khobza* (Captain Baguette) debuted on YouTube and social media. The revolutionary

Figure 6.3 *Al-Khubz al-Siyasiyy* (The Political Bread): animated Tunisian democracy. 2011 © Atelier 216.

superhero character fights against oppression with a French baguette in his hands, a cigarette dangling from his lips, wearing a traditional fez, a Zorro mask, a red Superman cape and the Arabic letter *kh* on his chest. The first video, *Ektob Dusturan* (Write a Constitution) was made up of a photograph montage and hand-drawn images animated by Flash. The accompanying song served as an introduction to the concept of Captain Khobza – initially presented in the form of animated photographs of a real person dressed as a superhero – describing him as the defender of the homeland and someone who will 'correct everything that was corrupted by time'. In the coming days, a second video, *Hal Sahadtom Lissan?* (Did You See a Thief?) followed. This one was a JibJab-style animation, featuring cut-out images of politicians failing to escape with stolen goods, as Captain Khobza knocks their heads off with his baguette in front of Tunis's iconic Bab el Bahr monument.

Soon afterwards, the creators launched a web series called *Al-Khubz al-Siyasiyy* (The Political Bread). In the two- to four-minute spots animated by Flash and After Effects, Captain Khobza was turned into a fully animated, drawn character and met with high-profile politicians and other prominent individuals of public life in the post-Ben Ali era, such as former president Moncef Marzouki who had just returned from exile, Beji Caid Essebsi, founder of the Nidaa Tounes secularist political party, temporary president

Fouad Mebazaa and many others, who all sought Khobza's support to boost their political career. Still, nobody was safe from scorching satire. The mockery of politicians and previously respected public figures came as a breath of fresh air in a country where political humour had been oppressed for many decades.

The creators of *Captain Khobza* particularly faced the wrath of supporters of the Islamist Al-Nahda Party, following a sarcastic spot about their leader, Rached Ghannoushi. The controversial piece shows Captain Khobza smoking his cigarette as a white limousine draws up beside him. As the car slows down, Ghannoushi's head appears in the window and offers vast sums of money for political endorsement from Captain Khobza. Khobza refuses the offer and the limousine drives off, leaving Khobza shocked to see four women in black burqas dragged behind the car, tied to the vehicle by leashes. This spot was a strong criticism not only of Ghannoushi's conservative approach to religion, but also of his well-known ties to Saudi Arabia and the Gulf.

In a short time, *Captain Khobza*'s official Facebook page, called *Captain 5obza*, gained over 200,000 followers. As its reputation grew, the project faced a similar media-hybridisation to Kharabeesh, as local television channels embraced the spots and aired them in different programmes. This success emboldened the 'Bakers' to step out of the shadows and reveal their true identity: Atelier 216, a Tunis-based communications and production company established in 2007 by Mohamed Trabelsi and Mehdi Larguech. The creators explained that they had decided to reveal their identity after rumours began circulating on the web, accusing them of being secret supporters of the Ben Ali regime and trying to defame politicians of the democratic transition (Horizon Médiatique 2012).

Atelier 216's general rhetoric was very much in line with the enthusiastic atmosphere of post-revolutionary Tunisia. Unlike many of Kharabeesh's animations, *Captain Khobza* remained local, given its narrow focus on domestic affairs and the exclusive use of Tunisian Arabic.

While they were releasing new episodes of *Al-Khubz al-Siyasiyy*, the team of Atelier 216 were simultaneously busy working on a one-hour film, *Captain 5obza Le Film* (Captain Khobza, the Movie), which they released online in January 2012, on the first anniversary of the revolution. The story takes place in a future Tunisia, where the economy is flourishing, after the discovery that prickly pears (*al-hindi* in Arabic), a popular fruit in Tunisia, are an energy source that can replace oil. Soon, reports emerge that prickly pears have also been found on the Moon, which inspires the unity government made up of politicians and public figures of the post-revolutionary political scene, each of them called 'President', to claim the resources. After several failed attempts to launch a spaceship, they seek the help of Captain Khobza. Meanwhile, a group of former dictators try but fail in their scheme to lay their hands on the prickly pears on the Moon, which they see as their opportunity to make their way back into power. Soon, Captain Khobza discovers that although the 'Presidents' all claim to be committed to serving the country, they are secretly all conspiring with a foreign power, France, the US, Saudi Arabia, China or Russia, to hand over the national wealth. Khobza helps the presidents to reach the Moon, where they are dumbfounded to discover that what the reports referred to as *al-hindi* was not the precious fruit, but an Indian man (which in Arabic is also *al-hindi*). In the end, Khobza refuses to show them how to return to Earth, and the Tunisian people are finally rid of all corrupt politicians.

The changing post-revolutionary Tunisian media landscape offered other promising opportunities, as in 2011 and 2012, several private satellite channels were launched, hungry for exclusive, locally relevant content. In early 2012, the newly established Tunisia World Television (TWT) approached Atelier 216. Soon, a new series, *Khobzoulougia* (Breadology), was launched, providing weekly animated commentaries on the country's political events and mocking Tunisian public figures from the worlds of politics, business and sport, for example President Moncef Marzouki, the sports minister and soccer player Tarek Diab, and the billionaire president of the Free Patriotic Union Party Slim Riahi, among others. For Ramadan 2012, TWT ordered thirteen episodes of *Tartouriyyat* (Tartar Sauces). The show was a comical account of Moncef Marzouki's path to the presidency, with each of the ten-minute episodes showing how he tried and failed in professions such as policeman, fruit vendor, soccer referee, and so on before he finally reached the presidential chair.

The next year, Atelier 216 signed a deal with Tunisian TV for a series of thirty episodes, each six minutes long, for Ramadan. Based on the popular American TV show *Lost*, *Da'na* (We Are Lost) starts in Tunis with members of the post-revolutionary Tunisian political elite attempting to flee by plane to escape the wrath of the people. While the plane is in the air, they start arguing about the destination and end up crashing on a deserted island. The real plot starts at this point, showing how rival politicians struggle to work together and to make compromises in order to survive, something to which none of them is accustomed. Though the show was well-received, for unknown reasons Atelier 216 released only eleven episodes. This incomplete project also marked Atelier 216's departure from political humour in order to focus on commercial projects. Soon, the company stopped releasing animations, as it signed contracts with mobile company Orange and Coca Cola Tunisia, owned by the Société Frigorifique et Brasserie de Tunis, headed by Hamadi Bousbia, a local businessman with close ties to the country's liberal elite.

The Tahrir of Animation

Despite barriers such as illiteracy and poverty, and infrastructural constraints, the use of the internet in Egypt has been increasing since the mid-2000s, especially among young people aged between twenty and thirty (Khamis et al. 2012). By 2005, Egypt was home to an active blogosphere, opening a new arena for discussing a variety of issues and for expressing opinions and criticisms on cultural, social and religious topics (Radsch 2008). A few years before the 2011 uprising, a small but influential group of urban, highly educated, middle-class, primarily young Egyptian activists had already formed an array of loosely affiliated networks.

Ashraf Hamdi was part of this new online elite, as he had established himself as an online cartoonist well before the Arab uprisings, and then became involved in animation production in May 2010. The visual style of his first online-distributed animation, *Rafaheyyat al-Sha'b al-Misriyy* (Prosperity of the Egyptian People), was based on his familiar technique of creating cartoons of real people with sharp contours and vivid colours, his signature style. In the two-minute animation, Hamdi ridiculed a notorious public statement made by steel magnate Ahmad 'Ezz, who in one of his speeches turned a blind eye to the harsh economic conditions and extolled the 'luxury of the Egyptian people' (BBC 2012). The video features the animated character of 'Ezz, dubbed by Hamdi, as he gives a PowerPoint presentation to the press,

Figure 6.4 Egyptoon: animating a time of political enthusiasm. 2011 © Egyptoon.

showing a set of photographs of the pitiful Egyptian streets and presenting them as an illustration of the wellbeing of Egyptians. While the severe mockery of such an influential businessman might at first glance be regarded as daring, Hamdi did not risk too much. By the time *Rafaheyyat al-Sha'b al-Misriyy* was released, 'Ezz's shady business of driving up steel prices that led in turn to a rise in property prices was already being widely discussed in Egyptian national media, which made mocking him safe.[14]

A month later, Hamdi released a similarly edgy animation called *Maslahatak Awwalan* (Your Interest First) featuring Boutros Boutros-Ghali, former UN Secretary-General and liberal Egyptian politician. The two-minute animation is a reflection on the *Al-Dara'eb: Maslahatak Awwalan* (Taxes: In Your Best Interest) campaign in which Boutros-Ghali appeared to convince Egyptians of the importance of paying taxes. However, at least in the case of Hamdi, Boutros-Ghali failed to do so, as in the animation spot he is dressed in a karate outfit and shown beating up a man representing the average Egyptian hanging from a rope tied to the ceiling. As a reference to popular fighting videogames, each time Boutros Ghali hits the man, coins fall out of his body and the name of a different type of tax appears on the screen in blood red. At the end of the animation, Boutros Ghali is shown swimming in coins resembling the Disney character Scrooge McDuck.

By late January 2011, upheaval had erupted in Egypt and Kharabeesh approached online animator Ashraf Hamdi in search of regional production partners. Soon, Kharabeesh Egypt had been set up by Hamdi and two of his colleagues, Amira Mustafa and Mustafa Ashri, as the Egyptian branch of the Jordanian company. This cooperation provided Hamdi with an opportunity to benefit from the growing popularity and wide distribution of Kharabeesh, while Kharabeesh gained a foothold on the Egyptian market.

Immediately after Mubarak's resignation on 11 February 2011, the Egyptian military, which had temporarily sided with the revolution, formed the Supreme Council of the Armed Forces (SCAF) and took over executive authority from the presidency to oversee a democratic election process (Darwisheh 2014). SCAF's Constitutional Declaration guaranteed media freedom and banned administrative censorship (Articles 12 and 13), heralding an age of media freedom that had been unknown to the Egyptian public for decades (El-Issawi 2014). Hamdi and his crew released animated commentaries on the transitional period, criticising the old and the emerging political actors using Hamdi's signature visual style.

The first and primary target of their ridicule was former president Hosni Mubarak, who appeared in more than one spot, and never in a positive light. In February 2012, Kharabeesh Egypt released an animation based on the idea of the then popular mobile app *Angry Birds*, presenting Mubarak as the green pig king of the game, quivering with fear as the other pigs are smashed one after the other by the colourful birds.

Kharabeesh Egypt released a dozen short animated productions, poking fun at emerging political actors such as the interim government that was installed following the fall of Mubarak. Although reflecting on actual political issues, Hamdi vehemently denied any kind of political sympathies, claiming to mediate the voice of the people on the street (MBC Live 2013).

Kharabeesh Egypt played its part in the democratic process. In a spot released in March 2011, they showed a poor man complaining about his lack of rights and dignity. The poor man is beaten up by a rich man, who is in turn knocked out by a ballot box falling on his head at the end of the spot. In another spot released in late May 2011, a man is shown tied to a chair, gagged and tortured. Another man comes in, calling the first man by the name Fawzi, and preparing instruments of torture. As soon as the gag is removed, the man reveals that his name is not Fawzi. At the end of the spot, we see a sign: 'Fawzi is not your enemy, know your real enemy. No to religious division'. This was a response to the increased violence against Egypt's Coptic Christian minority by Muslim radicals.

Like many upper-middle-class Cairenes, Hamdi and his crew were sceptical about the democratic commitment of the Islamists in general, and the Muslim Brotherhood in particular, who emerged as the most organised political force of the scene. This mistrust is best reflected in the one-minute video Kharabeesh Egypt released in March 2011, showing a bearded Islamist jumping up and down on the letters of the Arabic word *Deemuqratiyya* (Democracy) towards a presidential chair which is placed on the last letter. As he reaches the presidential chair, sits down and makes himself comfortable, the letter *m* changes into an *n*, turning the word into *Deenuqratiyya* (Religiocracy).

Although Kharabeesh Egypt's critical stance towards the Islamists did not change after Mohammed Morsi was elected president in June 2012, the company became increasingly cautious. Hamdi and his crew shifted their focus onto seemingly new, non-political projects such as *Samak fi-Mayya* (Fish in Water). The series of four-minute animated spots launched in April 2013 recounts the adventures of a small fish, narrated by Hamdi, and his quarrel with bigger fish. One of the episodes shows the small red fish arguing with a more aggressive fish about who has the right over the other to live in the sea. At the end the camera zooms out, and we see that what the fish perceived as a sea is actually a tiny aquarium, watched over by a cat, preparing for her meal. In light of Egypt's developing politics, one can assume that the quarrelling fish represent the country's rival political factions, while the cat embodies its most powerful organisation, the army, which will eventually have the upper hand in political conflicts.

Indeed, on 3 July 2013, following anti-government street protests, Egyptian army chief General 'Abdel Fattah el-Sisi led a coalition to remove President Morsi from power and suspended the Egyptian constitution. July 2013 brought changes not only for Egypt, but also for Hamdi and his crew, as they separated from Kharabeesh and started their own enterprise, Egyptoon, focusing exclusively on the Egyptian political scene.[15]

While both Hamdi and the other members of Kharabeesh denied that politics was the reason for their split, it is obvious that from July 2013 on,

Karabeesh and Egyptoon animations took different paths: Kharabeesh moved away from direct political involvement, while Egyptoon continued to release animated commentaries on actual events, with animated spots indicating Hamdi's support of General Sisi's power grab. On 9 July 2013, Egyptoon came up with an animation mocking ousted president Morsi, shown as giving a speech in which he repeats the word *shar'eyya* ('legitimacy') as many times as he can within a sentence. In various spots, Egyptoon ridiculed R4bia, a social media movement that appeared after the Rabaa massacre in August 2013 that involved 800–900 deaths. In September 2013, *Obama bin Laden* showed the then American president with an Islamist beard, speaking in *fusha* Arabic, as he vowed to help ex-president Morsi to regain his chair. This mockery could hardly be regarded as daring, as it was in line with the new government's official discourse on fighting against international challenges of its legitimacy.

While clearly siding with 'Abdel Fattah el-Sisi, Hamdi and his crew remained aware of the deepening divides in Egyptian political life. In August, they released a video featuring an Islamist, whose identity is indicated by his beard and green tie, as he cheers a policeman beating up a liberal activist, calling him a criminal who deserves punishment. In the next scene, we see the same Islamist being beaten up by the policeman, while the liberal activist, a young shaven man with a peace emblem on his shirt, cheers the policeman and reviles the Islamist.

In a short animation released in January 2014, the president is shown giving a talk, continuously interrupted by an over-enthusiastic supporter. In another spot, released in November 2014, five months after el-Sisi had assumed presidential office, we see a mild criticism of el-Sisi as he gives a lecture in chemistry and, despite warnings, throws sodium into water, leading to an explosion. While President el-Sisi made occasional appearances in various other spots, his character was never ridiculed in the way Mubarak's and Morsi's were, and his authority remained unchallenged.

Egyptoon's soft approach to el-Sisi can be explained not only by Hamdi's personal sympathy, but also by the government's strengthening grip on the Egyptian media. The coup was followed by a crackdown on independent media, and finding a place for critical voices in established outlets became increasingly difficult ('Abdulla 2014). The government's application of the

State of Emergency Law and other penal codes, including 'insulting the president' or 'insulting religions', resulted in the intimidation of journalists, bloggers and broadcasters (Freedom House 2014). Many journalists and artists adopted self-censorship in their productions (El-Issawi 2014). Egyptoon stopped direct political engagement in 2014. In a phone interview, Hamdi told me that the decision to avoid politics was made after he received serious threats from 'different factions of the Egyptian political spectrum', as he put it.[16]

Ever since then, Hamdi has maintained a profile in freelance graphic services and making cartoons for various Egyptian newspapers and online portals, among them Masrawy, a private news web portal where he works as the editorial cartoonist.[17] Their flagship YouTube series, *Aymoun al-Magnoun* (Aymoun the Crazy), features an animated character sitting behind a desk and talking about a variety of personal and social issues, while carefully avoiding sensitive political topics. Hamdi's productions are among the most popular Egyptian animations of their kind, often reaching more than 1 million viewers.

Syrian Mockers in Exile

The decades-long political repression by the Assad regime, coupled with a tightly controlled media and online sphere, was not conducive either to the emergence of a local public sphere of opposition groups in Syria, or to any significant alternatives to Baathism (Khamis et al. 2012). This changed in March 2011, when the first demonstrators took to the streets of Damascus, and then to the city of Deraa in the south. The uprising unfolding across the country led to the emergence of a revolutionary identity aiming to unite Syrians through slogans, political posters, performances, songs, theatre and videos (Díaz 2016). The Syrian government's response was amongst the harshest in the region, as it brutally cracked down on opposition artists and activists. On 4 July 2011, Ibrahim Qashoush, a young man from the city of Hama, and author of the protest anthem *Yalla Erhal Ya Bashar* (Come on Bashar, Leave) was found dead with his throat cut and vocal cords ripped out. On 25 August, renowned political cartoonist 'Ali Farzat was attacked by masked gunmen and left with broken fingers as a warning for drawing cartoons critical of the president (Camps-Febrer 2012; Wedeen 2013). These atrocities pushed many artists, including renowned animators Mwaffaq Katt and Sulafa Hijazi, to flee the country. As the uprising unfolded, diaspora activism increased (Andén-Papadopoulos and Pantti 2013).

After the protest turned into an insurgence and the regime lost ground to different rebel factions, revolutionary clusters with their own media production emerged (Howard and Hussain 2011). One creative centre of revolutionary art that immediately attained international fame was Kafranbel, a small town in the province of Idlib. When the regime forces pulled out in the summer of 2012 and the Free Syrian Army took control in Kafranbel, a creative hub emerged, where civil activists started to create political videos and to design humorous banners, distributing them through online social networks (Ramírez 2013).

As the ground war intensified, a struggle to shape the narrative of the Syrian uprising emerged (Andén-Papadopoulos and Pantti 2013: 2188). Soon, the inclusive revolutionary identity faded, giving way to a clash of rivalling notions of identities. In addition to graffiti, cartoons, songs and other forms of self-expression, animation also emerged as a popular format in mediating new Syrian identities and utilising humour as a tool of resistance.

Kharabeesh was the first to release animated commentaries on the Syrian uprising. The revolutionary climate of 2011, the mass demonstrations across Syria, the mass desertions of army personnel and the strong foreign support of the revolutionaries created a general sense that the regime of Bashar al-Assad would face a similar fate to its counterparts in Egypt and Libya. Starting from May 2011, this assumption inspired Kharabeesh to release a number of short animated cartoons mocking the Syrian dictator. One of these early animations portrayed him as a weak, voiceless lion (a reference to his name, which means lion in Arabic) surrounded by hyenas resembling al-Assad's Iranian and Lebanese allies.

However, this critical attitude did not last long. Unlike many other Middle Eastern governments that pushed for a regime change in Damascus, Jordanian leaders took a neutral position from the early days of the uprising, declaring that the events were a Syrian domestic affair (Al-Weshah 2014). When the uprising turned into a full-scale armed conflict in the spring of 2012 and Syrian refugees started to pour into neighbouring countries, the Jordanian government and the public alike became increasingly concerned that the conflict would possibly spill across the borders. Kharabeesh stopped mocking the Syrian president and his regime, and began to focus on the less controversial, humanitarian side of the Syrian tragedy, such as the suffering of civilians in the war. An animation released in August 2012, *Qissa 'an Suriyyeen Ma' al-Nizaam wa Diddahu* (Story of Syrians For and Against the Regime), introduced two rival narratives of the uprising. The first part features a man of lowly background, who recalls how he was humiliated at school and abused while serving in the army, and then failed to find a good job. His miserable life experience led him to take part in the demonstrations on which the regime eventually cracked down. He therefore glorifies the rebels whom he regards as saviours of the people. The other side of the coin is presented by a man of privileged birth, provided with a good education and then a well-paid job. As a loyal supporter of the regime, he blames a foreign conspiracy for his country's troubles and expresses his support for the army cracking down on opponents. In this video, Kharabeesh presented both the pro- and anti-government positions as having equal legitimacy, refusing to take a stand. The human side of the conflict is highlighted even more in *Al-Tareeq al-Asfar li-Genefa 2* (The Yellow Road To Geneva 2), released in August 2013. The one-minute, Flash-animated, cut-out and hand-drawn montage shows the death and sorrow in the wake of the chemical attack in Damascus's Ghouta suburb earlier that month. The spot avoids blaming either the government or the opposition, focusing instead on the victims' suffering.[18]

While Kharabeesh became increasingly cautious, Syrian producers affiliated to publish their short revolutionary animations. This was an integral element of the creative uprising represented by hundreds of revolutionary social network accounts, many with a satirical profile, that were opened from late 2011 onwards. For security reasons, the majority of artists and activists, especially those operating within the country, remained anonymous.

One of the most popular projects in terms of the number of Facebook followers was *Al-Thawra al-Siniyya didd Taghiya al-Sin* (The Chinese Revolution against the Chinese Tyrant) that boasted 100,000 followers in less than a year. Launched in June 2011 by two young men using the pseudonyms Hazem and Songa, the page's main profile was to gather news items concerning Syrian politics and to provide funny commentaries on them.

Songa, who later also used the pseudonym Samir al-Mufti, comes from the city of Homs, one of the first strongholds of the 2011 uprising. After two of his brothers were killed, he fled to Turkey via Egypt with his family.

The WikiSham animation project was one of the creative projects loosely tied to *Al-Thawra al-Siniyya*. The producers, whose identities are not known, started to release a series of one- to two-minute biting cartoon animations called *Qasr al-Sha'b* (The Palace of the People) in August 2011. The title was a reference to the presidential palace overlooking Damascus. It featured President Assad, his brother Maher, the head of the Republican Guard and Bouthania Sha'ban, a presidential spokesman, as well as many others. Some episodes also included Lebanese Hezbollah leader Hasan Nasrallah, whose image also appeared on the wall of Assad's office on a superhero-style poster, Iranian president Mahmoud Ahmadinejad and Ali Khamenei, the Supreme Leader of Iran, who in one clip was shown hiding in a cave where he offers advice to client dictators on how to repress the Middle Eastern revolts. One episode even features Ban Ki-moon, the then UN Secretary-General, who visits Syria after the massacre of Jisr al-Shoghour (Karouny 2011). As the plane approaches, Assad panics and orders his brother Maher to clean up the blood and ruins. When Assad and Ban Ki-moon walk along the empty streets, the president is dismayed to see that bloodstains can still be seen on the wall and that a severed hand is lying on the pavement. Luckily, Maher manages to hide the evidence at the last minute. When the UN Secretary-General asks where the people are, Assad explains that all the inhabitants have gone off to visit their relatives in Turkey, an old tradition of the people of the city.

In interviews, Songa admitted to receiving donations from friends, but denied that any funding had come from political entities (al-Haj 2015). Although neither the *Al-Thawra al-Siniyya* project nor WikiSham was officially affiliated with any political faction, several episodes of *Qasr al-Sha'b* showed the logo of The International Campaign in Support of the Syrian People, a Turkish-led initiative in support of the Free Syrian Army (FSA), and the Istanbul-based opposition coalition, the Syrian National Council (SNC). *Al-Thawra al-Siniyya* has also been cooperating with Shaam News Network (SNN), a loose network of Syrian activists who work with contacts outside Syria to disseminate videos recording protests. Even though, according to the statement posted on its Facebook page, it is 'unaffiliated to any group or

Figure 6.5   *Qasr al-Sha'b* (The Palace of the People): animation with real stakes. 2011 © Wikisham.

party', it is often sympathetic to both the FSA and SNC.¹⁹ In general, both *Al-Thawra al-Siniyya* and WikiSham advocate a narrative – shared not only by the SNC, but also by the majority of opposition factions – that blames the Syrian regime for brutality, sectarianism and serving the regional interests of Iran. Linguistically, WikiSham articulates a Syrian identity, as the characters speak colloquial Syrian Arabic. The president and his people, however, are narrated with a strong Alawite dialect, an allusion to Assad's family belonging to the Shiite Muslim minority. By May 2013, the WikiSham team had released around forty short animations, but then stopped their activity for unknown reasons.

Two years later, in May 2015, Songa and three other young Syrians using the pseudonyms Hazem, Khaled and Youssef launched a creative group called Online for Media Production, releasing animations of WikiSham's successor, *Siyasa Noss Komm* (Half-Sleeve Politics) on Facebook and YouTube. *Siyasa Noss Komm* focuses on the character of President Assad, who, as narrated by Songa, is ridiculed for his physical appearance, juxtaposing what the character says and what is actually happening. The other main characters include political figures in the Syrian arena such Hezbollah Secretary-General Hasan Nasrallah, Syrian National Coalition head Khaled Khoja and Louay Hussein, head of the Building the Syrian State movement.

In an episode released in April 2017, Assad is infuriated by Donald Trump calling him an animal for using chemical weapons against innocent people. Enraged, he calls his ally, President Putin, who calms him, explaining that the American president did not mean any harm, as Assad means 'lion', which is indeed an animal. Having regained his self-esteem, Assad sits back and watches a National Geographic documentary that shows videos of him, while the narrator speaks about donkeys.

Animation also became a popular format to mediate a revolutionary Syrian Islamist identity. The *Shazaya* (Shrapnel) project was released by a creative group called Backlight, located in the Ghouta suburb in the east of Damascus, a district that became a base of Jaysh al-Islam, one of the best-organised and strongest Islamist groups in the rebel camp (Bell 2014). According to the closing credits of *Shazaya*, which was the group's sole production, Backlight was operated by three young men, using pseudonyms. *Shazaya* is dubbed in a heavy Damascene accent, carrying a propaganda message for the inhabitants of eastern Ghoua to legitimise the presence of oppositional Islamist militias.

The four- to six-minute episodes are set in an unnamed rebel-held neighbourhood of Damascus enclosed by regime forces. The plots are almost entirely made up of the conversations between two characters: Abu Qasem, a middle-class man wearing a traditional dress called the *ghallabiyya*, vest and bandana, and a local militiaman, Abu Omar, whose Islamist identity is indicated by his facial hair – a beard but no moustache – and his self-identification as a mujahed. The plots mainly revolve around the harsh living conditions of the besieged neighbourhood, advocating the importance of solidarity between civilians and militants. Abu Qasem is often portrayed as a selfish, ignorant man who is lectured by Abu Omar in a friendly manner about his duties towards society, framed in an Islamic way.

One episode shows Abu Omar holding bags of food supplies he has received from the rebel command. When Abu Qasem enviously questions him about why the militants receive better supplies than the civilians, Abu Omar patiently explains that this is no more than compensation for their risking their lives for the good of their people. He then tells Abu Qasem that civilians too are entitled to aid. At the end of the episode, we see Abu Qasem bottling and selling the petrol he received as aid at cut-throat prices and he is lectured by Abu Omar about the immorality of his deed. The episode ends with a black screen and a quote from the Prophet Muhammad: 'He who prepares a Ghazi [Jihadist] going in Allah's cause is (given a reward equal to that of) Ghazi', providing a religious legitimacy for the episode's message.

Syrian revolutionary animators proved to be less lucky than their colleagues in other countries. While many Jordanian, Tunisian and even Egyptian authors turned their fame into profit, or at least maintained their production on a more modest level after a shift to politically less sensitive issues, very few of the animators in Syria consolidated their position because of the continuing turmoil. Meanwhile, the majority have given up animation production, keeping their identities hidden to the public.

Conclusion

During the Arab uprisings, national and transnational flows of creative content, including animation, challenged the cultural status quo of the Middle East and North Africa, and became a tool for political engagement and the mediation of revolutionary identities. While revolutionary discourse is usually full of promises of the future, these animations did not mention the future, as their primary goal was to comment on day-to-day issues and events.

Even though the Arab Spring turned into winter as hopes of democracy faded, many buds of the Arab animation spring turned into blossoming flowers. In Jordan, Kharabeesh consolidated its position by creating a new business model, and synchronising and hybridising with mainstream media. In Egypt, Ashraf Hamdi's Egyptoon worked out a sustainable business model by profiting from online advertisements placed alongside its socially critical animation content. In Tunisia, Atelier 216 turned its fame into profit by exchanging the political images of Captain Khobza for well-paying commercials for renowned companies. Meanwhile, as Syria descended into civil war, revolutionary animators within the country and in exile faced different fates, many giving up revolutionary activity as they struggled to make ends meet.

Although the changing political scene put an end to revolutionary animation production in the Middle East, forcing producers to embrace self-censorship, the genie was out of the bottle. Easy access to computers and animation software on the producers' side, and laptops, tablets and smartphones on the consumers' side, enabled creative individuals and groups from all over the Arab world to publish their short animation projects online. Emboldened by the example of the early revolutionaries, numerous projects emerged. In June 2011 Riyadh-based Myrkott Animation Studio launched *Masameer* (Screws), a YouTube comedy series touching upon sensitive domestic and regional issues, like sexual harassment, the indifference of citizens to social matters and more. Not much later, despite the chaos that followed the toppling of President Abdullah Saleh in February 2012, followed by a war with the Houthi rebels, Yemen, a country that had never before engaged in animation production, became home to *Hadramtoun*, a project comprising sharp-tongued sitcom animations distributed online, rich in references to the social characteristics of the Hadramout region.

Ultimately, the 'democratisation' of Arab animation has not taken place since the creation and distribution of online animation content largely remains the privilege of well-educated members of the middle and upper-middle classes with access to technological tools, production know-how and sufficient capital to create a sustainable business model, or at least to fund their hobby. Still, the occasional fresh, humorous animated voices that are re-emerging offer tiny specks of hope and relief for societies struggling with conflict and fragmentation.

Notes

1. A similar approach was taken by Díaz (2016).
2. In 1994, Zain (formerly Fastlink) was the first telecommunications company to introduce mobile services in Jordan.
3. In early 2010, Google launched a Middle East-focused online campaign called *Ahlan* to educate the public about the internet, with a focus on Google's internet products.
4. Personal interview with Omar al-'Abdallat (Amman, 8 February 2016).
5. In January 2011, Orange, Jordan's main telecommunications company, blocked a satirical blog that criticised the Jordanian regime without a formal blocking order. Orange's decision to do this was not backed by an official government request.
6. Kharabeesh's staff of five in 2008 grew to around thirty-five in 2013, while the number of total viewers increased from 1 million per month in 2011 to a total of 23 million in 2013.
7. Personal interview with Wafa Nabulsi (Amman, 6 February 2016).

8. The increased focus on live-action content could be also explained by Omar al-'Abdallat, the producer of many animations, leaving the Kharabeesh team.
9. The breakdown of Kharabeesh's audience is as follows: 27 per cent from the Gulf, 27 per cent from the Levant, 25 per cent from North Africa, 4 per cent from the United States and 8 per cent from Europe.
10. Personal interview with Wafa Nabulsi (Amman, 6 February 2016).
11. Personal interview with Omar al-'Abdallat (Amman, 8 February 2016).
12. BDS (Boycott, Divestment, Sanctions) is a Palestinian-led global campaign, established in 2005, whose goal is to increase economic and political pressure on Israel to end what it describes as violations of international law.
13. In January 2015, N2OComedy had over 550,000 subscribers and over 96 million views.
14. His story was later covered in an episode of the renowned sitcom animation, *Bsant wa Dyasty* (Chapter 3, n. 30).
15. Telephone interview with Ashraf Hamdi (1 March 2016).
16. Telephone interview with Ashraf Hamdi (28 February 2016).
17. Masrawy is an Arabic Egyptian web-based news portal that covers a wide range of news, including political, economic, artistic and technology-related news. It was founded in 1999 by Ehab Heikal, Gamal Selim and Wael Salah, and is currently owned by LinkOnLine, an online media company and subsidiary of OTventures.
18. The Ghouta chemical attack of 21 August 2013 was the deadliest use of chemical weapons since the Iran–Iraq War, with an estimated death toll ranging from at least 281 people to 1,729.
19. Sham News Network was established by a group of Syrian activists in March 2011.

7

Epilogue: Can Arab Animation Go Global?

In May 1976, for the very first time in its seven-decade history, Arab filmmaking experienced a global moment. *Al-Risalah* (The Message), a historical epic about the life of the Prophet Muhammad, debuted in New York, and was then screened in cinemas across the United States and Europe. Syrian-American director Moustapha Akkad became the first Arab filmmaker to create a cinematic production that transcended the national and geolinguistic borders of the Arab world, reaching out to an audience that otherwise shared little cultural understanding with Arabs and Muslims. The global moment faded quickly. Ever since then, with a few exceptions, the distribution of Arab cultural and media productions has largely remained within the geolinguistic boundaries of the Arab and Muslim world.

At present, Arab animated cartoons are also little known beyond the Arab and Muslim world. Like Arab film in general, Arab animation was also born of the desire of local elites to create an alternative to the one-way flow of foreign productions. By adopting a Western format and using Western technology since the 1930s, Arab producers – operating within local political and media hierarchies and dependent on local and regional financial sources – have been successful in mediating and negotiating rivalling notions of national, pan-Arab and Islamic identities. On their own turf, Arab animated cartoons even fulfilled their producers' ambitions to counter the assumed cultural imperialism of foreign productions, and consolidated their position as 'local champions'.

Meanwhile, despite the tremendous growth that Arab animated cartoon production has experienced since the mid-1990s, only a few studios and production companies have reached beyond the borders of the Arab world. Even when they do, their global outreach has been largely restricted to international festivals, Muslim markets and immigrant communities of the West, who share some basic religious or cultural identities with the producers.

The absence from the global scene can in part be attributed to the producers' deliberate aim of articulating an 'own' identity through the text. True enough, some Arab animation producers claim a universal, humanist, or even global identity for their productions. Still, most productions are predestined not to reach a wider global audience, as producers tend to set their sights on the primary audience and articulate an 'own' identity through visuals, language and narrative, which is hard for outsiders to decode.

Despite 'Disney's menu for global hierarchy' (Artz 2005) that continued to maintain its hegemony well into the first decade of the twenty-first century, national animation still has the potential to go global. Japanese anime's worldwide popularity is also a counter-Disney phenomenon that moves beyond national and cultural borders through viewer engagement (Napier 2007: 150). As Iwanbuchi noted, when creating their globally distributed animations, Japanese media industries use 'hybridism' as one of the strategies to repackage American media products for the Asian market while simultaneously creating 'culturally odourless' products that are easily consumed in America (Iwabuchi 2002). By now, Japanese anime has articulated transnational subcultures that are seen as a 'strong grassroots activity' in the counter-Disney vein (Napier 2007: 150).

Considering anime's success outside Japan, notions of dividing the global animation scene into a centre and periphery may be outdated (Annett 2011). Still, the gates are not wide open, and anime's strategies towards a global presence are not entirely applicable to Arab animation. Unlike anime, Arab animation is far too heterogeneous in style, visual practices and narrative as well as too small in volume to articulate a core for a transnational subculture.

Global trends might offer opportunities for Arab animation. In 2016, a full four decades after Arab filmmaking became the subject of a global

Figure E.1 *Bilal*: an Arab animation going global. 2015 © Barajoun Entertainment.

phenomenon with the release of *Al-Risalah*, Arab animation's moment finally arrived. *Bilal*, a 113-minute Saudi-Emirati film was premiered in Cannes.¹ The film was created in a Pixar style, and was produced by Saudi national Ayman Jamal, who set up the Barajoun studio in Dubai solely for the *Bilal* project, with the goal of reaching a global audience. The $30 million budget film production was sponsored by private equity investors in the Gulf as well as by the Doha Film Institute, and was produced by a crew of over 327 people of twenty-four nationalities.

The plot is loosely based on the life of Bilal ibn Rabah, an Ethiopian slave in pre-Islamic Mecca who became Islam's first muezzin and a close adviser to the Prophet Muhammad. Despite these historical references, Ayman Jamal, who co-directed the film with Khurram H. Alavi, consistently denies *Bilal*'s religious identity. Pointing to the fact that not a single word refers to Islam in the movie, he claims that the story is a universal one, recounting Bilal's journey from slave to free man (Vivarelli 2015). In interviews, Ayman Jamal has argued that, in his eyes, Bilal is not a Muslim hero, but a universal one, representing values such as love for the family and freedom (McMahon 2016).

The story takes us to the sixth-century Abyssinian desert, the home of Bilal, a seven-year-old boy living with his mother and his little sister

Ghufaira. Bilal's childhood is destroyed when marauders kill his mother. The raiders take the children to Mecca, where they are enslaved by the evil idol seller 'Umayya Ibn Khalaf and his son Safwan. Haunted by nightmares and plagued by doubts, Bilal is determined to be free. To reach this goal, he struggles to cast off the inner chains of anger and fear. After years of captivity, Bilal, now an adult, meets a renowned warrior, Hamza, who shares with him the words of wisdom that no man was born a slave.[2] Under Hamza's spiritual guidance, Bilal is able to regain his dignity. By using the leitmotif of a leaf unfurling in the desert, the film suggests that life can spring anew and flourish even after apparent devastation. After being bought from his owner and set free, Bilal joins the forces of Mohamed – who is not explicitly named – and fulfils his dream of becoming a great warrior in an epic battle between good and evil.

Bilal is stripped of religious identities and contains barely any decipherable national characteristics. Visually, it does not articulate a unique style, but instead aims for a realistic representation of both environments and characters. *Bilal*'s representation of both Ethiopians and Arabs strives for realism, and it is the evil and comical characters who are caricatured. In its representation of racial characteristics, *Bilal*'s striving for globalness clearly differs from many anime creators' technique of erasing ethnic characteristics as a key to the global market (Iwabuchi 2002: 28). Bilal and his family members resemble Ethiopians, with their large, dark eyes and dark skin, while the Arab characters have lighter brown skin and dark eyes and hair, similar to people of the Arabian peninsula.

The dialogues are simple, and despite the philosophical content and the issues addressed, Bilal essentially remains light-hearted as it is consistently cut with comic relief from the supporting characters.

The potential of *Bilal* to reach an audience beyond the Arab and Islamic world is partly attributed to the fact that the hero's historical character is also known in the United States' African-American community, for whom Bilal, a freed African slave who becomes a famous warrior, is of great symbolical value (Curtis 2005). In 2013, African-American actor Will Smith visited the Barajoun studio, directing American attention to the project (Levine 2015). It was also Will Smith who suggested that the story's hero should have an African accent and proposed Nigerian-British actor Adewale Akinnuoye-

Agbaje for the voice of adult Bilal. In order to find the best voices, Ayman Jamal signed with an American casting agency, which suggested British actor Ian McShane, for the voice of 'Umayya Ibn Khalaf, the evil Arab trader. Thus, in *Bilal*, a dramatic British accent is also an indicator of evilness, in line with similarly evil characters like Disney's Scar in *The Lion King* and Jaffar in *Aladdin* (Wenke 2008; Fattal 2018). The Arabic version of *Bilal* was dubbed in non-accented *fusha*, and it was also translated into Turkish, Russian, French, Chinese and Urdu.

Operating in a transnational space and primarily targeting a global audience, Ayman Jamal stressed the universal value of the production. Therefore he did not turn to religious authorities for advice when preparing the script (Hia Magazine 2016). Indeed, in the English, French and Russian versions, *Bilal* only obliquely mentions the Prophet Muhammad (and usually as references to 'this man' or 'the noble man'), instead emphasising the socially just origins of the Prophet's message. The opening titles, too, highlight the universal aspect by indicating 'humanity's struggle for freedom and equality' along with the line 'inspired by a true story'. The Arabic, Turkish and Urdu versions of the film, however, targeting a niche market, articulate a definite Islamic identity: The dubbing includes explicit mentions of the name Mohamed, direct references to Islam and even prayer scenes. The call to prayer (*adhan*) at the end of the film (cut from the English, French and Russian versions) finally overrides the universal humanist identity in favour of an Islamic one.

Bilal received mainly positive reviews. In 2016 it was officially selected at the Annecy International Animated Film Festival under Best Feature Film, and was nominated for the Asia Pacific Screen Awards, after winning the 'Best Inspiring Movie' award in Animation Day at the Cannes Festival in 2016 and the 'Best Innovative Movie' at the BroadCast Pro Middle East Awards.[3] However, unsurprisingly, the first success came in a Muslim country.

Yet it is hard to tell if *Bilal*'s *Al-Risalah* moment will break the ice for Arab animations, mediating global identities and globalising Arab and Islamic stories for a transnational audience. New means of distribution certainly offer Arab producers opportunities like never before. In 2020 Netflix signed a five-year exclusive partnership with Myrkott, a Riyadh-based studio and creator of *Masameer*, a popular YouTube series, to produce Saudi-focused animated shows for worldwide distribution.[4] It is clear that international collaborations, transfer of know-how and creative workers offer opportunities for Arab animation to circulate between cultures and nations, challenging the Disney model and telling stories of universal validity for a broader audience around the globe.

Notes

1. The film was first screened at the Ajyal Youth Film Festival in Doha, Qatar, on 9 November 2015, then premiered at the 12th Annual Dubai International Film Festival on 9 December 2015, before being released in cinemas across the Middle East.
2. This is probably a reference to Hamza, the uncle and one of the first followers of the Prophet Muhammad, since his identity is not revealed.
3. In Turkey, the premiere was attended by President Recep Tayyip Erdogan, who praised the film highly.
4. See https://english.alarabiya.net/en/News/gulf/2020/09/16/Netflix-signs-deal-with-Saudi-Arabia-animator-Myrkott-creator-of-Masameer-cartoons

Bibliography

Abbassi, Driss (2005) *Entre Hannibal et Bourguiba: identité tunisienne et histoire depuis l'indépendance*, Paris: Karthala-IREMAM.

'Abdulla, Rasha (2014) 'Egypt's Media in the Midst of Revolution', *Carnegie Endowment for International Peace*, July, http://carnegieendowment.org/files/egypt_media_revolution.pdf

Abu Amr, Ziad (1994) *Islamic Fundamentalism in the West Bank and Gaza*, Bloomington, IN: Indiana University Press

Abu-Lughod, Lila (1993) 'Finding a Place for Islam: Egyptian Television Serials and the National Interest', *Public Culture* 5.3, pp. 493–513.

Abu-Lughod, Lila (1995) 'The Objects of Soap Opera: Egyptian Television and the Cultural Politics of Modernity', in Daniel Miller (ed.), *Worlds Apart: Modernity Through the Prism of the Local*, London: Routledge, pp. 190–210.

Abu-Lughod, Lila (2005) *Dramas of Nationhood. The Politics of Television in Egypt*. Cairo: The American University in Cairo Press.

Abu-Lughod, Lila (2006) *Local Contexts of Islamism in Popular Media*, Amsterdam: Amsterdam University Press.

AFP (2013) 'High Hopes for Palestinian 3-D Animated Film The Scarecrow', 18 May, http://www.thenational.ae/arts-culture/film/high-hopes-for-palestinian-3-d-animated-film-the-scarecrow

Aksoy, Asu and Kevin Robins (2000) 'Thinking Across Spaces: Transnational Television from Turkey', *European Journal of Cultural Studies* 3.3, pp. 343–65.

Aksoy, Asu and Kevin Robins (2003) 'Banal Transnationalism: The Difference that

Telelevision Makes', in Karim H. Karim (ed.), *The Media of Diaspora*, London: Routledge, pp. 89–104.

ʿAli, Mohammad (2015) 'Tadsheen Musalsal "Badr" Lil-rusuum al-Mutaharrika ʿala Tilfizyoon "Jeem"', *Sharjah* 24, 8 October.

Alrimawi, Tariq (2013) 'The Arab Animation Spring: How Have Arab Animation Artists Used the Power of YouTube and Social Media in Response to the Recent Arab Revolution?', *CONFIA 2nd International Conference on Illustration and Animation, Porto, Portugal, December 2013*, pp. 303–16, https://www.uop.edu.jo/download/research/members/901_3179_T_Al.pdf

Alshaer, Atef (2012) 'Hamas Broadcasting: Al-Aqsa Channel in Gaza', in Khalid Hroub (ed.), *Religious Broadcasting in the Middle East*, London and New York: Hurst and Columbia University Press, pp. 237–61.

Amitai-Preiss, Reuven (1995) *Mongols and Mamluks: The Mamluk-Ilkhanid War, 1260–1281*, Cambridge: Cambridge University Press.

Amos, Deborah (2010) 'Confusion, Contradiction and Irony: The Iraqi Media in 2010', Joan Shorenstien Center on the Press, Politics and Public Policy Discussion Paper Series D-58, John F. Kennedy School of Government, Harvard University, https://dash.harvard.edu/handle/1/4421401

Andén-Papadopoulos, Kari and Mervi Pantti (2013) 'The Media Work of Syrian Diaspora Activists: Brokering Between the Protest and Mainstream Media', *International Journal of Communication* 7.22, pp. 2185–206.

Anderson, Benedict (1991) *Imagined Communities: Reflections on the Origin and Spread of Nationalism*, London: Verso.

Annett, Sandra (2011) 'Imagining Transcultural Fandom: Animation and Global Media Communities', *Transcultural Studies* 2, pp. 164–88.

Aouragh, Miriyam and Anne Alexander (2011) 'The Egyptian Experience: Sense and Nonsense of the Internet Revolution', *International Journal of Communication* 5, pp. 1344–58.

Arabian Business (2012), 'Best of 2012: Rubicon Group interview', 21 October, https://www.arabianbusiness.com/best-of-2012-rubicon-group-interview-476827.html

Al-Arabiya (2008) 'Sudaniyyoun Ghadeboun min "Super Henedy" li Wasfihim ʿal-Shaʿb Al Mutakhallif' Mukhrij al-ʿamal Qaddam Eʿtizar', 8 October, http://www.alarabiya.net/articles/2008/10/08/57896.html

Al-Arabiya News (2012) 'Egypt Steel Magnate Ahmed Ezz Sentenced for 7 Years, Fined $3 Bln', 4 October, http://english.alarabiya.net/articles/2012/10/04/241798.html (web page expired).

Armbrust, Walter (2000) 'The Golden Age Before the Golden Age: Commercial Egyptian Cinema Before the 1960s', in Walter Armbrust (ed.), *Mass Mediations: New Approaches to Popular Culture in the Middle East and Beyond*, Berkeley, CA: University of California Press.

Armbrust, Walter (2002) 'Islamists in Egyptian Cinema', *American Anthropologist*, New Series, 104.3, pp. 922–31.

Armbrust, Walter (2006) 'Synchronizing Watches: The State, the Consumer, and Sacred Time in Ramadan Television', in Birgit Meyer and Annalies Moors (eds), *Religion, Media, and the Public Sphere*, Bloomington, IN: Indiana University Press, pp. 207–26.

Artz, Lee (2002) 'Animating Hierarchy: Disney and the Globalization of Capitalism', *Global Media Journal*, http://www.globalmediajournal.com/open-access/animating-hierarchy-disney-and-the-globalization-of-capitalism.php?aid=35055

Artz, Lee (2004) 'The Righteousness of Self-Centred Royals: The World According to Disney Animation', *Critical Arts: A Journal of South-North Cultural and Media Studies* 18.1, pp. 116–46.

Artz, Lee (2005) 'Monarchs, Monsters, and Multiculturalism: Disney's Menu for Global Hierarchy', in Mike Budd and Max H. Kirsch (eds), *Rethinking Disney: Private Control, Public Dimensions*, Middletown, CN: Wesleyan University Press, pp. 75–98.

Al-Ashraf, Hassan (2010) 'Kuwait Channel Apologizes for Animated Series', *Al Arabiya News*, 22 August, http://www.alarabiya.net/articles/2010/08/22/117298.html

Aziz Sahar F. (2017) 'De-Securitizing Counterterrorism in the Sinai Peninsula', *Policy Briefing, Brookings Institution*, April, https://www.brookings.edu/wp-content/uploads/2017/05/de-securitizing-counterterrorism-in-the-sinai-peninsula_aziz_english.pdf

Baatout, Faisal and Christian Chaise (2005) 'Al-Jazeera Starts Kids Channel – with a Difference', *AFP*, 10 September, https://www.arabnews.com/node/272791

Bachy, Victor (1978) *Le Cinéma de Tunisie*, Tunis: Societe Tunisienne de Diffusion.

Baldwin, Derek (2010) 'Freej Creator Partners with Cartoon Network', *gulfnews.com*, 22 July, http://gulfnews.com/business/features/freej-creator-partners-with-cartoon-network-1.657482

Al-Bannay, 'Abd al-Muhsin (2009) *Jadeeduna al-Musalsal al-Kartouniyy « Ahmad wa Kan'aan »*, 25 December, http://www.alqabas.com.kw/node/562436

Barber, Brian K. and James Youniss (2013) 'Egyptian Youth Make History: Forging a Revolutionary Identity Amid Brutality', *Harvard International Review* 34.4, pp. 68–72.

Barraclough, Steven (1998) 'Al-Azhar: Between the Government and the Islamists', *The Middle East Journal* 52.2, pp. 236–49.

Bashkin, Orit (2011) 'Hybrid Nationalisms: Waṭanī and Qawmī Visions in Iraq under ʿAbd al-Karim Qasim, 1958–61', *International Journal of Middle East Studies* 43.2, pp. 293–312.

Batkin, Jane (2017) *Identity in Animation: a Journey into Self, Difference, Culture and the Body*. New York: Taylor & Francis.

Bátora, Jozef (2006) 'Public Diplomacy Between Home and Abroad: Norway and Canada', *Hague Journal of Diplomacy* 1, p. 55.

Bátora, Jozef and Frank Van de Craen (2006) 'Public Diplomacy Between Home and Abroad: Norway and Canada', *The Hague Journal of Diplomacy* 1.1, pp. 53–349.

Al-Bayan (2008) '"Sha'beyyat al Kartoun 3" Tunaqishu Qadaya Ijtima'iyya Muta'addidat al Thaqafaat Wal-lahajat Nylyfat Kumydyat', *al-bayan*, 3 September, http://www.albayan.ae/five-senses/1220107098507-2008-09-03-1.671680

BBC (1999) 'Malaysia Bans Spielberg's Prince', 27 January, http://news.bbc.co.uk/2/hi/entertainment/263905.stm

BBC (2009a) 'Why I Based Superheroes on Islam', 2 July, http://news.bbc.co.uk/2/hi/8127699.stm

BBC (2009b) 'Egypt-Algeria World Cup Anger Turns Violent in Cairo', 20 November, http://news.bbc.co.uk/2/hi/8369983.stm

BBC (2012) 'Egyptian Steel Magnate Ahmed Ezz Convicted', 4 October, https://www.bbc.com/news/world-middle-east-19830922

BBC (2013) 'Gaza Firm Produces First Palestinian 3D Animated Film', 12 January, http://www.bbc.com/news/world-middle-east-20993135

Beinin, Joel (1998) *The Dispersion of Egyptian Jewry: Culture, Politics and the Formation of a Modern Diaspora*, Berkeley, CA: University of California Press.

Belkhyr, Souad (2012) 'Disney Animation: Global Diffusion and Local Appropriation of Culture', *International Journal of Human Sciences* 9.2: 704–14.

Bell, Theodore (2014) 'Increased Rebel Unity Threatens Assad in Damascus and Southern Syria', *Institute for the Study of War*, 28 October, http://www.understandingwar.org/sites/default/files/Theo_Damascus_Backgrounder.pdf

Bendazzi, Giannalberto (1995) *Cartoons: One Hundred Years of Cinema Animation*, Bloomington, IN: Indiana University Press.

Bendazzi, Giannalberto (2015) *Animation: A World History: Volume II: The Birth of a Style – The Three Markets*, Boca Raton, FL: CRC Press.

Bengio, Ofra (1998) *Saddam's World. Political Discourse in Iraq*, Oxford: Oxford University Press.

Bennington, Geoffrey (1990) 'Postal Politics and the Institution of the Nation', in Homi K. Bhabha (ed.), *Nation and Narration*, London: Methuen, pp. 121–37.

Bhabha, Homi K. (1990) 'Introduction: Narrating the Nation', in Homi K. Bhabha (ed.), *Nation and Narration*, London: Routledge, pp. 1–8.

Bhabha, Homi K. (1994) *The Location of Culture*, New York: Routledge.

Bladd, Joanne (2010), 'Cartoon Network Set to Launch Free Arabic channel', *Arabian Business*, 4 July, http://www.arabianbusiness.com/cartoon-network-set-launch-free-arabic-channel-304175.html

Boëx, Cécile (2011) 'The End of the State Monopoly over Culture: Toward the Commodification of Cultural and Artistic Production', *Middle East Critique*, 20.2, pp. 139–55.

Booker, M. Keith (2006) *Drawn to Television: Prime-time Animation from The Flintstones to Family Guy*, Westport, CN: Praeger.

Boyd, Douglas A. (1999) *Broadcasting in the Arab World*, Aimes, IA: Iowa State University Press.

Brahimi, Denise (1997) *Cinemas d'Afrique francophone et du Maghreb*, Paris: Nathan.

Branche, Raphaëlle (2011) 'The Martyr's Torch: Memory and Power in Algeria', *The Journal of North African Studies* 16.3, pp. 431–43.

Brockelmann, Carl (1978) 'Kalila wa-Dimna', *The Encyclopaedia of Islam* 2, pp. 503–6.

Byrne, Eileen (2011) 'Maghreb's New TV Stations Face Commercial Realities', *Financial Times*, 21 November, http://www.ft.com/intl/cms/s/0/fa52562e-1414-11e1-b07b-00144feabdc0.html#axzz3RMJs6gLo

Cambie, Silvia (2012) 'Lessons from the Front Line: The Arab Spring Demonstrated the Power of People and Social Media', *Communication World* 29.1, pp. 28–32.

Camps-Febrer, Blanca (2012) 'Political Humor as a Confrontational Tool against the Syrian Regime; A Study Case: Syria, 15th March 2011–15th May 2012', https://papers.ssrn.com/sol3/papers.cfm?abstract_id=2205200

Chaker, Mohammad Naim (2003) 'The Impact of Globalization on Cultural Industries in United Arab Emirates', *Journal of American Academy of Business* 3.1–2, pp. 323–6.

Chalaby, Jean K. (2005) *Transnational Television Worldwide*, London: I. B. Tauris.

Charif, Maher (2000) *Rihanat al-nahda fi' l-fikr al-ʿarabi*, Damascus: Dar al-Mada.

Charter of the Gulf Cooperation Council (GCC) (1981), 25 May, https://www.gcc-sg.org/en-us/AboutGCC/Pages/Primarylaw.aspx

Cherian, Vijaya (2007) 'Jordan's Rubicon to Co-produce Pink Panther', *arabianbusiness.com*, 2 July, http://www.arabianbusiness.com/jordan-s-rubicon-co-produce-pink-panther-201200.html

Collins, Jim (1992) 'Postmodernism and Television', in Robert C Allen (ed.), *Channels of Discourse, Reassembled*, Chapel Hill: University of North Carolina Press, pp. 327–353.

Contadini, Anna (2007) *Arab Painting: Text and Image in Illustrated Arabic Manuscripts*, Leiden: Brill.

Costello, Matthew J. (2009) *Secret Identity Crisis: Comic Books and the Unmasking of Cold War America*, New York and London: Continuum.

Crafton, Donald (2012) *Shadow of a Mouse: Performance, Belief, and World-Making in Animation*. Berkeley, CA: University of California Press.

Curtis, Edward E. IV (2005) 'African-American Islamization Reconsidered: Black History Narratives and Muslim Identity', *Journal of the American Academy of Religion* 73.3: 659–84.

Darwisheh, Housam (2014) 'Trajectories and Outcomes of the "Arab Spring": Comparing Tunisia, Egypt, Libya and Syria', *Institute of Developing Economies, Japan External Trade Organization (JETRO)* 456, http://www.ide.go.jp/English/Publish/Download/Dp/456.html

Dasqupta, Samir (2004) 'Globalization, Altruism, and Sociology of Humanity', in Samir Dasqupta (ed.), *The Changing Face of Globalization*, New Delhi: Sage Publications, pp. 125–50.

Deeb, Mary-Jane (2012) 'The 99: Superhero Comic Books from the Arab World', *Comparative Studies of South Asia, Africa and the Middle East* 32.2, pp. 391–407.

De Swaan, Abram (1991) 'Notes on the Merging Global Language System: Regional, National, and Supranational', *Media, Culture and Society* 13: 309–23.

Díaz, Naomí Ramírez (2016) 'Against All Odds: Defining a Revolutionary Identity in Syria', *Mediated Identities and New Journalism in the Arab World*, Basingstoke: Palgrave Macmillan, pp. 83–99.

Dick, Marlin (2005) 'The State of the Musalsal: Arab Television Drama and Comedy and the Politics of the Satellite Era', *Transnational Broadcasting Studies* 15, pp. 1–19.

Dittmer, Jason (2014) 'Towards New (Graphic) Narratives of Europe', *International Journal of Cultural Policy* 20.2, pp. 119–38.

Djeflat, 'Abdelkader (2009) 'Building Knowledge Economies for Job Creation, Increased Competitiveness, and Balanced Development: Individual Country Overviews', *Worldbank Report* 42, https://tinyurl.com/ybstakbb

Dobrow, Julia R. and Calvin L. Gidney (1998) 'The Good, the Bad, and the Foreign:

The Use of Dialect in Children's Animated Television', *Annals of the American Academy of Political and Social Science* 557.1, pp. 105–19.

Dobson, Nichola (2003) 'Nitpicking The Simpsons: Critique and Continuity in Constructed Realities', *Animation Journal* 11, pp. 84–93.

Douglas, Allen and Fedwa Malti-Douglas (1994) *Arab Comic Strips: Politics of an Emerging Mass Culture.* Bloomington, IN: Indiana University Press.

Dubai Press Club (2010) *Arab Media Outlook 2009–2013,* Dubai: Dubai Press Club, http://fas.org/irp/eprint/arabmedia.pdf

Dubai School of Government (2013), 'The Arab World Online: Trends in Internet Usage in the Arab Region', Arab Social Media Report 2.1, https://www.arabsocialmediareport.com/News/description.aspx?NewsID=11

Edwardson, Ryan (2003) 'The Many Lives of Captain Canuck: Nationalism, Culture, and the Creation of a Canadian Comic Book Superhero', *The Journal of Popular Culture* 37.2, pp. 184–201.

Elsayed, Yomna (2016) 'Laughing Through Change: Subversive Humor in Online Videos of Arab Youth', *International Journal of Communication* 10, pp. 5102–22.

Elseewi, Tarik Ahmed (2011) 'The Arab Spring: A Revolution of the Imagination', *International Journal of Communication* 5, p. 1198–206.

Elsheshtawy, Yasser (2010) *Dubai: Behind an Urban Spectacle,* New York: Routledge.

Engle, Gary (1987) 'What Makes Superman So Darned American?' in Dennis Dooley and Gary Engle (eds), *Superman at Fifty,* New York: Collier, pp. 80–3.

Erdle, Steffen (2010) *Ben Ali's 'New Tunisia' (1987–2009): a Case Study of Authoritarian Modernization in the Arab World,* Berlin: Klaus Schwarz.

Eskandar, Rashed and Kamal al-Mallah (1962) *Khamsuna Sana Min al-Fann,* Cairo: Dar al-Maarefa bi-Misr.

Farouk-Sluglett, Marion and Peter Sluglett (2001) *Iraq Since 1958: From Revolution to Dictatorship,* London: I. B. Tauris.

Fattal, Isabel (2018) 'Why Do Cartoon Villains Speak in Foreign Accents?', *The Atlantic,* 4 January, www.theatlantic.com/education/archive/2018/01/why-do-cartoon-villains-speak-in-foreign-accents/549527

Findlow, Sally (2000) *The United Arab Emirates: Nationalism and Arab Islamic Identity,* Abu Dhabi: ECSSR.

Fingeroth, Danny (2007) *Disguised as Clark Kent: Jews, Comics, and the Creation of the Superhero,* New York: Continuum.

Foucault, Michel (1975) 'Film and Popular Memory: an Interview with Michel Foucault', *Radical Philosophy* 11, pp. 24–9.

Freedom House (2014) 'Press Freedom in 2013: Media Freedom Hits Decade Low', https://freedomhouse.org/sites/default/files/FOTP_2014.pdf

Fuccaro, Nelida (2005) 'Mapping the Transnational Community: Persians and the Space of the City in Bahrain, c. 1869–1937', in Madawi al-Rasheed (ed.), *Transnational Connections and the Arab Gulf*, New York: Routledge, pp. 29–58.

Galal, Ehab (2017) 'Domestication and Commodification of "the Other" on Children's TV', in Tarik Sabry, Naomi Sakr and Jeanette Steemers (eds), *Children's Television and Digital Media in the Arab World*, London: I. B. Tauris, pp. 163–81.

Gall, Carlotta (2014) 'Tunisian Discontent Reflected in Protests That Have Idled Mines', *The New York Times*, 13 May, https://www.nytimes.com/2014/05/14/world/africa/tunisian-discontent-reflected-in-protests-that-have-idled-mines.html

Gelvin, James (1999) 'Modernity and Its Discontents: On the Durability of Nationalism in the Arab Middle East', *Nations and Nationalisms* 5.1, pp. 71–89.

Ghabra, Shafeeq (1997), 'Kuwait and the Dynamics of Socio-economic Change', *The Middle East Journal* 51.3, pp. 358–72.

Ghaibeh, Lina and George Khoury (2017) 'Cultivating an Arthouse Viewership: Lebanese Animation Audiences Grow Up', in Stefanie Van de Peer (ed.), *Animation in the Middle East: Practice and Aesthetics from Baghdad to Casablanca*, London: I. B. Tauris.

Al-Ghazzi, Omar (2018) 'Grendizer Leaves for Sweden', *Middle East Journal of Culture and Communication* 11.1, pp. 52–71.

Giroux, Henry A. and Grace Pollock (2010) *The Mouse that Roared: Disney and the End of Innocence*, Plymouth: Rowman & Littlefield.

Gournelos, Ted (2009) *Popular Culture and the Future of Politics: Cultural Studies and the Tao of South Park*, Lanham, MD: Lexington Books, pp. 20–9.

Gray, Jonathan (2006) *Watching with The Simpsons: Television, Parody, and Intertextuality*, New York: Routledge.

Gruber, Christiane (2009) 'Between Logos (*kalima*) and Light (*nūr*): Representations of the Prophet Muhammad in Islamic Painting', *Muqarnas* 26, pp. 229–62.

Gulf Information and Research Centre (1983) *The GCC*, London: n.p.

Haeri, Niloofar (2000) 'Form and Ideology: Arabic Sociolinguistics and Beyond', *Annual Review of Anthropology* 29, pp. 61–87.

Haeri, Niloofar (2003) *Sacred Language, Ordinary People: Dilemmas of Culture and Politics in Egypt*, New York: Palgrave Macmillan.

al-Haj, Mustafa (2015) 'Syrian Online Satirical Show Gains Popularity', *al-Monitor*,

10 August, www.al-monitor.com/pulse/originals/2015/08/syria-opposition-satirical-online-series.html

Al-Harthy, Nasser (2010) 'Saladin Premiere a Major Hit', *The Peninsula*, 19 September, http://www.thepeninsulaqatar.com/qatar/126630-saladin-premiere-a-major-hit.html (web page expired).

Haugbølle, Rikke Hostrup and Francesco Cavatorta (2012) '"Vive la grande famille des médias tunisiens". Media reform, authoritarian resilience and societal responses in Tunisia', *The Journal of North African Studies* 17.1, pp. 97–112.

Havens, Timothy (2006) *Global Television Marketplace*, London: British Film Institute.

Heard-Bey, Frauke (2001) 'The Tribal Society of the UAE and its Traditional Economy', in Ibrahim Al Abed and Peter Hellyer (eds), *United Arab Emirates: a New Perspective*, London: Trident, pp. 98–116.

Hia Magazine (2016), Interview with Ayman Jamal, 27 November, https://www.youtube.com/watch?v=TmPRCzIC3gU

Higson, Andrew (2005) 'The Limiting Imagination of National Cinema', in Mette Hjort and Scott Mackenzie (eds), *Cinema and Nation*, London and New York: Taylor and Francis, pp. 63–74.

Hijazi, Sulafa (2012) 'al-Hawiyya al-mahalliyya fil-rusuum al-mutaharrika al-dramiyya', unpublished paper.

Hitti, Philip Khuri (1956) *History of the Arabs: From the Earliest Times to the Present*, London: Macmillan.

Holm, Ulla (2005) 'Algeria: President Bouteflika's Second Term', *Mediterranean Politics* 10.1, pp. 117–22.

Holt, Peter Malcolm, Ann Lambton and Bernard Lewis (1977) 'The Central Islamic Lands from Pre-Islamic Times to the First World War', *The Cambridge History of Islam, Vol. 1A*, Cambridge: Cambridge University Press.

Horizon Médiatique (2012) *Captain 5obza: de Facebook à la célébrité*, 4 February, https://horizonsmediatiquesmondearabe.wordpress.com/2012/02/04/captain-5obza-de-facebook-a-la-celebrite

Hoskins, Colin and Rolf Mirus (1988) 'Reasons for the US Dominance of the International Trade in Television Programmes', *Media, Culture and Society* 10: 499–515.

Hourani, George F. (1956) 'The Principal Subject of Ibn Tufayl's Hayy Ibn Yaqzan', *The Journal of Near Eastern Studies* 15.1, pp. 40–6.

Howard, Philip N. and Muzammil M. Hussain (2011) 'The Role of Digital Media', *Journal of Democracy* 22.3, pp. 35–48.

Hoy, Norman Emberson (1969) 'Report on Mission in Iraq, December 26th 1968 to February 24', *UNESDOC Digital Library*, http://unesdoc.unesco.org/images/0015/001582/158205eb.pdf

Human Rights Watch (2012) 'Jordan: A Move to Censor Online Expression', 10 September, https://www.hrw.org/news/2012/09/10/jordan-move-censor-online-expression

Hunebelle, Guy (1980) 'Introduction aux cinémas du Maghreb', *Ciném'Action*, special issue, 67, n. 3.

Hurriez, Sayyid Hamid (2002) *Folklore and Folklife in the United Arab Emirates*, London: Routledge Curzon.

Hutcheon, Linda (2006) *A Theory of Adaptation*, New York: Routledge.

Inge, Thomas M. (2004) 'Walt Disney's Snow White and the Seven Dwarfs: Art Adaptation and Ideology', *Journal of Popular Film and Television* 32.3: 132–42.

Isakhan, Benjamin (2009) 'Manufacturing Consent in Iraq: Interference in the Post-Saddam Media Sector', *International Journal of Contemporary Iraqi Studies* 3.1, pp. 7–25.

Ismail, Salwa (1999) 'Religious "orthodoxy" as public morality: The state, Islamism and cultural politics in Egypt', *Critique: Critical Middle Eastern Studies* 8.14, pp. 25–47.

El-Issawi, Fatima (2014) 'Egyptian Media under Transition: in the Name of the Regime . . . in the Name of the People?', *POLIS – Media and Communications London School of Economics 'Arab Revolutions: MediaRevolutions' Project*, http://eprints.lse.ac.uk/59868/

ITP (2005) 'Al Jazeera Children's Channel Goes on Air', 2 October, http://www.itp.net/484287-al-jazeera-childrens-channel-goes-on-air

Iwabuchi, Kochi (2002) *Recentering Globalization: Popular Culture and Japanese Transnationalism*, Durham, NC: Duke University Press.

Jamal, Amal (2000) 'The Palestinian Media: An Obedient Servant or a Vanguard of Democracy?', *Journal of Palestine Studies* 29.3, pp. 45–59.

Jaseen, Amjad (2006) 'Ibn al-Ghaba fi Sitt Duwal Khaleejiyyah', *Elaph*, 6 September, www.elaph.com/ElaphLiterature/2004/9/8388.htm

Al Jazeera (2006) 'Ibn al-Ghaba fi Bath Oula wa Hasriyy 'ala al-Jazeera lil-Atfal', 31 August, https://tinyurl.com/y8wx8a8m

Jensen, Eric (2012) 'Mediating Social Change in Authoritarian and Democratic States – Irony, Hybridity, and Corporate Censorship', in Brady Wagoner, Eric Jensen and Julian A. Oldmeadow (eds), *Culture and Social Change: Transforming*

Society Through the Power of Ideas, Charlotte, NC: Information Age Publishing, pp. 212–17.

Karouny, Mariam (2011) 'Syria to Send in Army After 120 Troops Killed', *Reuters*, 6 June, https://ca.reuters.com/article/topNews/idCATRE7553AI20110606

Kaylani, Nabil (1972) 'The Rise of the Syrian Ba'th, 1940–1958: Political Success, Party Failure', *International Journal of Middle East Studies* 3.1, pp. 3–23.

Kchir-Bendana, Kmar (2003) 'Ideologies of the Nation in Tunisian Cinema', *The Journal of North African Studies* 8.1, pp. 35–42.

Khalaf, Sulayman (2002) 'An Anthropological Look at Dubai Heritage Village', *Journal of Social Affairs* 19.75, pp. 13–42.

Khalaf, Sulayman (2006) 'The Evolution of the Gulf City Type, Oil and Globalization', in John Fox, Nada Mourtada-Sabbah and Mohammed al-Mutawa (eds), *Globalization and the Gulf*, London: Routledge, pp. 244–65.

Khalaf, Sulayman and Saad Alkobaisi (1999) 'Migrants' Strategies of Coping and Patterns of Accommodation in the Oil-Rich Gulf Societies: Evidence from the UAE', *British Journal of Middle Eastern Studies* 26.2, pp. 271–98.

Al-Khalidi, Ashraf, Sophia Hoffmann and Victor Tanner (2007) 'Iraqi Refugees in the Syrian Arab Republic: A Field-Based Snapshot', *Brookings Institution-University of Bern Project on Internal Displacement*, https://www.brookings.edu/research/iraqi-refugees-in-the-syrian-arab-republic-a-field-based-snapshot/

Khalifa, Aisha Bilkhair (2006) 'Spirit Possession and its Practices in Dubai', *International Journal of Ethnomusicological Studies* 1.2, pp. 43–64.

Khalil, Joe and Marwan Kraidy (2017) *Arab Television Industries*, London: Bloomsbury Publishing.

Khallaf, Rania (2000) 'A Token of Respect', *Al-Ahram Weekly* 463, 6–12 January.

Khamis, Sahar, Paul B. Gold and Katherine Vaughn (2012) 'Beyond Egypt's "Facebook Revolution" and Syria's "YouTube Uprising": Comparing Political Contexts, Actors and Communication Strategies', *Arab Media & Society* 15, http://www.arabmediasociety.com/index.php?article=791&printarticle

Khamis, Sahar and Vit Sisler (2010) 'The New Arab Cyberscape Redefining Boundaries and Reconstructing Public Spheres', *Annals of the International Communication Association* 34.1, pp. 277–315.

Khlifi, Omar (1970) *L'Histoire du cinéma en Tunisie*, Tunis: Societe Tunisienne de diffusion.

Kim, Hun Shik (2011) 'Redefining Press Freedom: A Survey of Iraqi Broadcasters in Political Transition and Conflict', *Journal of Broadcasting & Electronic Media* 55.4, pp. 431–47.

Kishtainy, Khalid (1985) *Arab Political Humor*, London: Quartet Books.
Kraidy, Marwan M. (1999) 'The Local, the Global and the Hybrid: A Native Ethnography of Glocalization', *Critical Studies in Media Communication* 16.4, pp. 456–77.
Kraidy, Marwan M. (2002) 'Arab Satellite Television Between Regionalization and Globalization', *Global Media Journal* 1.1, https://repository.upenn.edu/cgi/viewcontent.cgi?article=1192&context=asc_papers
Kraidy, Marwan M. (2005) *Hybridity, or the Cultural Logic of Globalization*, New Delhi: Temple University Press.
Kraidy, Marwan M. (2006) 'Hypermedia and Governance in Saudi Arabia', *First Monday*, https://www.firstmonday.dk/ojs/index.php/fm/article/view/1610/1525
Kraidy, Marwan M. (2016a) *The Naked Blogger of Cairo*, Cambridge, MA: Harvard University Press.
Kraidy, Marwan M. (2016b) 'Revolutionary Creative Labor', in Michael Curtin and Kevin Sanson (eds), *Precarious Creativity: Global Media, Local Labor*, Oakland, CA: University of California Press, pp. 231–40.
Krämer, Gudrun (1982) *Minderheit, Millet, Nation? Die Juden in Agypten 1914–1952*. Minderheiten Prolem im Islam 7, Wiesbaden: Verlag Otto Harrassowitz.
Kunkel, Dale and Bruce Watkins (1987) 'Evolution of Children's Television Regulatory Policy', *Journal of Broadcasting & Electronic Media* 31.4, pp. 367–89.
La Bourse égyptienne (1935) 'Mickey Mouse a un frère égyptien', 24 May.
La Bourse égyptienne (1936) 'Mish-Mish Effendi a fait ses débuts', 17 December.
Larson, Allen (2003) 'Re-drawing the Bottom Line', in Carol A. Stabile and Mark Harrison (eds), *Prime Time Animation: Television Animation and American Culture*, New York: Routledge, pp. 55–73.
Lawrence, Elizabeth A. (1986) 'In the Mick of Time: Reflections on Disney's Ageless Mouse', *The Journal of Popular Culture* 20.2: 65–72.
Lawson, Fred H. and Hasan M. al-Naboodah (2008) 'Heritage and Cultural Nationalism in the United Arab Emirates', in Alanoud Alsharekh and Robert Springborg (eds), *Popular Culture and Political Identity in the Arab Gulf States*, London: SAQI in association with London Middle East Institute SOAS, pp. 15–30.
Lee, Hye-Kyung (2010) 'Introduction: Animation Industries at a Crossroads', *Creative Industries Journal* 3, pp. 183–7.
Le Tallec, Camille (2011), 'En Tunisie, Captain Khobza garde la transition démocratique à l'œil', *La Croix*, 22 December, https://www.la-croix.com/Actualite/

Monde/En-Tunisie-Captain-Khobza-garde-la-transition-democratique-a-l-aeil-_NG_-2011-12-22-749961
Lybarger, Loren D. (2007) *Identity and Religion in Palestine: The Struggle between Islamism and Secularism in the Occupied Territories*. Princeton, NJ: Princeton University Press.
McDougall, James (2003) 'Myth and Counter-Myth: "The Berber" As National Signifier in Algerian Historiographies', *Radical History Review* 86.1, pp. 66–88.
McGlennon, David (2006) 'Building Research Capacity in the Gulf Cooperation Council Countries: Strategy, Funding and Engagement', Second International Colloquium on Research and Higher Education Policy 29, http://citeseerx.ist.psu.edu/viewdoc/download?doi=10.1.1.485.2284&rep=rep1&type=pdf
McGuire, Sara (2017) 'What Disney Villains Tell Us About Color Psychology', *Venngage*, 28 July, https://venngage.com/blog/disney-villains/
Macleod, Dianne Sachko (2003) 'The Politics of Vision: Disney, Aladdin, and the Gulf War', in Brenda Ayres (ed.), *The Emperor's Old Groove: Decolonizing Disney's Magic Kingdom*, New York: Peter Lang, pp. 179–92.
McMahon, Vanessa (2016) 'Interview with Ayman Jamal on Bilal', *filmfestivals.com*, 31 May, https://www.youtube.com/watch?v=Zjvf0FLsFAA
Maddy-Weitzman, Bruce (2011) *The Berber Identity Movement and the Challenge to North African States*, Austin, University of Texas Press.
Al-Mahadin, Salam (2003) 'Gender Representations and Stereotypes in Cartoons: a Jordanian Case Study', *Feminist Media Studies* 3.2, pp. 131–51.
Mango, Mutaz (2004) 'Art Imitates Life', *JO Magazine*, March, pp. 76–9.
Masmoudi, Mustapha (2006) 'The Arab Child and the Information Society', in Ulla Carlsson and Cecilia Von Feilitzen (eds), *In the Service of Young People Yearbook 2005/2006*, Gothenburg: Gothenburg University.
al-Masri, Hanada (2016) 'Jordanian Editorial Cartoons: A Multimodal Approach to the Cartoons of Emad Hajjaj', *Language & Communication* 50, pp. 45–58.
Matheson, Carl (2001) '*The Simpsons*, Hyper-irony, and the Meaning of Life', in William Irwin, Mark T. Conrad and Aeon J. Skolbe (eds), *The Simpsons and Philosophy: The D'oh! of Homer*, Chicago: Open Court, pp. 108–25.
Mayer, Vicki (2009) 'Bringing the Social Back In: Studies of Production Cultures and Social Theory', in Vicki Mayer, Miranda J. Banks and John T. Caldwell (eds), *Production Studies: Cultural Studies of Media Industries*, New York: Routledge, pp. 15–24.
MBC Live (2013) Interview with Ashraf Hamdi, 18 September, https://www.youtube.com/watch?v=BfhGxbf9m2Q

Menoret, Pascal (2014) *Joyriding in Riyadh: Oil, Urbanism, and Road Revolt*, Cambridge: Cambridge University Press.

Micaud, Charles Antoine (1964) *Tunisia: The Politics of Modernization*, New York: Praeger.

Miller, Toby, Nitin Govil, John McMurria and Richard Maxwell (2001) *Global Hollywood*, London: British Film Institute.

Al Mir'at (Mirror) Media Monitoring Network (2010) 'Balanced Media Coverage for Fair Voting: Media Monitoring during the Iraqi Parliamentary Elections in 2010 (Media Monitoring Period November 15, 2009–March 6, 2010)'.

Al-Mirsal (2016) 'Musalsal Khousa Bousa Yatasabbab fi Azma Bayna al-Misriyyeen wa al-Imaratiyyeen', 22 August, https://www.almrsal.com/post/373193

Mittell, Jason (2001a) 'Cartoon Realism: Genre Mixing and the Cultural Life of The Simpsons', *Velvet Light Trap* 47, pp. 15–28.

Mittell, Jason (2001b) 'A Cultural Approach to Television Genre Theory', *Cinema Journal* 40.3, pp. 3–24.

Montauk, Iliana (2014) 'Kharabeesh's Path to Scale: How a Jordanian New Media Production and Distribution Company Harnessed the Arab Digital Renaissance', *Wamda*, static.wamda.com/web/uploads/resources/wamda_kharabeesh.pdf (web page expired).

Moran, Albert (1998) *Copycat Television: Globalisation, Program Formats and Cultural Identity*, Luton: University of Luton Press.

Moran, Albert (2009) *TV Formats Worldwide: Localizing Global Programs*, Chicago: Intellect books, 2009.

Moore, Clement Henry (1988) 'Tunisia and Bourguibisme: Twenty Years of Crisis', *Third World Quarterly* 10, pp. 176–90.

Mourtada-Sabbah, Nada, Mohamed al-Mutawa, John W. Fox and Tim Walters (2008) 'Media as Social Matrix in the United Arab Emirates', in Alanoud Alsharekh and Robert Springborg (eds), *Popular Culture and Political Identity in the Arab Gulf States*, London: SAQI in association with London Middle East Institute SOAS, pp. 121–42.

Mujtaba, Syed Ali (2008) '"The 99" – A World Class Brand with Muslim Values', *Dinar Standard*, 28 May, http://mujtabas-musings.blogspot.com/2008/06/99-comic-books-world-class-brand.html

Murray, Christopher (2011) *Champions of the Oppressed: Superhero Comics, Popular Culture, and Propaganda in America during World War Two*, New York: Hampton Press.

Mutaharrika, Humoum (2007) 'Tajreba Filastiniyya Jadeeda fi Intag al Rusum al

Mutaharrika', Reuters, 22 March, http://www.elaph.com/ElaphWeb/Politics/2007/3/220707.htm

Al-Musawi, Muhsin Jassim (2003) *The Postcolonial Arabic Novel: Debating Ambivalence*, Leiden and Boston: Brill.

Al-Mutawa, Naif (2010) 'Superheroes Inspired by Islam', *TED Talk*, 20 July, http://www.youtube.com/watch?v=_K095wuE_eE

Najjar, Orayb Aref (1997) 'The 1995 Palestinian Press Law: A Comparative Study', *Communication Law and Policy* 2.1, 41–103.

Napier, Susan Jolliffe (2007) *From Impressionism to Anime: Japan as Fantasy and Fan Cult in the Mind of the West*, New York: Palgrave Macmillan.

News24 (2011), 'New Tunisia in Facebook "Crosshairs"', *News24.com*, 18 June 2011, https://www.news24.com/africa/news/new-tunisia-in-facebook-crosshairs-20110718

Nichols, Bill (1981) *Ideology and the Image*, Bloomington, IN: Indiana University Press.

Nossek, Hillel and Khalil Rinnawi (2003) 'Censorship and Freedom of the Press under Changing Political Regimes: Palestinian Media from Israeli Occupation to the Palestinian Authority', *Gazette* 65.2, pp. 183–202.

Obama, Barack, 'A New Beginning', The President's Speech in Cairo, https://obamawhitehouse.archives.gov/cairo-speech

Ostman, Ronald E. (1996) 'Disney and its Conservative Critics: Images Versus Realities', *Journal of Popular Film and Television* 24.2, pp. 82–9.

Ozersky, Josh (1991) 'TV's Anti-Families: Married . . . with Malaise', *Tikkun* 6.1, pp. 11–14.

Patrick, Steven (2006), 'Weaving the Magic of Saladin', *The Star Online*, 31 May, http://saladinayyubi.blogspot.com/2007/01/blog-post.html

Peek, Lori (2011) *Behind the Backlash: Muslim Americans after 9/11*, Philadelphia: Temple University Press.

Peterson, John E. (2006) 'Qatar and the World: Branding for a Micro-state', *The Middle East Journal* 60.4, pp. 732–48.

Peterson, Mark Allen (2005) 'The JINN and the Computer: Consumption and Identity in Arabic Children's Magazines', *Childhood*, 12.2, pp. 177–200.

Pierret, Thomas (2013) *Religion and State in Syria: the Sunni Ulama from Coup to Revolution*, Cambridge: Cambridge University Press.

Pieterse, Jan Nederveen (2004) *Globalization and Culture: Global Mélange*, Oxford: Rowman & Littlefield.

Powers, Shawn and Eytan Gilboa (2007) 'The Public Diplomacy of Al-Jazeera', in

Philip Seib (ed.), *New Media and the New Middle East*, New York: Palgrave, pp. 53–80.

Prager, Laila (2014) 'Bedouinity on Stage. The Rise of The Bedouin Soap Opera (Musalsal Badawi) in Arab Television', *Nomadic Peoples* 18.2, pp. 53–77.

Al-Qassemi, Sultan Sood (2009) 'Our Cartoon Heroes – Now That They Are Really Our Own', *Arab News*, 7 September, http://www.arabnews.com/node/327794

Al-Quds al-'Arabi (2013) 'Najla' al-Shey: Musalsal "Khousa Bousa" waqa' fi akhta' bisabab dayq al-waqt', 5 September, http://www.alquds.co.uk/?p=81146

Radsch, Courtney (2008) 'Core to Commonplace: The Evolution of Egypt's Blogosphere', *Arab Media & Society* Fall 6, pp. 1–14.

Ramírez, Naomí (2013) 'Kafranbel: Esos de las pancartas', *Entretierras*, 19 May, http://entretierras.net/2013/05/20/kafranbel-esos-de-laspancartas (web page expired).

Raphaeli, Nimrod (2005) 'Demands for Reforms in Saudi Arabia', *Middle Eastern Studies* 41.4, pp. 517–32.

El-Rayyes, Thoraya (2014) 'Enchanting Internet Media Freedom in Jordan: International Lessons for Progressive Internet Regulation', *7iber media*, 11 April, http://7iber.com/wp-content/uploads/2015/04/Enhancing-Internet-Media-Freedom-in-Jordan-Research-Project-FINAL.pdf

Regalado, Aldo (2005) 'Modernity, Race, and the American Superhero', in Jeff McLaughlin (ed.), *Comics as Philosophy*, Jackson, MS: University Press of Mississippi, pp. 84–99.

Rehman, Nadia (2008) 'Place and Space in the Memory of United Arab Emirates Elders', in Alanaud Alsharek and Robert Springborg (eds), *Political Culture and Political Identity in the Arab Gulf States*, London: SAQI in association with London Middle East Institute SOAS, pp. 31–9.

Renard, John (1999) *Islam and the Heroic Image: Themes in Literature and the Visual Arts*, Macon, GA: Mercer University Press.

Reynolds, Richard (1992) *Super Heroes: A Modern Mythology*, London: B. T. Batsford.

Ricks, Thomas M. (1988) 'Slaves and Slave Traders in the Persian Gulf, 18th and 19th Centuries: An Assessment', *Slavery & Abolition: A Journal of Slave and Post-Slave Studies* 9.3, pp. 60–70.

Rinnawi, Khalil (2006) *Instant Nationalism: McArabism, Al-Jazeera, and Transnational Media in the Arab World*, Lanham, MD: University Press of America.

Rizvi, Hasan-Askari (1982) 'Gulf Cooperation Council', *Pakistan Horizon* 35.2, pp. 29–38.

Rosenstone, Robert (1995) *Revisioning History: Film and the Construction of a New Past*, Princeton, NJ: Princeton University Press.

Rubin, Barry M. (1994) *Revolution until Victory?: The Politics and History of the PLO*. Cambridge, MA: Harvard University Press.

Ryan, Curtis R. (2004) '"Jordan First": Jordan's Inter-Arab Relations and Foreign Policy under King Abdullah II', *Arab Studies Quarterly* 26.3, pp. 43–62.

Ryzova, Lucie (2005) 'Social and Cultural Constructions of the Middle Class in Egypt under the Monarchy', in Arthur Goldschmidt, Amy J. Johnson and Barak A. Salmon (eds), *Re-envisioning Egypt 1919–1952*, Cairo: University of Cairo Press, pp. 124–63.

Sadiki, Larbi (2002) 'The Search for Citizenship in Bin Ali's Tunisia: Democracy versus Unity', *Political Studies* 50, pp. 497–513.

Saffarini, Reema (2006) 'Students Help Bring Cartoon to life', *gulfnews.com*, 14 October, http://gulfnews.com/about-gulf-news/al-nisr-portfolio/notes/articles/students-help-bring-cartoon-to-life-1.260499

Sakr, Naomi (2001) *Satellite Realms: Transnational Television, Globalization and the Middle East*, London: I. B. Tauris.

Sakr, Naomi (2004) 'Maverick or Model? Al-Jazeera's Impact on Arab Satellite Television', in Jean K. Chalaby (ed.), *Transnational Television Worldwide: Towards a New Media Order*, London: I. B. Tauris, pp. 66–95.

Sakr, Naomi (2007a) *Arab Television Today*, London: I. B. Tauris.

Sakr, Naomi (2007b) 'Egyptian TV in the Grip of Government: Politics before Profit in a Fluid Pan-Arab Market', in David Ward (ed.), *Television and Public Policy: Change and Continuity in an Era of Global Liberalization*, New York: Taylor & Francis, pp. 265–81.

Sakr, Naomi (2008) 'Egyptian TV in the Grip of Government: Politics before Profit in a Fluid Pan-Arab Market', in David Ward (ed.), *Television and Public Policy: Change and Continuity in an Era of Global Liberalization*, New York: Lawrence Erlbaum Associates, pp. 265–81.

Sakr, Naomi (2013a) 'Social Media, Television Talk Shows, and Political Change in Egypt', *Television & New Media* 14.4, pp. 322–37.

Sakr, Naomi (2013b) '"We Cannot Let it Loose": Geopolitics, Security and Reform in Jordanian Broadcasting', in Tourya Guaaybess (ed.), *National Broadcasting and State Policy in Arab Countries*, London: Palgrave Macmillan, pp. 96–116.

Sakr, Naomi and Jeanette Steemers (2017) 'Rebranding Al-Jazeera Children's Channel', in Naomi Sakr and Jeanette Steemers (eds), *Children's TV and Digital*

Media in the Arab World: Childhood, Screen Culture and Education, London: I. B. Tauris, pp. 99–121.

Salama, Vivian (2006) 'Hamas TV: Palestinian Media in Transition', *Arab Media & Society* 16, https://www.arabmediasociety.com/hamas-tv-palestinian-media-in-transition/.

Salamandra, Christa (2004) *A New Old Damascus: Authenticity and Distinction in Urban Syria*, Bloomington, IN: Indiana University Press.

Salamandra, Christa (2005) 'Television and the Ethnographic Endeavor: The Case of Syrian Drama', *Transnational Broadcasting Studies* 14, pp. 1–22.

Salloukh, Bassel F. (1996) 'State Strength, Permeability, and Foreign Policy Behavior: Jordan in Theoretical Perspective', *Arab Studies Quarterly* 18.2, pp. 37–65.

Salti, Rasha (2006) 'Critical Nationals: the Paradoxes of Syrian Cinema', in Rasha Salti (ed.), *Insights into Syrian Cinema: Essays and Conversations with Contemporary Filmmakers*, New York: AIC Film Editions/Rattapallax Press, pp. 21–44.

Sanders, Julie (2006) *Adaptation and Appropriation*, New York and London: Routledge.

Santo, Avi (2013) 'Is It a Camel? Is It a Turban? No, It's The 99': Branding Islamic Superheroes as Authentic Global Cultural Commodities', *Television New Media*, 30 December, pp. 679–95.

Sayfo, Omar (2014) 'The Emergence of Arab Children's Television and Animation Industry in the Gulf States', in Mazhar Al-zo'oby and Birol Baskan (eds), *State-society Relations in the Arab Gulf States*, Berlin: Gerlach Press, pp. 77–101.

Sayfo, Omar (2015) 'Arab Sitcom Animations as Platforms of Satire', in Sonja de Leeuw (ed.), *The Power of Satire*, Amsterdam: Benjamins.

Sayfo, Omar (2017a) 'Arab Animation: Between Business and Politics', in Naomi Sakr and Jeanette Steemers (eds), *Children's Television and Digital Media in the Arab World*, London: I. B. Tauris.

Sayfo, Omar (2017b) 'From Kurdish Sultan to Pan-Arab Champion and Muslim Hero: The Evolution of the Saladin Myth in Popular Arab Culture', *The Journal of Popular Culture* 50.1, pp. 65–85.

Sayfo, Omar (2018) 'Mediating a Disney-style Islam: The Emergence of Egyptian Islamic Animated Cartoons', *Animation* 13.2, pp. 102–15.

Schlee, Günther (2004) 'Taking Sides and Constructing Identities: Reflections on Conflict Theory', *Journal of the Royal Anthropological Institute* 10.1, pp. 135–56.

Seale, Patrick (1995) *Asad: Struggle for the Middle East*, Berkeley, CA: University of California Press.

Selvik, Kjetil (2011) 'Elite Rivalry in a Semi-Democracy: The Kuwaiti Press Scene', *Middle Eastern Studies* 47.3, pp. 477–96.

Shafik, Viola (2007a) *Popular Egyptian Cinema: Gender, Class, and Nation*, Oxford: Oxford University Press.

Shafik, Viola (2007b) *Arab Cinema: History and Cultural Identity*, Cairo: The American University in Cairo Press.

Shaheen, Jack (2012) *Reel Bad Arabs: How Hollywood Vilifies a People*, New York: Interlink Publishing.

Shamir, Shimon (1987) *The Jews of Egypt*, Boulder, CO: Westview Press.

Al-Sharq al-Awsat (2004) 'Fannan Khaleegiyyun wa Mukhrij Iraqiyy fi Film lil-Rusuum al-Mutaharrika', 29 November, https://archive.aawsat.com/details.asp?article=268137&issueno=9498#.X9dG7JNKg1I

Al Sharqiya (2011) 'Interview with Ali Abu Khumra and Muhaned Abu Khumra', 18 September, https://www.youtube.com/watch?v=zyCnvlolzlE

Shields, Amber (2017) 'Restoring Cultural Historical Memories: Animating Folktales to Form New Iraqi Identities', in Stefanie Van de Peer (ed.), *Animation in the Middle East: Practice and Aesthetics from Baghdad*, London: I. B. Tauris, pp. 29–50.

Siddiq, Muhammad (2007) *Arab Culture and the Novel: Genre, Identity and Agency in Egyptian Fiction*, London: Routledge.

Sinclair, John, Elizabeth Jacka and Stuart Cunningham (1996) *New Patterns in Global Television: Peripheral Vision*, Oxford: Oxford University Press.

Smith, Elizabeth A. (2006) 'Place, Class, and Race in the Barabra Café. Nubians in Egyptian Media', in Diane Singerman and Paul Amar (eds), *Cairo Cosmopolitan. Politics, Culture, and Urban Space in the New Globalized Middle East*, Cairo: The American University in Cairo Press, pp. 399–413.

Sraieb, Noureddine (1987) 'Élite et Société: l'Invention de la Tunisie', in Michel Carnau (ed.), *Tunisie au présent*, Paris: CNRS, pp. 65–95.

Steemers, Jeanette and Naomi Sakr (2015) 'Co-producing Content for Pan-Arab Children's TV: State, Business, and the Workplace', in Miranda Banks, Bridget Conor and Vicki Mayer (eds), *Production Studies, the Sequel!: Cultural Studies of Global Media Industries*, London: Routledge, pp. 238–50.

Steinberg, Jacques (2006), 'A Children's Cartoon From the Middle East Has a New Mideast Peace Plan', *The New York Times*, 30 April, http://www.nytimes.com/2006/04/30/arts/television/30stei.html?pagewanted=all

Straubhaar, Joseph (2007) *World Television: From Global to Local*, Thousand Oaks, CA: Sage.

Street, John (1997) *Politics and Popular Culture*, Philadelphia: Temple University Press.

Sulayman, Fawzi (1975) "al-Fann al-Thamin-Nahwa cartoon qawmiyy tatamassalu fihi al-shakhsiyya al-misriyya', *Magallat al-Cinema* II.1.

Suleiman, Yasir (1994) 'Nationalism and the Arabic Language: A Historical Overview', in Yasir Suleiman (ed.), *Arabic Sociolinguistics: Issues and Perspectives*, Richmond: Curzon, pp. 3–23.

Suleiman, Yasir (2003) *The Arabic Language and National Identity: A Study in Ideology*, Washington, DC: Georgetown University Press.

Tabar, Tania (2009), 'Fatenah: Palestine's First 3D Animation', 6 July, , http://www.menassat.com/?q=en/news-articles/6777-fatenah-palestines-first-3d-animation

Tam, Alon (2020) 'Blackface in Egypt: the Theatre and Film of Ali al-Kassar', *British Journal of Middle Eastern Studies*, 15 January 2020, https://doi.org/10.1080/13530194.2020.1714427

Tarawnah, Nasim (2011) 'Kharabeesh: Creativity Unbound', *Jordan Business*, May, pp. 42–4.

Tawil-Souri, Helga (2012) 'Digital Occupation: Gaza's High-tech Enclosure', *Journal of Palestine Studies* 41.2, pp. 27–43.

Teshkeel Media Group (2005), 'Teshkeel Media Group Brings Marvel Comics to the Middle East', press release, 21 October 2005, updated 23 February 2006, marvel.com/news/story/172teshkeel__media_group_brings_marvel_comics_to_the_middle_east

The 99 Newsletter (2012) 19 July.

The 99 Newsletter (2013) 1 February.

Tibi, Bassam (1997) *Arab Nationalism between Islam and the National State*, London: Macmillan.

UNICEF (2006) 'L'UNICEF s'associe au lancement du premier film d'animation tunisien, « Les Naufragés de Carthage »', 12 September, http://www.unicef.org.tn/html/alliance_cinetelefilms.htm

Van de Peer, Stefanie (2013) 'Fragments of War and Animation: Dahna Abourahme's Kingdom of Women and Soudade Kaadan's Damascus Roofs: Tales of Paradise', *Middle East Journal of Culture and Communication* 6.2, pp. 151–77.

Van de Peer, Stefanie (2017) 'From Animated Cartoons to Suspended Animation: A History of Syrian Animation', in Stefanie Van de Peer (ed.), *Animation in the Middle East: Practice and Aesthetics from Baghdad to Casablanca*, London: I. B. Tauris.

Van Nieuwkerk, Karin (2008) 'Creating an Islamic Cultural Sphere: Contested Notions of Art, Leisure and Entertainment. An Introduction', *Contemporary Islam* 2.3, pp. 169–76.

Vivarelli, Nick (2015) 'Dubai Festival: Animated "Bilal" Draws Attention to Middle East Animation', *Variety*, 11 December, variety.com/2015/film/global/diff-co-director-ayman-jamal-on-bilal-the-most-ambitious-cg-animated-pic-ever-made-in-the-middle-east-1201659097

Waisbord, Silvio (2004), 'McTV: Understanding the Global Popularity of Television Formats', *Television & New Media* 5.4, pp. 359–83.

Watts, Steven (1995) 'Walt Disney: Art and Politics in the American Century', *The Journal of American History* 82.1, pp. 84–110.

Wedeen, Lisa (1999) *Ambiguities of Domination: Politics, Rhetoric, and Symbols in Contemporary Syria*, Chicago: University of Chicago Press.

Wedeen, Lisa (2013) 'Ideology and Humor in Dark Times: Notes from Syria', *Critical Inquiry* 39.4, pp. 841–73.

Wells, Paul (1998) *Understanding Animation*, London: Routledge.

Wells, Paul (2002) *Animation: Genre and Authorship*, London: Wallflower Press.

Wenke, Eric (2008) 'Accents in Children's Animated Features as a Device for Teaching Children to Ethnocentrically Discriminate', Paper submitted to Conference on Language and Popular Culture, http://ccat.sas.upenn.edu/~haroldfs/popcult/handouts/wenkeric.htm

al-Weshah, 'Abdellateef (2014) 'Jordan Diplomacy Towards Syria and the 2011 Syrian Crisis (2011–2013)', *Śodkowoeuropejskie Studia Polityczne* 3, pp. 197–214.

Wheeler, Deborah (2000) 'New Media, Globalization and Kuwaiti National Identity', *The Middle East Journal*, 54.3, pp. 432–44.

Wildermuth, Norbert (2005) 'Defining the "Al-Jazeera Effect": American Public Diplomacy at a Crossroad', *In Medias Res* 1.2, http://www.medievidenskab-odense.dk/index.php?

Wright, Bradford W. (2001) *Comic Book Nation: The Transformation of Youth Culture in America*, Baltimore: The Johns Hopkins University Press.

Yom, Sean L. (2009) 'Jordan: Ten More Years of Autocracy', *Journal of Democracy* 20.4, pp. 151–66.

Yoshida, Kaori (2008) 'Animation and "Otherness": The Politics of Gender, Racial, and Ethnic Identity in the World of Japanese Anime', Unpublished PhD thesis, University of British Columbia.

Zghal, 'Abdelkader (1991) 'The New Strategy of the Movement of the Islamic Way: Manipulation or Expression of Political Culture?' in I. William Zartman (ed.), *Tunisia: the Political Economy of Reform*, Boulder, CO: Lynne Rienner Publishers, pp. 205–17.

Index

2D, 38, 42, 54, 95, 114, 129, 130, 153, 199
3D, 2, 7, 15, 38, 41, 42, 43, 48, 49, 57, 91, 96, 114, 115, 119, 148, 153, 165, 171, 180, 199, 206, 212, 227
3D Studio, 217

'Abbas ibn 'Abbas, 196
ABC News, 225
'Abd al-Hamed, 'Issa, 32
al-'Abdallat, Omar, 223, 227–8
'Abdel Nasser, Gemal, 33, 42, 139, 194
  Nasser era, 34, 35
'Abdul-Fattah, Ahmad, 32
Abu al-Nasr, Mona, 36–7, 42, 199
Abu Dhabi, 44, 97, 162, 175
Abu Dhabi Authority for Culture and Heritage, 46
Abu Dhabi Channel, 115
Abu Dhabi Media 55, 166
Abu Mahjoub, 111–14, 223
Adrar (1979), 77
Agha, Akram, 153
A Hero from Port Said (*Batal min Boursa'eed*, 2011), 42
A Hero from the Sinai (*Batal min Seena'*, 2007), 42
al-Ahram, 26
al-Ahram Studio, 33
Ah, s'il savait lire (1963), 77
Aladdin, 144
Aladdin (1992), 5, 16, 132, 251
Ali Baba, 35, 191
Ali Baba and the Forty Thieves (*'Ali Baba wal-Arba'ina Lissan*, 1996), 191
Ahmad and Kan'aan (*Ahmad wa Kan'aan*, 2009), 165
'ajam, 45, 51, 117, 127
Ajyal, 168
Alawite, 149, 242
Alexandria, 6, 24, 25, 32, 203

Algeria, 2, 70, 74–83, 98, 99, 120,
Algeria History and Civilization (*Al-Jaza'ir Tarikh wa Hadarah*, 2012) 78–83, 99,
Al Jazeera Children's Channel (JCC) 19, 21, 53, 140, 153, 165, 168, 169, 170–2, 176, 198, 205
Allawi, Iyad, 121
Almajd TV Network, 168
L'Ambouba (2009), 68
American animation, 6, 8, 28, 36, 58
American Football (*al-Kurat al-Qadam al-Amreekiyya*, 1972), 142–3
Amman, 7, 111, 130, 168, 221, 223, 224, 225, 226, 227
'ammiyya, 16, 99, 197
anasheed (*nasheed*), 168, 180, 181, 185, 187, 188, 189, 191, 193, 196, 213
Andalus (Andalusia) 75, 126, 164, 189, 190, 209
Andoni, Sa'eed, 96,
Animal Stories in the Qur'an (*Qisas al-Hayawan fil-Qur'an*, 2011) 198–201
Anime 3, 6, 7, 50, 73, 79, 152, 160, 174, 182, 248, 250
Anything For You, (*'Ala Ra'si*, 2007), 223
A Peasant's Dream (*Hilm Fallah*, 1938), 32
al-Aqsa TV, 87, 88, 90, 91
Arab Awakening (*al-Nahda*), 9, 134, 138
Arab Centre for Animation, 144
al-Arabiyya, 220
Arabsat, 124
'Aram, Mohammed, 77–8
ART 167, 196
Artiste comme la cigale (1981), 67
al-Assad, Hafez, 149
al-Assad, Bashar, 239, 241, 242, 243
Association of Young Tunisian Filmmakers (AJCT), 62, 65
A Story of Nails (*Hikaya Mismariyya*, 1991), 150
Atelier 216, 231–3, 244

Al-'Ataak (2011), 122–3
Attention (*Intibah*, 2005), 153
'Attia, Mohamed Habib, 70
Attili, Wael 221, 224, 229
Aymoun the Crazy (*Aymoun al-Magnoun*, 2013) 238
Ayyoubi, Randa, 57
al-Azhar, 40, 194, 195, 197, 198, 199, 201, 202,

Baathist, 19, 21, 121, 139, 140, 141, 142, 143, 145, 147, 148, 149, 156, 157, 158, 160, 175, 176
Baath Party, 138, 141, 142
Babylon, 144
Badr (2017), 174–5
Baghdad Night (2013) 148
Bakkar (1998)1, 37–41, 198
Banque Misr, 24
Baraem, 168
Barajoun, 249–50
al-Bargheeneyy, 'Abd al-Haleem, 33–4
Bargouth, Fatma, 95
Basma, 168
Bazzaz, Sa'd, 121
BBC, 220
Bedouin, 17, 42, 50, 51, 55, 117, 123, 127, 130–2, 223
Bein Media Group, 174
Ben Ali, Zine al-Abidine, 62, 63, 68, 69, 70, 73, 132, 133, 134, 217, 224, 230, 231
Ben and Izzy (*Ben wa 'Esam*, 2006), 57–60
Besbes, Samir, 67
Betty Boop, 28
Bilal (2016) 249–51
Block 13 (2000) 124–5
Bon Appetit (*Bil-Hana wal-Shifa'*, 1946), 27
Bosko and Buddy, 30
Bourguiba, Habib, 61, 62, 63, 64, 65, 66, 67, 68, 70
Bouteflika, Abdelaziz, 81
Breadology (*Khobzoulougia*, 2012), 233
British Council, 86

Cable Vision, 165
Cairo, 6, 7, 24, 25, 27, 30, 32, 38, 39, 40, 118, 121, 167, 188, 189, 196, 199, 207,
Cairo Cartoon, 36–7, 41, 118, 198–9
Cannes, 249, 251
Cars (2006), 7
Carthage International Film Festival, 62
CartooNile, 41, 199
Cartoon Network, 167
Cartoon Network Arabic, 57, 169
Captain Baguette (*Captain Khobza*, 2012) 218, 229–32, 244
Captain Majid (*Captain Tsubasa*), 1, 7
CGI, 36, 180
Chaplin, Charlie, 30
Charbagi, Mohamed, 65
Châteaux de sable (2010), 68
Chicago International Cinema Festival, 36
Christian, 9, 74, 81, 97, 138, 168, 186, 187, 190, 236
Cinétéléfilms, 70, 71, 72
Civilisation Makers (*Sunna' al-Hadarah*, 2005), 164
Cohl, Émile, 64
Cold War, 6

Colloquial Arabic, 16, 18, 33, 38, 97; *see also* '*ammiyya*
Comments of the Day (Ta'aleeq al-Yaoum, 1995), 109
Count it Well (*Ehsebha Shahh*, 2010), 222
Cowan, Paul, 96
Crusaders, 172, 173, 185

Dana Film Studio, 143, 165
Daqdaq (1940), 32
Damascus, 7, 152, 154, 190, 238, 239, 240, 241, 243
Darwish, Mahmoud, 228
Data City (*Madeenat al-Ma'loomaat*, 2004), 153
Dayton's Gangs ('*Esabaat Dayton*, 2010), 88–90
DC Comics, 205, 207
al-Deen, Hosaam, 34
Directorate of Television Production, 152
Disney, 1, 3, 6, 8, 9, 15, 25, 28, 36, 38, 43, 50, 99, 147, 152, 156, 157, 161, 167, 172, 181, 182, 186, 201, 213, 234, 248, 252
Disney Channel Middle East (DCME), 169
Disneyesque, 41, 199
Doha Film Institute, 249
Douieb au Sahara (1967), 77
DreamWorks, 7, 158
Dubai 20, 44–50, 114, 116, 117, 121, 122, 128, 152, 249
Dubai Heritage Villages, 47
Dubai Media City (DMC), 47
Dubai Media Incorporated (DMI), 114, 166
Dubai Society for Heritage Revival, 47
Dubai TV, 120

East Germany, 144
Education City, 160
Egypt 1, 2, 3, 5, 6, 8, 16, 18, 20, 21, 23, 24–44, 53, 69, 78, 85, 93, 98, 99, 108, 114, 115, 116, 118–21, 139, 143, 149, 156, 166, 167, 181, 182, 188, 194–9, 204–5, 213, 218, 219, 233–8, 241, 244
Egyptian Companies Law, 31
Egyptian Radio and Television Union, 33
Egyptian Television, 33, 34, 35, 37, 40, 41, 43, 108, 119, 194, 195, 196, 204
Egyptoon, 218, 236–8, 244,
E-junior, 167
Ella, 21, 183, 188–93,
EmariToons, 152
Emberson Hoy, Norman, 142,
Enterprise Nationale de Télévision (ENTV), 78
Etana Productions, 122
Etisalat, 57, 116
European Commission, 71, 73, 86
European Union, 56
Eve (*Hawwa'*, 2010), 222
Everyday Stories of Bou Qatada and Bou Nabeel (*Youmiyyat Bou Qatada wa Bou Nabeel*), 42, 125–8
Everyday Stories of Mr Sahlawi (2008), 41
Everyday Stories of Mnahy (*Youmiyyat Mnahy*, 2006), 129
E-Vision, 167
'Ezz, Ahmad, 120, 233, 234

Facebook, 220, 223, 226, 231, 240, 241, 242
Faculty of Fine Arts, 32, 33, 34, 36
al-Fakharani, Yahya, 199,
Family Business (*Taish 'Eyal*, 2012), 129–30
Family Guy, 58, 107, 110
Fanar Production, 116
Faraj, Bassam, 142, 143
al-Faramawy, Mustafa, 8, 41, 199–200,
Fares, Diana, 158
Faour, Sami, 133
Farooha Media Productions, 124
Fatenah (2009), 95–6
Felix the Cat, 6, 25, 28
Fertoh et le singe (1971), 77
Film and Theatre Organisation, 141
Fish in Water (*Samak fi-Mayya*, 2012), 236
Flash, 217, 221, 230, 240
Fleur de pierre (1992), 67
France24, 225
Frankenstein (1931), 30
Franklin the Turtle (1997–2003), 41
Freej, 2, 48–53, 110, 114, 115, 116, 117, 182
Free Syrian Army, 239, 241
Frenkel Brothers, 8, 25–32, 39,
fusha, 16–20, 27, 38, 70, 73, 92, 93, 99, 111, 138, 145, 151, 152, 154, 156, 157, 158, 159, 160, 163, 164, 170, 171, 172, 175, 176, 187, 196, 197, 199, 203, 213, 222, 237, 251

Galal, Sherif, 41
Gaza, 85–92, 95, 96
General Organisation for Cinema, 152
Guerbagi (1984), 67
Ghannoushi, Rached, 231
Ghariani, Riad, 110, 133
globalisation, 47, 139,
Google, 222, 226
Google Ahlan, 222
Gulf Cooperation Council (GCC), 21, 140, 161, 162,

Habash, Ahmad, 96
Haboub and Haboubah (*Haboub wa Haboubah*, 1938), 32
Hadi TV, 168, 181
Haidar, Mohammed, 110, 116
Hajjaj, Emad, 111–13
Hakeem, Mohamed, 33
Half-Sleeve Politics (*Siyasa Noss Komm*), 242
Hamas, 85, 87–91, 93, 95
Hamdi, Ashraf, 233–8, 244
Hammad, Fathi Ahmad, 88
Hanna-Barbera, 107, 152
Hannibal TV, 105, 132, 133
Harbaoui, 'Erzeddine, 67
Harib, Mohammed Sa'eed, 48, 49, 50, 110
Hatem, Abdelkader, 34
Helwan University, 32, 36
Henedy, Mohammad, 120
heritage revival *(ihya' al-turath)*, 46, 47, 50, 53, 115
Hezbollah, 241, 242
High School of Fine Arts, 32
Hijazi, 'Abdel-Nabiyy, 151, 158
Hijazi, Mannaa', 151, 152

Hijazi, Razam, 158
Hijazi, Sulafa, 153, 154, 156, 161, 177, 239
H'Mimo et les allumettes (1965), 77
Hodhod TV, 168, 169, 180
Hollywood, 30
humour, 52, 58, 110, 118, 123, 125, 127, 130, 134, 135, 220, 227, 231, 233, 239
Hungary, 143, 165
Hussein, Habib, 165
Hussein, Mustafa, 33
Hussein, Saddam, 20, 121, 142, 144, 146, 148
hybrid identity, 9, 12, 21, 54, 124, 205, 207, 209, 214
hybridisation, 11, 12, 13, 180, 231,
hybridity, 11, 12, 13, 209,
hyper-reflexivity, 107

Ibn Tufayl, 165, 192
al-Ibrahim, Faysal, 125, 165
al-Ibrahim, Walid, 128
infitah, 35, 198
I Love You, Oh Our Country (*Bhibbak ya Baladna*, 2008), 87
Investment Law 10, 151
Iraq, 2, 6, 16, 19, 20, 56, 58, 60, 105, 121–3, 125, 127, 139–48, 160–3, 172, 175, 176
Iraqi TV, 144
Iskandar Nadheer Studio, 34
Islamic Action Front, 56
Islamism, 9, 11
Island of Adventures (*Jazeerat al-Mughamarat*, 2004) 152
Island of the Light (*Jazeerat al-Nur*, 2000), 192
al-Ittihad, 54
al-Ittijah TV, 147
Izzedeen al-Qassam Brigades, 88

Jabr, Samir, 150
Jahjouh, Il était une fois (1986), 67
al-Jama'a al-Islamiyya, 194
Jamal, Ajman, 249, 251
al-Jamil, Furat, 148
Jasmine Birds (*Tuyur al-Yasmeen*, 2009), 20, 154–6, 158, 160, 177
Jeem TV, 140, 170–1, 174
Jewish, 9, 25, 31, 56, 89, 90, 93, 94, 208
JibJab, 224, 230,
jihad, 83, 126, 185,
Joint Programme Production Institution (JPPI), 21, 140, 143, 153, 154, 161–6, 175, 176
Jordan, 2, 20, 21, 55–60, 85, 88, 98, 99, 105, 111–14, 130–1, 139, 168, 172, 211, 217, 218, 221–9, 235, 239, 244,
Jordanian TV, 112, 113
Juha at the Court (*Juha fil-Mahkameh*, 1985), 150

Kafranbel, 239
Kalil and Dimn (*Kalil wa Dimn*, 1993), 109
Kamel, Saleh, 37, 167, 196
Kani and Mani (*Kani wa Mani*, 1989), 36, 199
Karadsheh, Zaidoun, 130
Karamesh TV, 168, 169
Katt, Mwaffaq, 150, 152, 161, 239,
Kélibia International Festival, 62

Al-Khalifa, ʿAli, 125
Khalifa, Osama, 84, 183, 191, 193,
Khalila and Dimna, 191
Kharabeesh, 217, 221–9, 231, 234, 235, 236, 237, 238–44
Khemir, Nacer 65
Khomeini, 144, 211,
Khoury, George, 109,
Khousa Bousa (2009) 115, 116, 118
King Abdullah II, 56, 57
King Abdullah II Fund for Development, 57
King Hussein 56, 57, 229
Kuwait, 2, 42, 105, 108, 123–8, 140, 148, 161–5, 175, 205
Kuwait Media Group Company, 125

La Bourse égyptienne, 26, 27
La Calligraphie arabe (1970), 66
La Cigale (1986), 67
La Fête de l'arbre (1963), 77
La Fleur (1970), 65
La Goutte miraculeuse (2009), 67
La Rentrée des classes (1965) 63
Lagardère International Images, 170
Lammtara Pictures, 48, 116
Larguech, Mehdi, 231
Laurel and Hardy, 30
Le Bûcheron (1972), 65
Le Calligraphe (1987), 67
Le Chien intelligent (1966), 64
Le Déluge (1992), 67
Le Guerbagi (1984), 67
Le Magicien (1965), 78
Le Marchand de Fez (1967), 64
Le Mulet (1975), 65
Le Petit Hibou (1982), 66
Le Rêve du beau Danube bleu (1964), 31
Le Soulier (1989), 67
Le Sous-Marin de Carthage (1999), 68
L'enfant et l'avion (1981), 67
Les Aventures de Hatem, le courageux cavalier Zlass (1992), 67
Les Aventures de Jahjou (1983), 67
Les Couleurs du diable (1975), 77
Les Deux souris blanches (1974), 66
Les Ficelles (1995), 68
Les Naufragés de Carthage (2008), 70–3
L'histoire d'un oeuf (1976), 66
L'homme et le rocher (1969), 64
L'homme qui dort (1971), 65
Liberated Drawings (*Rusuum Mutaharrira*, 2001), 109
Libya, 6, 35, 218, 219, 224, 225, 226, 239
localisation, 8, 12, 13, 15, 25, 182
localised, 13, 25, 36, 38, 40, 77, 96, 124, 158, 193
L'olivier justicier (1978), 77

McArabism, 10, 19
McLaren, Norman, 34
Madagascar (2005), 7
al-Majd Kids Channel, 168, 169,
Majid (2015), 53–4
Majid TV, 55
al-Maktoum, Rashid bin Saʿeed, 47

Mahjoub, Zouhair, 66
al-Maleki, Fayez, 129
Maʿrouf, Ahmad, 152
Marco Monkey (1935), 25–6, 32
Al-Masageel (2011–13), 130–2
Al-Maliki, Nuri, 123
Malsoun.org (2010), 154
Mariage (1966), 78
Screws (*Masameer*, 2011), 245, 251
Masrour on the Pearl Island (*Masrour fi Jazirat al-Luʾluʾ*, 1998), 193
al-Mazen, Khalil, 95
MBC, 119, 128, 129, 130, 166, 167, 225
MBC3, 19, 21, 53, 167, 169
Mecca, 82, 93, 130, 203, 249, 250
Media Plus, 87
Mesopotamia, 142, 145, 147
Mickey Mouse, 25, 26, 27, 28, 32
Microbes des poubelles (1964), 78
Ministry of the Mujahedeen, 75, 79
Miracle Stories in the Qurʾan (*Qisas al-ʿAjaʾib fil-Qurʾan*, 2014), 199
Mish Mish Effendi, 26–31, 39, 43
Misr Company for Cinema and Performance, 24
Modern Standard Arabic (MSA), 7, 59
Mohammad the Conqueror (*Mohammad al-Fatih*, 1995), 185–7
Mohammedia (1991), 65, 68
Moheeb, ʿAli, 34, 36
Moheeb, Husaam, 34
Monsters, Inc., 120
Morocco, 40, 70, 126, 128
Mounir, Mohamed, 29
Moving Issues (*Humum Mutaharrikah*, 2007) 86–7
L'Mrayet (2011), 68–9
Mubarak, Hosni, 39, 42, 43, 194, 198, 204, 225, 235, 237,
Mubarak era, 44, 108, 118, 120; *see also* Mubarak regime
Multimedia Development Corporation (MDeC), 171
Muslim Brotherhood, 56, 87, 194, 204, 236
al-Mutawa, Naif, 205, 206, 207, 208, 210, 212
Muzna and Fami (*Muzna wa Fami*, 2007), 129
My Arab House (*Bayti al-ʿArabi*, 2007), 153

Nabulsi, Wafa, 121, 125,
Al-Nahda Party, 134, 231
Nahhas, Gabriel, 32,
al-Namr, Husayn, 164
Nasser era, 34, 35
Nasser, Gemal ʿAbdel, 33, 42, 139, 194
National Defence (*al-Difaʾ al-Wataniyy*, 1938), 29–30
National Film Board of Canada, 97
National Film Organisation (NFO), 149, 150, 152, 153
Nationalism, 9, 11, 16, 17, 45–6, 61, 80, 87
National Organisation of Mujahedeen, 75
Neilson Hordell Ltd, 150
Netflix, 206, 251
Nickelodeon Arabia, 167, 168
Nidaa Tounes, 230
Nile Family, 167
Nile Life, 119
Nilesat, 118, 124

No Big Deal (*Tash ma Tash*, 1992–2010), 108
Nubian, 28–9, 37–9

Obama, Barack, 207, 237
Of God's Most Beautiful Names (*Min 'Asma' Allah al-Husna*, 2007), 196
OK Toons, 84, 183
Oman, 52, 108, 161, 162
Omran, Bechir
Open Sesame! (*Iftah Ya Simsim*) 154, 163
Organisation of Radio and Television, 151
Oslo Accords, 85, 98
Ottomans, 74, 75, 81, 123, 185

Pain (1972), 64
Palestine Liberation Organization (PLO), 85, 86, 87, 88
Palestinian Authority, 85, 88
Palestinian Territories, 2, 20, 58, 83–7, 98, 99
Palmer, John, 144
pan-Arab, 10, 11, 16, 18, 19, 20, 21, 22, 33, 35, 55, 61, 70, 78, 134, 135, 138–77, 180, 184, 201, 213, 222, 225, 247
Pasin, Dervis, 187
Post Productions
Prosperity of the Egyptian People (*Rafaheyyat al-Sha'b al-Misriyy*, 2010), 233–4
Pritchard, David, 58
Propaganda, 10, 20, 30, 34, 75, 79, 88, 90, 99, 121, 142, 144, 145, 156, 243

al-Qaddafi, Muammar, 211, 225
Qadisiyya (*Al-Qadisiyya*, 1981) 1941
Qatar, 2, 162, 168, 170, 175
Qatar Foundation for Education, 168, 170
Queen Rania, 58
Qur'an, 19, 21, 41, 93, 168, 180, 183, 187, 188, 196, 197, 198, 199, 200, 201, 202, 207, 213

Rais, Nadia, 68, 69
Rajae the Space Creature (*Rajae al-Ka'en al-Fada'eyy*, 2012), 227
Ramadan, 49, 52, 105, 110, 112, 113, 115, 115, 125, 133, 174, 199, 232
The President (*al-Rayes*, 2013), 122–3
Red Line (*Khatt Ahmar*, 2008), 221
Required Vision, 89
Al-Ribat Communications and Artistic Productions, 88
Rotana, 166
Roya TV, 105, 114
Rubicon Group Holding, 57
Ruya Foundation, 148

Al-Sadat, Anwar, 35, 194
Saddam Hussein, 20, 121, 142, 144, 146, 148
Sa'eed Harib, Mohammed, 48, 49, 50, 110
al-Sahy, Neyla, 115
Saladin: the Animated Series (2009) 171–4, 177
Salafi, 92, 124, 126, 168, 181, 182
Salim, Ahmad, 32
Salim, Antoine, 32
Sama Dubai, 49, 105, 114, 115
Sancho, Mongi, 63–6, 68, 69

SAT-7 Kids, 168
SATPEC, 62, 64, 67
Saudi Arabia, 2, 6, 82, 92, 107, 118, 128–32, 162, 166, 175, 181, 182, 196, 197, 211, 212, 223, 231, 232
Saudi TV Channel 1, 129
Al-Sayegh Group, 113
Sayf al-Qutuz 'ayn Jalout (1998) 188–9
Scientists of the Muslims ('Ulama' al-Muslemeen, 2013), 198
Supreme Council of the Armed Forces (SCAF), 235
Seddik, Tayeb Cherif, 79
Sema (1983), 77
Secourez-là (1986), 67
Shaam News Network (SNN), 241
Shaabiat Al Cartoon, 110, 116–18
al-Shahar, 195–6
Shaker (*Hazzaz*, 2010), 222
al-Shakhs, Hashem Muhammad, 164
al-Shammari, Nawaf Salem, 124
al-Sha'rawi Hazem, 91
al-Sharbaji, Ammar, 156
Sheikh of the Mujaheds – Ahmad Yassin (*Shaykh al-Mujahedeen – Ahmad Yassin*, 2013), 91–4
Shia, 9, 81, 121, 123, 124, 142, 168, 181, 182, 197
al-Shmemri, 'Abdulrahman, 168
Shomali, Amer, 96, 98
Shrapnel (*Shazaya*, 2012), 243–4
el-Sisi, 'Abdel Fattah, 226, 236, 237
Six-Day War, 139
Sketch in Motion, 87, 113, 130
Snow White and the Seven Dwarfs (1938), 106
Son of the Forest (*Ibn al-Ghaba*, 2006), 165
Songa, Samir Al-Mufti, 240, 241, 242
Soviet Union, 34
Spacetoon TV, 152, 153, 167, 169
Star Animation for Artistic Production, 152, 156
Stories of the Animals in the Qur'an, 199–201
Stories of the People in the Qur'an (*Qisas al-Insan fil-Qur'an*, 2012), 199, 201
Stories of Sindbad the Seaman (*Hekayat Sindbad al-Bahreyy*, 1996), 36
From the Stories of the Prophets (*Min Qisas al-Anbiya'*, 1999), 196
Stories of Women in the Qur'an (*Qisas al-Nisa' fil-Qur'an*, 2013) 201–4
Story of the Ayah (1995) 195–6
Story of Syrians For and Against the Regime (*Qissa 'an Suriyyeen Ma' al-Nizaam wa Diddahu*, 2012), 240
Studio El Bouraq, 79
Sudan, 40, 115, 121
Sufi, 182
Sunni, 9, 81, 82, 121, 123, 138, 142, 150, 160, 182, 194, 197
Super Henedy (2008), 120–1
Superman, 132, 207, 208, 211, 230
Syria, 2, 6, 19, 20, 21, 40, 78, 138, 139, 140, 143, 149–61, 176, 183, 218, 219, 226, 238–44

Taieb, Mustafa, 67, 69
Tal'at Harb, 24
Talhimi, Michel, 32
Taha TV, 168

Tarek Rashed Studio, 41–2, 115, 125,
Tartar Sauces (*Tartouriyyat*, 2012), 232
Teshkeel Media, 205, 206
Tete (1958), 34
The 99 (2011) 21, 205–12, 214
The Arabian Nights, 5, 36, 147, 191, 193, 222
The Bat Sheikh (*Al-Shaikh Khaffash*, 2010), 223
The Boy and the King (*Rihlat al-Kholoud*, 1996), 187–8
The Conquest of Andalusia – Tareq ibn Ziyad (*Fath al-Andalus – Tareq ibn Ziyad*, 1999) 21, 189–90
The Epic of Gilgamesh (*Malhamat Gilgamesh*, 1986), 147–8
The Family of Mr Ameen ('*Aelat al-Ustaz 'Ameen*, 2008), 118–19
The Flintstones, 4, 107
The General's Boot (*Hidha' al-Jenral*, 2008), 153
The Jasmine Birds (*Tuyur al-Yasmeen*, 2009), 20, 154–56, 160
The Jug (*Al-Jarrah*, 2001), 20, 156–58
The Leader (*Al-Za'eem*, 2013), 227
The Lion King (1994), 120, 251
The Message (1976), 247
The Mice of Corruption in Gaza (*Fe'ran al-Fasad fi Ghazza*, 2007), 90
The Miraculous Journey to the Past (*Al-Rehlah al-'Ajeebah ilal-Madee*, 1985), 147
The Occasions of Revelation (*Asbab al-Nuzul*, 2005), 196
The Palace of the People (*Qasr al-Sha'b*, 2011), 241
The Prince of Egypt (1998), 158, 179
The Princess and the River (*Al-'Amirah wal-Nahr*, 1982), 20, 144–7
The Scarecrow (*Khayal al-Haql*, 2013), 95
The Simpsons, 4, 58, 106, 107, 110
The Song of Hope (*Nashid al-Amal*, 1937), 27
The Survival (*Al-Muntaser*, 1989), 36
The Return of the Magic Lantern ('*Oudat al-Misbah al-Sehriyy*, 1984), 147
The Royal Automobile Club, 31
The Wanted 18 (2014), 96–8
The White Line (*Al-Khatt al-Abyad*, 1962), 34
The Yarn of Life (*Khait al-Hayat*, 2007), 20, 158–60
The Yellow Road to Geneva (*Al-Tareeq al-Asfar li-Genefa*, 2013), 240
There's No Benefit (*Mafish Fa'ida*, 1936), 27
ThinkArabia, 221
Tiger Production, 152, 154, 158
Tom and Jerry, 1, 6, 36, 64, 144,
al-Tourjuman, Ahmad, 164
Toy Story (1995), 7

Toyour al-Jannah TV
Trabelsi, Mohamed, 231
Tunis 2050, 110, 133–4
Tunisia, 2, 20, 21, 53, 61–73, 98, 99, 133–6, 217, 218, 219, 224, 229–33, 244
Tunisian Ministry of Culture, 62, 69
Tunisia World Television (TWT), 232
Turner, 57
Tyba, Robert, 32

UFO Robo Grendizer, 6
UNESCO, 142
UNICEF, 71, 72
United Arab Emirates, 2, 44–55, 99, 114–18
United Arab Republic, 139, 149
United Nations, 40, 71, 148
United States, 35, 36, 56, 60, 113, 126, 145, 156, 206, 207, 208, 209, 210, 221, 226, 247, 250
USAID, 86, 87

Venus for Art Production (al-Zahra), 151–2, 153
Viva Carthago (2005), 70–3, 98

Wamda, 86
Warner Bros., 30
al-Watan, 125, 128
al-Watan TV, 124, 125
We are lost (*Da'na*, 2013), 232–4
West Bank, 85–8, 89, 90
WikiSham, 218, 241–2
With Contentment and Healing (*Bil-Hana wal-Shifa'*, 1946), 30
World Health Organization (WHO), 95
World War II, 29, 138

X-Men, 205, 208, 210

Yarn of Life (*Khait al-Hayat*, 2007), 20, 158–60
al-Yasseri, Faissal, 144, 147
Yemen, 40, 218, 245
You Stay Safe (*Dumtom Salemeen*, 2002), 153
YouTube, 132, 219, 220, 222, 223, 224, 226, 229, 238, 242, 245, 251

al-Zaidi, Thamer, 143, 165
Zain 221, 222
Zaitoon Animation & Games 95
Zamzam Media, 42–3, 196, 197
Zamzam, Zainab, 42, 196
Zan Studio, 86–7
Za'toor (1995) 163–4, 165, 166, 177
Zuhra (1922), 61

EU representative:
Easy Access System Europe
Mustamäe tee 50, 10621 Tallinn, Estonia
Gpsr.requests@easproject.com

www.ingramcontent.com/pod-product-compliance
Lightning Source LLC
Chambersburg PA
CBHW051604230426
43668CB00013B/1980